Child Protection Systems

International Policy Exchange Series

Published in collaboration with the
Center for International Policy Exchanges
University of Maryland

Series Editors
Douglas J. Besharov
Neil Gilbert

United in Diversity?
Comparing Social Models in Europe and America
Edited by
Jens Alber and Neil Gilbert

The Korean State and Social Policy:
How South Korea Lifted Itself from
Poverty and Dictatorship to Affluence and Democracy
Stein Ringen, Huck-ju Kwon, Ilcheong Yi,
Taekyoon Kim, and Jooha Lee

Child Protection Systems:
International Trends and Orientations
Edited by
Neil Gilbert, Nigel Parton, and Marit Skivenes

SCHOOL of
PUBLIC POLICY

Child Protection Systems

International Trends and Orientations

Edited by

NEIL GILBERT
NIGEL PARTON
MARIT SKIVENES

OXFORD
UNIVERSITY PRESS

Published in the United States of America by Oxford University Press, Inc.,
198 Madison Avenue, New York, NY, 10016
United States of America

Oxford University Press, Inc., publishes works that further Oxford University's
objective of excellence in research, scholarship, and education

Oxford is a registered trade mark of Oxford University Press
in the UK and in certain other countries

Library of Congress Cataloging-in-Publication Data

Child protection systems : international trends and orientations / edited by Neil Gilbert,
Nigel Parton, Marit Skivenes.
   p. cm. — (International policy exchange series)
 Includes bibliographical references and index.
 ISBN 978-0-19-979335-8 (hardcover : alk. paper)
 1. Child welfare. 2. Child abuse. I. Gilbert, Neil, 1940- II. Parton, Nigel. III. Skivenes, Marit.
 HV713.C38266   2011
 362.76—dc22

                                                            2010054150

CONTENTS

CONTRIBUTORS

PETER ADRIAENSSENS
Catholic University of Leuven
Leuven, Belgium

JILL DUERR BERRICK
School of Social Welfare
University of California, Berkeley
Berkeley, California

DAVID BERRIDGE
Centre for Family Policy and Child
    Welfare
University of Bristol
Bristol, United Kingdom

KAY BIESEL
Alice-Salomon University
    of Applied Sciences
Berlin, Germany

MADELEINE COCOZZA
Division of Child and Adolescent
    Psychiatry
Linköping University
Linköping, Sweden

KRISTOF DESAIR
Catholic University of Leuven
Leuven, Belgium

NEIL GILBERT
School of Social Welfare
University of California, Berkeley
Berkeley, California

STEFAN HEINITZ
Alice-Salomon University
    of Applied Sciences
Berlin, Germany

ANNE-DORTHE HESTBÆK
Research Unit on Child & Family
The Danish National Centre
    for Social Research
Copenhagen, Denmark

SVEN E.O. HORT
Södertörn University College
Södertörn, Sweden

TRUDIE KNIJN
Faculty of Social
    and Behavioural Sciences
Utrecht University
Utrecht, The Netherlands

NIGEL PARTON
School of Human and Health Sciences
University of Huddersfield
Huddersfield, United Kingdom

TARJA PÖSÖ
School of Humanities and
    Social Sciences
University of Tampere
Tampere, Finland

MARIT SKIVENES
Faculty of Health and Social Sciences
Bergen University College
Bergen, Norway

KAREN J. SWIFT
School of Social Work
York University
Toronto, Canada

CAROLUS VAN NIJNATTEN
Utrecht University
Utrecht, The Netherlands

REINHART WOLFF
Alice-Salomon University
    of Applied Sciences
Berlin, Germany

ACKNOWLEDGMENTS

The overall project for this book was sponsored by the Norwegian Ministry of Children and Equality and the National Society for the Prevention of Cruelty to Children (NSPCC), the largest nongovernmental child protection agency in the U.K. The research group conducting this study met three times over the course of two years to develop the framework that would guide the analyses of the different countries. An opportunity to explore some of the initial findings was presented at a conference sponsored by the Center for Child and Youth Policy at the University of California, Berkeley, from which the research group gained constructive feedback.

The editors would like to thank the members of the research group, all of whom have contributed to this volume. Throughout they have been a delight to work with and without them the project would not have been possible.

Neil Gilbert, Nigel Parton, and Marit Skivenes

Child Protection Systems

1

INTRODUCTION

NEIL GILBERT, NIGEL PARTON, AND MARIT SKIVENES

This volume builds upon and advances the comparative analysis of child protection systems that was conducted in the mid-1990s and presented in *Combatting Child Abuse: International Perspectives and Trends* (Gilbert, 1997). Prompted by the rapid increase in reports of child maltreatment from 1980 to the early 1990s, that study compared social policies and professional practices in nine countries, examining differences as well as common problems and policy orientations. One of the key findings revealed important variations among the countries concerning the extent to which their child abuse reporting systems were characterized by a *child protection* or a *family service orientation*.

The two orientations were distinguished along four dimensions. First, and perhaps most significant, was the way the problem of child abuse was framed. In child protection–oriented systems, abuse was conceived of as an act that demanded the protection of children from harm by "degenerative relatives"; whereas, in other systems, abuse was conceived as a problem of family conflict or dysfunction that arose from social and psychological difficulties but which responded to help and support. Second, and depending on how child abuse was framed, the response operated either as a mechanism for investigating deviance in a highly legalistic way or as a service-oriented, often therapeutic response to a family's needs, in which the initial focus involved the assessment of need. As a result, third, the child welfare professionals functioned either in the child protection orientation, in a highly adversarial way, or, in the family service orientation in a spirit of partnership—particularly with the parents. Finally, although there seemed to be a high rate of voluntary arrangements with parents in making out-of-home placements with the family service orientation, in the child protection orientation, the majority of out-of-home placements were compelled through the coercive powers of the state, usually in the form of court orders.

The analysis suggested that the countries under investigation could be clustered into three groups with Anglo-American countries oriented toward child protection, while the Continental European and Nordic countries approached the problem of maltreatment from a family service orientation but differed on the policy of mandatory reporting. As it happens, this grouping parallels Esping-Andersen's (1990) oft-cited classification of liberal (Anglo-American), conservative (Continental), and social democratic (Nordic) welfare state regimes. Despite these distinguishing characteristics, however, there seemed no apparent link between placement rates and the orientation of reporting systems. The United States, with a child protection orientation, and Denmark, with a family service orientation, had the highest out-of-home placement rates in 1992–93, whereas the lowest placement rates were in family service–oriented Netherlands and child protection–oriented England.

Combatting Child Abuse illuminated the alternative perceptions of child abuse and varied policy and practice arrangements in place in different countries. Although primarily focused on the details of different programs and policies, this comparative analysis inevitably drew attention to broader social conditions that influence the scope of the problem and the character of public and professional responses, thus illustrating the potential to deepen our understanding of the problem and develop new possibilities. This work was followed by a flurry of publications that looked at how different countries defined and responded to child abuse and the ways in which different systems operated (Harder & Pringle, 1997; Pringle, 1998; Khoo, Hyvönen, & Nygren, 2002; May-Chahal & Herezog, 2003; Freymond & Cameron, 2006; Cameron, Coady, & Adams, 2007). In most cases, the overriding concern was for researchers and policy makers to look to other countries for practices or ideas they could learn from, to help reform their own systems, which were not coping well with the demands made of them. These efforts had a distinctly normative tendency to be more prescriptive than analytic.

There was a particular interest in comparing European approaches to those employed in Anglo-American countries. The distinction between the *child protection* and *family service orientations* was often adopted (sometimes in a slightly revised way), almost as received wisdom, as the way to represent alternative approaches. The two orientations seemed to provide something of a touchstone for debates in both research-based studies and official, often governmental, reports. The essential features of these orientations are clearly evident; as, for example, in providing a basis for differentiating the "UK/North American" and "continental western European" systems in a report by the Scottish Executive (2002).

Since the mid-1990s, however, much has changed in the realm of child welfare and how states define and deal with their responsibilities for children at risk. This book sets out to identify and analyze these changes and their implications, with a particular focus on assessing the extent to which the child protection and family service orientations continue to provide a helpful framework for understanding and comparing systems in different countries. The chapters in this volume, which includes the nine countries previously studied, as well as Norway, examine efforts to ensure the well-being of children from several perspectives. First, the text describes the basic features of child protection systems in a group of countries that represent the conventional typology of liberal (Anglo-American), conservative/corporatist (Continental European), and social democratic (Nordic) regimes, which has framed much of the field of inquiry on comparative welfare state analyses (Esping-Andersen, 1990). Bringing us up to date, the second objective of this book is to review the current legislative reforms related to child abuse prevention, the definitions of maltreatment, legal criteria for intervention, and administrative processes of referral, along with the empirical picture of current levels of child abuse reporting and placement arrangements. Finally, the chapters analyze the overarching policy developments and trends since the mid-1990s and their implications for reorienting child protection systems and promoting child welfare.

In the course of this study, we struggled with the challenges of formulating common definitions and understanding the various cultural perspectives and different measures used in the countries. Generally, unless otherwise specified, when we speak of children in this volume, the reference is to young people under 18 years of age. The exact connotations of child welfare activities and institutions, such as abuse reporting, investigations, out-of-home placements, and residential settings sometime vary among the countries, and will be specified in such cases. One of the issues that arose was how to convey a perspective on the larger social context in which the ten child welfare systems were embedded. In response to this issue, and as a backdrop to the country-specific analyses of child protection arrangements and trends, we begin with a comparative picture of the broader social policy context that frames the systems in which they operate.

ANALYSIS OF THE BROADER CONTEXT

The promotion of child welfare is a significant political and social challenge in modern democratic states. What are the best methods to guarantee the well-being for children at risk of abuse, neglect, and other dangers that might inflict harm? From a political perspective, the challenge is to craft those public measures to provide for and protect children which do not tread heavily on their parents' rights of privacy and their right to a family life of their own choosing. This issue is accentuated by the fact that children are ascribed strong individual rights in the Convention of the Rights of the Child (CRC) and in national laws, while at the same time being highly dependent on their caregivers to fulfil their rights. What is the appropriate level of public effort to ensure children's rights and safeguard them from harm? States may answer this question differently by taking a narrow or broad responsibility for children's upbringing and education.

Those states that take a narrow range of responsibility tend to focus on protecting children from the risk of harm and providing basic social safety nets; those that take a broad degree of responsibility also protect children from the risk of unequal life outcomes as a result of their social standing or upbringing. The way in which responsibility is constructed (narrowly or broadly) is related to how the child welfare system defines responsibility between the private and the public spheres, and to cultural views on children and the family. That is to say, these systems are nested within a broader policy context, which helps to define the role of the state vis-à-vis the family and the child. The changing balance among these parties is reflected in the 1990s policy debates in England.

There, it was argued that the state's focus on safeguarding children needed to be shifted from a forensic approach to protection toward policies that emphasize participation, prevention, and family support. "The priority," as Parton (1997) explains, "should be kept on helping parents and children in the community in a supportive way and should keep notions of policing and coercive intervention to a minimum."

In constructing the well-known classification of liberal, conservative, and social democratic welfare state regimes, the decommodification of labor was one of the central characteristics initially used to classify social welfare policies linked to each type of welfare state. Later analyses, however, argued that these regimes also varied in their approaches to role of the state, vis-à-vis the family, particularly in the degree to which social welfare family benefits reduced the individual's dependence on kinship—a process known as *defamilialization* (Esping-Andersen, 1999). Family policy expenditures are one of the major measures used to operationally define the degree of defamilialization. Based on a cross-sectional analysis of early 1990 data on family policy spending, for example, Esping-Andersen found a general consistency among the three standard welfare regimes and the degree of defamilialization. That is, in social democratic welfare state regimes, family policies exhibit the highest degree of defamilialization, emphasizing a strong government role, stressing the goal of gender equity and child well-being. There is somewhat less spending on family policies in the conservative (Continental European) regimes, which stress the role of traditional family and discourage female labor force participation—reflecting a modest level of defamilialization. The liberal regimes' approach to family policy has the lowest levels of spending and defamilialization.[1]

To place the child welfare systems of the ten countries in this study within this broader context, we analyze their levels of social expenditures on family policy over several decades. As illustrated in Table 1.1 social expenditures on family policy, which encompass both cash benefits and services, are employed as an analytic lens through which to compare levels of state responsibility for the daily welfare and caring functions of family life. In contrast to Esping-Andersen's

Table 1.1: Social Expenditure on Family Policy: Range of Benefits Covered

New Social Expenditure Database Structure	Old Social Expenditure Database Structure
Family cash benefits	**Family cash benefits**
Family allowances	Family allowances for children
	Family support benefits
Maternity and parental leave	Maternity and parental leave
Other cash benefits	Lone parent cash benefits
	Family other cash benefits
Benefits in kind	**Family services**
Day cares/home-help services	Family day care
	Personal services
	Household services
Other benefits in kind	Household other benefits in kind

Source: The OECD Social Expenditure database (1980–2001).

(1999) cross-sectional study of 1992 data, our analysis presents longitudinal comparisons among the individual countries and among groups of countries clustered within their welfare state regime types. It will also look at the relationships between the levels of expenditure and several measures of child maltreatment and well-being.

But, first let us offer a caveat on comparative data. It has long been recognized that, in addition to the benefits and services distributed directly by government, comprehensive measures of welfare effort should include other sources of social expenditure that promote individual and family well-being. In the mid-1990s, as additional data became available, Adema (1996) and his colleagues at the Organization for Economic Cooperation and Development (OECD) developed a new ledger for social accounting that controls for the effects of costs and benefits from various sources, thus introducing the most rigorous and comprehensive measures of social spending to date. Their net total expenditure index represents the cumulative value of benefits distributed through direct public expenditures, tax expenditures, and publicly mandated private expenditures, reduced by direct and indirect taxes on these benefits, and it adds in the value of voluntary private expenditures, reduced by direct and indirect taxes. Later, they added data that allow analysis of family policy expenditures based on the gross measure of total direct spending and mandated benefits, but without controlling for taxes, tax expenditures, and voluntary spending.[2] All this is to say that the data on total direct spending on family policies offer a rough, but reasonable, estimate for comparisons of the public welfare efforts in this area.

Figure 1.1: Family spending per gross domestic product (GDP) by country 1980–2005

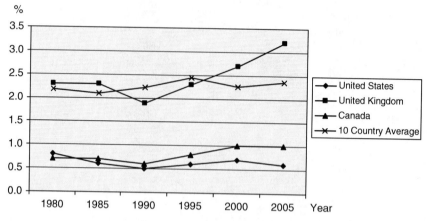

Source: OECD Stat Extracts: 8/25/09.

With this qualification in mind, the data in Figures 1.1 through 1.4 illustrate the pattern of social expenditures on family policy benefits over the 25 years since 1980. The data compare the individual levels of spending for each of the ten countries studied in this volume and the average rates of spending for these countries grouped within the welfare state regime typology.

The first three figures reveal several patterns. Overall, the average spending on family benefits as a percent of gross domestic product (GDP) for the ten countries increased from 1980 to 1995, after which is has slightly declined; but the level of spending in 2005 as a proportion of GDP was still about 10% higher than in 1980. Over the decade from 1995 to 2005, the levels of spending on family policy benefits in the United States, Canada, Germany and the Netherlands were below the ten-country average. The patterns of spending fluctuated over the 25 years in

Figure 1.2: Family spending per gross domestic product (GDP) by country 1980–2005

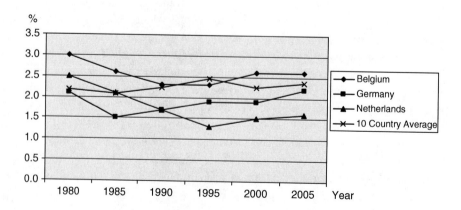

Figure 1.3: Family spending per gross domestic product (GDP) by country 1980–2005

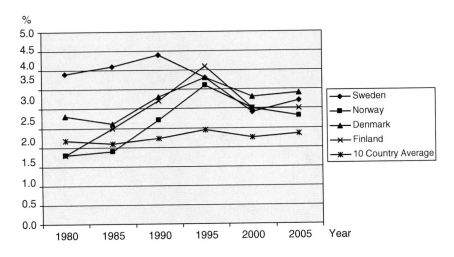

most of the countries. By 2005, Sweden, Denmark, and the U.K. had the highest levels of spending as a percent of their GDPs.

Figure 1.4 presents the patterns of average spending on family policy benefits when the countries are grouped by the types of welfare regimes they are supposed to represent. The findings here indicate shifting patterns of expenditure among these groups. In 1980, there was very little difference in family policy expenditures between the social democratic and the conservative continental European countries. At that time, the countries in both these groups spent as a proportion of GDP almost twice as much as the liberal Anglo-American countries. Evidence of three distinct regimes based on substantially different

Figure 1.4: Average spending per gross domestic product (GDP) by welfare regimes 1980–2005

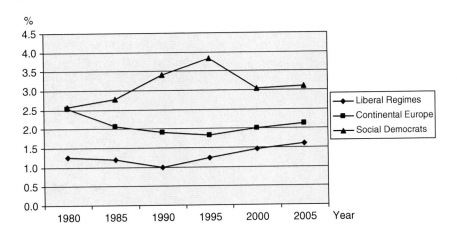

levels of expenditure began to emerge over the period from 1990 to 1995. However, over the decade from 1995 to 2005, the differences have diminished as levels of spending began to converge.[3] Whether the trend toward convergence continues awaits further verification and more detailed analysis of family policy expenditures from all sources.

Aside from signifying a welfare state typology based on varying degrees of defamilialization, to what extent are the different levels of social expenditure on family benefits associated with measures of child welfare? Examining the correlation between family benefit expenditures and measures of child well-being Figure 1.5 shows that the countries' levels of spending on family policy is somewhat related (R sq. = .33; p <.10) to their overall rank (the lower the ranking, the better the health and safety score) on the UNICEF index of health and safety of children, which draws on data about health at birth, immunization rates for children aged 12–23 months, and deaths from accidents and injuries among those from 0 to 19 years of age (UNICEF, 2007).

Measures of child health and safety reflected in Figure 1.5 express broader concerns for child well-being that go beyond immediate protection from physical abuse. On the narrower issue of child abuse, data in Figure 1.6 suggest that a moderate inverse relationship exists (R sq. = .42; p <.05) between family policy expenditures and the most extreme form of child abuse, deaths from child maltreatment. However, in this case the United States is a conspicuous outlier. When the relationship is calculated among the nine other countries (excluding the U.S.) it declines appreciably and is no longer statistically significant (R sq. = .05; p = .58).

Figure 1.5: Spending as % of gross domestic product (GDP) with child well-being ranking (health and safety)

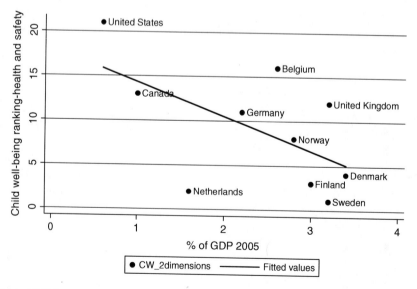

Figure 1.6: Spending as % of gross domestic product (GDP) with child maltreatment deaths

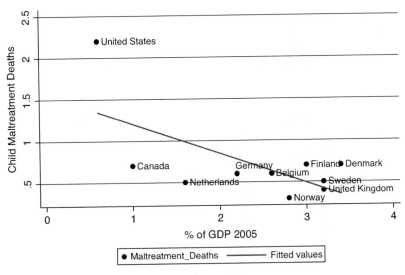

Source: OECD.

Although deaths from maltreatment are sometimes assumed to mirror a society's overall level of child abuse and the effectiveness of its child protection system, there is evidence that these tragic events often occur as a single assault in the absence of a pattern of escalating violence and neglect. Rather than the extreme end of a continuum of abuse and neglect, evidence suggests that infant maltreatment deaths may represent a special category of abuse that occurs within a distinct context, which includes severely mentally disturbed parents (UNICEF, 2003). This may help to explain the lack of relationship between spending on family benefits and the levels of maltreatment deaths among the nine countries. Family benefits may reduce some of the financial stress and pressures of parenting, but they are not designed to treat severe mental illnesses.

Child welfare systems are nested within this macro context of state expenditures on family benefits. However, children's positions in a society and the willingness of states to intervene in the family to protect children and ensure their individual rights do not necessarily correspond to levels of state expenditure and general trends of defamilialization. Narrowing the frame on child welfare, the following chapters offer nuanced and detailed analyses of how the child protection systems in ten countries operate, and the trends and changes that have shaped them since the mid-1990s. The important developments during this period include an emerging tendency to recognize children as independent beings and not only as future adults or as the property of their parents, which raises the issue of how best to achieve an appropriate balance between children's rights and parents' rights. We are conscious that the period since 1994 has seen a wide range of important changes to combat child abuse outside or on the edge of child welfare. These include major developments in criminal justice laws and policies to monitor and provide surveillance for "violent and sex offenders" and a range of new systems to assess the suitability of adults to work with children, a process that in the U.K. is referred to as "vetting and barring." However, these developments are not our focus. The focus of this volume is to examine a range of developments concerning the organizational character and types of intervention that depict the essential features of child welfare systems and the directions in which they are headed, such as movements toward privatization and devolution of child welfare service delivery. In the concluding chapter, we analyze the emerging policies and practice orientations, seeking to provide an in-depth understanding of the different ways in which modern welfare states assume the sensitive and immensely difficult responsibility of intervening in families to advance the well-being of children and to protect those who are at risk.

NOTES

1 Esping-Andersen (1999) suggests that the level of defamilialization based on public provisions showed such a huge gap between the social democratic regimes and all the others, as to form a bimodal distribution. In addition to these three regimes, the study introduces a fourth regime—Southern Europe—which on the measure of public spending on family services as a percent of GDP, falls at the very bottom of the list, with a level of defamilialization below that of the liberal regimes.

2 We did examine the data available on family benefits, which included mandated benefits in addition to direct expenditure. Since the differences here were so small that the outcomes paralleled those based on the analysis of total direct spending, the latter were taken as the final unit for analysis.

3 Analysis of variance among the welfare regimes in the average family spending as a percent of GDP show that the Social Democratic regime spending was significantly higher than the Liberal ($p < .01$) and Continental European ($p < .10$) regimes in 1990 and in 1995 ($p < .1$; $p < 0.01$). By 2005, however, none of the differences in spending among these regimes was statistically significant.

REFERENCES

Adema, W., Einerhand, M., Eklind, B., Lotz, J., & Pearson, M. (1996). *Net public social expenditure*. Labour market and social policy occasional papers no.19. Paris: OECD.

Esping-Andersen, G. (1990). *The three worlds of welfare capitalism*. Princeton, NJ: Princeton University Press.

Cameron, G., Coady, N., & Adams, G.R. (Eds.). (2007). *Moving towards positive systems of child and family welfare: Current issues and future direction.* Waterloo: Wilfrid Laurier University Press.

Freymond, N., & Cameron, G. (Eds.). (2006). *Towards positive systems of child and family welfare: International comparisons of child protection, family service, and community caring systems.* Toronto: University of Toronto Press.

Gilbert, N. (Ed.). (1997). *Combatting child abuse: International perspectives and trends.* New York: Oxford University Press.

Harder, M., & Pringle, K. (Eds.). (1997). *Protecting children in Europe.* Aalborg: Aalborg University Press.

Khoo, E.G., Hyvönen, U., & Nygren, L. (2002). Child welfare protection: Uncovering Swedish and Canadian orientations to social intervention in child maltreatment. *Qualitative Social Work, 1*(4), 451–71.

May-Chahal, C., & Herezog, M. (Eds.). (2003). *Child sexual abuse in Europe.* Strasburg: Council of Europe Publishing.

Parton, N. (1997). *Child protection and family support: Tensions, contradictions and possibilities.* London: Routledge.

Pringle, K. (1998). *Children and social welfare in Europe.* Buckingham: Open University Press.

Scottish Executive. (2002). *'It's everyone's job to make sure I'm alright: Report of the Child Protection Audit and Review.* Edinburgh: Scottish Executive.

UNICEF. (2007). *Child Poverty in perspective: An overview of child well-being in rich countries.* Innocenti Report Card #7. Florence: UNICEF Innocenti Research Centre.

UNICEF. (2003). *A league table of child maltreatment deaths in rich countries.* Innocenti Report Card #5. Florence: UNICEF Innocenti Research Centre.

PART I

ANGLO-AMERICAN SYSTEMS

2

TRENDS AND ISSUES IN THE U.S. CHILD WELFARE SYSTEM

JILL DUERR BERRICK

There is no single child welfare system in the United States. The federal government sets legal standards for establishing roughly similar systems across the 50 states, the District of Columbia, and the U.S. Territories, but state and local variation is significant. Child maltreatment reporting laws, system response activities, social worker practice, and standards for care all vary substantially depending on local law and custom. Within federal minimum standards, states have mandatory reporting laws that identify the types of professionals and/or citizens who are responsible for reporting child maltreatment. All states accepting federal funds must also establish a system for responding to child maltreatment reports; these systems have many similar contours, yet variation is typical. And, when children are separated from parents, states, tribes, and local governments must follow federal criteria for ensuring parents' and children's rights in the legal system. The federal law is clear: For example, agencies must show that "reasonable efforts" are made to prevent child removal, services must be offered to families to support reunification, children must be placed in settings that are the "least restrictive" and, if the child will benefit, close to the birth parent's home (U.S. Department of Health and Human Services [USDHHS], 2009). How closely states and localities adhere to these federal standards varies dramatically; practice variations across jurisdictions abound. This chapter offers general information about the nature of the child welfare system at the federal level, and offers insight at the state level to illustrate these local variations.

CHILD MALTREATMENT

Child maltreatment affects a large number of U.S. children. Of the approximately 82 million children in the U.S. in 2007, an estimated 3.5 million children were reported and assessed for maltreatment. (Table 2.1 provides information on maltreatment reporting and out-of-home placement information for the past decade.) School teachers, police officers, and social service staff made the largest number of maltreatment referrals. Many other professionals are mandated to report suspected child maltreatment depending on state law. These might include medical professionals, therapists, day care providers, fire fighters, clergy, or camp counselors. In some states, animal protection officers and photographic film processors are included among mandated reporters (Reed & Karpilow, 2002). And in two states (Wyoming and New Jersey), all citizens are mandated to report should they harbor a reasonable suspicion of maltreatment (Child Welfare Information Gateway, 2008).

Each state has an established "child abuse hotline" that accepts reports of maltreatment. Staffed by social workers in public agencies, these professionals ask a range of questions of the reporter to help determine the nature of the caller's concern and/or the severity of the maltreatment. State law specifies how quickly staff must respond to the call. In some cases, social workers are required to attempt contact with the family within hours; in cases identified as lower risk, staff may have up to several days to try to meet with the family.

Of all referrals, approximately one-third are "screened-out" by the child welfare agency as inappropriate for a service response. The remaining 62% of reports are "screened-in" and either offered an "assessment" or an "investigation," depending on the state or local jurisdiction. Of the cases "screened-in," approximately one-quarter are ultimately "substantiated," indicating that child protective services (CPS) staff are relatively confident that the circumstances fall under the local jurisdiction's definition of maltreatment.

Each state has great latitude to define child maltreatment, but the federal law sets minimum standards. According to federal law, child maltreatment includes:

> Any recent act or failure to act on the part of a parent or caretaker which results in death, serious physical or emotional harm, sexual abuse or exploitation; or
> An act or failure to act which presents an imminent risk or serious harm.
> (Child Abuse Prevention and Treatment Act, 1974)

In 2007, CPS agencies determined that approximately 800,000 children were victimized by maltreatment. Following patterns from previous years, the large majority of these children were victims of child neglect (59%). Approximately 11% of children suffered from physical abuse, 8% were victims of sexual abuse, and about 4% of children suffered from psychological or emotional maltreatment.[1]

Some evidence suggests that maltreatment in the United States may be declining (Finkelhor & Jones, 2006); in particular, rates of child physical and sexual abuse have declined by over 40%. Other indicators remain constant. Child neglect remains persistently high. Children from low-income families are

Table 2.1

	1994	1997	2004	2007
Rate of child maltreatment reports	43 children per 1,000; 1,988,514 reports [1a]	42 reports per 1,000[2]	42.6 reports per 1,000 children[3]	47.2 per 1,000; 3.2 million[4]
Number of child maltreatment victims and rate per 1,000	938,695 victims[5] 15 victims per 1,000 children	13.9 per 1,000; 984,000 victims[6]	11.9 per 1,000; 872,000 victims[7]	800,000 victims[8] 10.6 per 1,000
Number of children receiving prevention services	—	716,512[9b] or 10.1 per 1,000 children[10]	26.7 children per 1,000; nearly 2,000,000[11]	3.8 million;[12] 50.7 children per 1,000
Number of children placed in care (entries) and rate per 1,000	Data unavailable	299,000[13c] 4.2 per 1,000	268,000 removed from their home[14] 3.6 per 1,000	303,000[15] 4 per 1,000
Number of children in out-of-home care and rate per 1,000	Data unavailable	559,000[16] 8 per 1,000	517,000 in foster care[17] 7.15 per 1,000	6 per 1,000;[18] 510,000
Average age of children in care	Data unavailable	9.6 years[19]	10.1 years[20]	9.8 years[21]
Number of children in regular foster care and rate per 1,000	Data unavailable	48% of all children in care; 266,183[22]	238,084; 46% of all children in out-of-home care[23]	46% or 236,911[24]
Number of children in kinship foster care and rate per 1,000	Data unavailable	28% or 158,611[25]	122,528; 24% of all children in out-of-home care[26]	124,571; 24% of all children in out-of-home care[27]
Number of children in group and/or residential care and rate per 1,000	Data unavailable	7% or 41,223[28]	97,194; 19% of all children in out-of-home care[29]	86,475; 17% of all children in out-of-home care[30]
Proportion of children of color in out-of-home care	Data unavailable	61%[31]	64%[32]	63.9%[33]

(Continued)

Table 2.1 *(contd.)*

	1994	1997	2004	2007
Number of child deaths relating to maltreatment and rate per 1,000	996[34] 2 per 100,000	1,197[35] 1.7 children per 100,000 children in the general population or 123 child fatalities per 100,000 victims of maltreatment	1,490 2.03 deaths per 100,000[36]	1,760 2.35 deaths per 100,000[37]
U.S. median income	$ 34,027[38]	$ 37,005[39]	$ $44,389[40]	$50,233[41]

Sources:

[1] U.S. Department of Health and Human Services, National Center on Child Abuse and Neglect, Child Maltreatment 1995: Reports from the States to the National Child Abuse and Neglect Data System (Washington, DC: U.S. Government Printing Office, 1997).

[a] Number shown is for 1995 as a close approximation to the likely 1994 figures, individual children may have been counted more than once.

[2] U.S. Department of Health and Human Services, Administration on Children, Youth and Families, Child Maltreatment 1997: Reports from the States to the National Child Abuse and Neglect Data System (Washington, DC: U.S. Government Printing Office, 1999).

[3] U.S. Department of Health and Human Service, Administration for Children and Families, Administration on Children, Youth and Families, Children's Bureau. Preliminary Estimates for FY 2004 as of June 2006 (11). Retrieved from www.acf.hhs.gov/programs/cb/stats_research/afcars/tar/report11.htm

[4] U.S. Department of Health and Human Services, Administration on Children, Youth and Families. Child Maltreatment 2007 (Washington, DC: U.S. Government Printing Office, 2009). Retrieved from http://www.acf.hhs.gov/programs/cb/pubs/cm07/index.htm.

[5] U.S. Department of Health and Human Services, National Center on Child Abuse and Neglect, Child Maltreatment 1995: Reports from the States to the National Child Abuse and Neglect Data System (Washington, DC: U.S. Government Printing Office, 1997).

[6] Same as source number 2.

[7] Same as source number 3.

[8] Same as source number 4.

[9] U.S. Department of Health and Human Services, Administration on Children, Youth and Families, Child Maltreatment 1997: Reports from the States to the National Child Abuse and Neglect Data System (Washington, DC: U.S. Government Printing Office, 1999).

[b] Only 28 states reporting.

[10] U.S. Bureau of the Census, Current Population Reports, Series P23–194, Population Profile of the United States: 1997, p. 48. U.S. Government Printing Office, Washington, DC, 1998. Retrieved from http://www.census.gov/prod/3/98pubs/p23–194.pdf retrieved 8/3/09.

[11] Same as source number 3.

[12] Same as source number 4.

[13] U.S. Department of Health and Human Services, Administration for Children and Families, Administration on Children, Youth and Families, Children's Bureau, Preliminary Estimates for FY 2005 as of September 2006 (12). Retrieved from www.acf.hhs.gov/programs/cb/stats_research/afcars/tar/report12.htm

[c] 1998 figures used as a likely approximation.

[14] Same as source number 3.

[15] U.S. Department of Health and Human Services (2008). Trends in foster care and adoption. AFCARS Report #14. Washington, D.C.: U.S. DHHS Administration for Children and Families. Retrieved from http://www.acf.hhs.gov/programs/cb/stats_research/afcars/tar/report14.htm.

[16] U.S. Department of Health and Human Services, Administration for Children and Families, Administration on Children, Youth and Families, Children's Bureau, Preliminary Estimates for FY 2005 as of September 2006 (12). Retrieved from www.acf.hhs.gov/programs/cb/stats_research/afcars/tar/report12.htm.

Table 2.1 (*contd.*)

[17] U.S. Department of Health and Human Service, Administration for Children and Families, Administration on Children, Youth and Families, Children's Bureau. Preliminary Estimates for FY 2004 as of June 2006 (11). Retrieved from www.acf.hhs.gov/programs/cb/stats_research/afcars/tar/report11.htm.
Source: U.S. Census Bureau, Census 2000 Summary File 1, Matrices P13 and PCT12. Retrieved from http://factfinder.census.gov/servlet/QTTable? bm=y&-geo_id=01000US&-qr_name=DEC_2000_SF1_U_QTP1&-ds_name=DEC_2000_SF1_U. Based on 2000 census of 72,293,812 total children under 18 years old.
[18] Same as source number 15.
[19] Same as source number 16.
[20] Same as source number 3.
[21] Same as source number 15.
[22] Same as source number 16.
[23] Same as source number 3.
[24] Same as source number 15.
[25] Same as source number 16.
[26] Same as source number 3.
[27] U.S. Department of Health and Human Services. (2008). Trends in foster care and adoption. AFCARS Report #14. Washington, D.C.: U.S. DHHS Administration for Children and Families. Retrieved from http://www.acf.hhs.gov/programs/cb/stats_research/afcars/tar/report14.htm. (Figures are for 2006).
[28] Same as source number 16.
[29] Same as source number 3.
[30] U.S. Department of Health and Human Services (2008). Trends in foster care and adoption. AFCARS Report #14. Washington, D.C.: U.S. DHHS Administration for Children and Families. Retrieved from http://www.acf.hhs.gov/programs/cb/stats_research/afcars/tar/report14.htm (Figures are for 2006.)
[31] Same as source number 16.
[32] Same as source number 3.
[33] U.S. Department of Health and Human Services. (2008). Trends in foster care and adoption. AFCARS Report #14. Washington, D.C.: U.S. DHHS Administration for Children and Families. Retrieved from http://www.acf.hhs.gov/programs/cb/stats_research/afcars/tar/report14.htm (Figures are for 2006.)
[34] Same as source number 34.
[35] Same as source number 2.
[36] Same as source number 3.
[37] Same as source number 4.
[38] U.S. Census Bureau, Housing and Household Economic Statistics Division. Last Revised: May 13, 2005 Retrieved from http://www.census.gov/hhes/www/income/mednhhld/ta5.html.
[39] Source: U.S. Census Bureau Public Information Office. Last Revised: April 12, 2001. Retrieved from http://www.census.gov/Press-Release/cb98-175.html.
[40] Source: U.S. Census Bureau, Public Information Office, Last Revised: April 17, 2009 Retrieved from http://www.census.gov/Press-Release/www/releases/archives/income_wealth/005647.html
[41] Source: U.S. Census Bureau, Public Information Office, Last Revised: April 17, 2009. Retrieved from http://www.census.gov/Press-Release/www/releases/archives/income_wealth/012528.html

five times more likely to be maltreated than other children. And African American and American Indian children are overrepresented as victims of maltreatment (Sedlak et al., 2010).

WHAT IS THE SYSTEM RESPONSE?

The traditional CPS response to an allegation of maltreatment includes an investigation of the referral, evidence-gathering pertaining to the allegation of maltreatment, and a determination of the perpetrator of harm. Children's safety and future risk of harm is then assessed to determine the level of services and/or degree of state intervention required. Determining risk is, of course, tricky business. In California, for example, each of the 58 counties uses distinctive strategies for training their social workers in assessing risk; about half of the counties use a research-based *structured decision making* tool to guide decision making, and many counties rely on worker judgment, consensus-based tools, or other strategies to determine each child's current safety and future risk of harm. The development of evidence-based strategies for determining risk remains one of the signature areas for child welfare reform in the United States, as one strategy to better promote fairness and equitable services to children and families of diverse racial, ethnic, and socioeconomic backgrounds (see Gambrill & Shlonsky, 2000).

Recent initiatives in over 20 U.S. states involve the use of *differential response* as an alternative to the traditional CPS investigation. Under differential response, families reported for child maltreatment and identified as low- to moderate-risk are offered an *assessment* rather than an *investigation*. Families' circumstances are examined for their needs; *perpetrators*, *victims*, and notions of *substantiation* are eliminated. The purpose of the new approach is to develop a response to families that is nonadversarial and that invites families' voluntary cooperation with services without the heavy hand of the state (Kaplan & Merkel-Holguin, 2008). In cases of high risk or serious cases of harm, the traditional CPS response is invoked. In these cases, maltreatment reports may be cross-referred to local police officials depending on the type of maltreatment (e.g., sexual abuse is more likely to be cross-referred) or the severity of the harm (Cross, Finkelhor, & Ormrod, 2005). Although gaining ground in its popularity, differential response is as yet an untested child welfare strategy. Studies of the approach's effectiveness are equivocal, at best (see Conley & Berrick, 2008 for a review).

The large majority of families reported for maltreatment receive short-term, in-home services delivered by social workers who are employed by public or private nonprofit agencies (USDHHS, 2007). These services are designed to assess family needs, shore up family strengths, and connect parents and children to useful services. In some jurisdictions, services may be more or less available, waiting lists may or may not exist, and some families may be matched with services that offer limited benefits. Some families receive services mandated by the courts and some receive assistance under voluntary agreements. Voluntary services are usually time-limited (typically up to 6 months) and may include services provided in the home or voluntary placement of children outside of the home.

According to a nationally representative study of children who were investigated for maltreatment (some of whose cases were later substantiated and others whose cases were closed), about one-half had been reported previously to the child welfare system for maltreatment. Child welfare workers interviewed for the study indicated that among children's primary caregivers, about one in ten were abusing alcohol, one in ten were abusing drugs, 12% had been arrested within the previous 3 months (and one-third had been arrested at some point in their lifetime), 15% had a serious mental health problem, 7% had a cognitive impairment, and 5% had a physical disability. One-third of children had witnessed intimate partner violence in the home, and approximately one-half of all families had incomes below the federal poverty line (NSCAW, 2005). Other research indicates that families experiencing significant economic hardships such as food or housing insecurity, diaper shortages, or utilities recently shut off are at particularly high risk for child welfare involvement (Shook, 1999).

Children in these families presented numerous risks. Among very young children (aged 0–3), over half were at risk for developmental delay; their cognitive and language abilities were well below norms for the general population. Children aged 4 and older faced challenges in their social functioning, with behavior problems, and depression at rates well above that found among children in the general U.S. population (NSCAW, 2005).

Some children live in substantially risky homes. Indeed, in 2007, over 1,500 children died as a result of maltreatment. Whether due to better reporting systems or an actual increase in the incidence of fatalities, the number and rate of child fatalities has increased over the past 5 years (USDHHS, 2007). More than half of these children were under the age of 1 year, and the vast majority of perpetrators were these children's parents. About 12% of children had had previous contact with a child welfare agency (another 2% of children were victimized after they were returned to their parents following a stay in foster care).

OUT-OF-HOME CARE

The large majority of children reported for maltreatment either receive no services (because their report is screened out at the hotline) or voluntary preventive services. One estimate suggests that almost 4 million children received some child abuse prevention services during 2007 (USDHHS, 2007). But a rather smaller number of children live in family situations that are so harmful or pose such extreme risk that they are separated from their parents, either temporarily or permanently, by the state. Some evidence indicates that the characteristics of children and families involved in out-of-home care are an important yet distinctive subgroup of those families reported for maltreatment. Children placed in foster care are more likely to come from families with single parents, with very low incomes, with mothers who are either very young or older than 40, and who are single parents. At birth, children are more likely not to have benefited from prenatal care, and to be born with low birthweight (Needell & Barth, 1998).

From 1999 to 2008, the number of children in out-of-home care declined from about 560,000 to approximately 460,000. This decline translates into approximately .6% of U.S. children living in state-sponsored out-of-home care (down from about .7% a decade earlier) (USDHHS, 2008). Estimates indicate that approximately 300,000 children are removed from their homes every year and placed in out-of-home care (USDHHS, 2008). Some children remain in care for very short stays. In California, for example, of the approximately 33,000 children who entered care in 2007, about 13% remained in care for only 1 week or less (Needell et al., 2009). But for others, their stay in care may be longer. According to the U.S. Department of Health and Human Services (USDHHS), the average length of stay for children in foster care is 28 months; about one-quarter of children stay for 3 years or more (USDHHS, 2008).

When an involuntary placement is recommended, social workers must present evidence to a judicial officer in dependency court demonstrating the child's harm or risk of harm. (In cases of serious harm, the perpetrator may be arrested and may also face prosecution in criminal court.) Court officials make the determination to detain the child and, based upon the recommendation of the social worker, decide where a child will be placed. Detention hearings must occur within a short timeframe following the child's removal from his or her parent's home; subsequent court hearings occur regularly (every 3–6 months, depending on the state or county) to assess the child's circumstances and the parents' progress toward reunification with the child.

POLICY BACKDROP

Federal laws developed over the past 40 years have helped to shape the scope and nature of the child welfare system in the United States. The Child Abuse Prevention and Treatment Act (1974: P.L. 93–247) provided federal funding to help support the development of child abuse reporting systems and procedures for managing incoming maltreatment reports. In 1980, the Adoption Assistance and Child Welfare Act (P.L. 96–272) specified the procedures for determining when and if children could be involuntarily separated from parents and the obligations of the state to support parents in their efforts to care for their children safely at home or, if impossible to do so, to regain custody of their children rapidly following family separation. Federal funds were made available to support children's out-of-home placements and their adoption. Modest funding was also made available to develop maltreatment prevention efforts, and courts were required to first determine whether agencies had made reasonable efforts to maintain children in their birth parents' homes prior to an involuntary separation.

In contrast to the provisions of the 1993 federal legislation (referred to generally as the Family Preservation and Family Support provisions of P.L. 103–66), which offered a mechanism for funding support services to birth families, federal policy in 1994, 1996, and 1997 was concerned less with children's birth families and more with children's opportunities to live in new families created through adoption. The Multi-Ethnic Placement Act (1994: P.L. 103–382) and the

Interethnic Adoption provisions (1996: P.L. 104–188) were designed to make it easier to carry out transracial adoptive placements for children of color. The Adoption and Safe Families Act of 1997 (ASFA—P.L. 105–89) made it easier to expedite adoption when reunification was not feasible. In addition to its adoption provisions, ASFA included other components designed to give shape and substance to the child welfare system. That law specified the overarching goals of the child protection system in the United States and reduced the time available to birth parents to reunify with their children. According to the law, the fundamental goal of the child protection system is ensuring child safety, followed by supporting permanency for children, and finally securing children's well-being. In the context of child welfare, *permanency* refers to children's permanent, life-long connections with a secure, adult caregiver. In ideal circumstances, this would include children's opportunities to secure both legal and affective connections to a primary caregiver. The federal law also specifies the optimal order of children's permanency arrangements including, first and foremost, children's reunion with their birth parent (referred to as reunification), whenever the parent can provide a safe home environment for the child. If, after offered services and time, a child's parent is unable to provide permanent care, child welfare workers must seek alternative permanent arrangements for the child either in the home of a relative, in an adoptive home, or through legal guardianship.

While separated from their child, parents are given 12 months (with a possible extension of up to 6 additional months) to make changes in the circumstances that placed the child at risk of harm. The child welfare agency is also under obligation to refer parents to services that will support them in their efforts to make these changes. A court-ordered case plan is usually developed that specifies the obligations of the agency to provide or to refer to services, and the obligations of the parent to seek out and engage in services. During the child's stay in care, the parent is offered legal services to help give voice to his or her concerns within the courtroom, and judges regularly review the case to determine the parent's progress in meeting the case plan.

The child placed in out-of-home care may live in one of an array of different placement settings. Federal law prioritizes placement with a relative. About one-quarter of all children in out-of-home care in 2007 were living with relatives (USDHHS, 2008). If an appropriate relative is not available or able to provide care, the child must be placed in the least restrictive setting available. For almost half of U.S. children (46%), this means a nonrelative foster home. Depending on the child's needs and challenges, more restrictive placements may be necessary, such as a group home or institution. Nationally, these placement settings are used for 7% and 10% of children, respectively, but great variation exists across all of these placement types depending upon local practice. Payments to children's care providers vary greatly by jurisdiction and by placement type. On average, nonrelative foster parents receive approximately $400 per month, per child (U.S. Ways and Means Committee, 2004). This represents an income of approximately 9% of the U.S. median income. Importantly, according to the federal government, this amount is 37% below the minimum required to raise a child in a low-income family (Lino, 2006).

Incorporated into the concept of permanency is the notion of stability. While children reside in out-of-home care, however, a relatively small proportion experience stability of care. In California, for example, among children who were in care for 1 year, about one-third (29%) lived in a single care setting for the duration of that 12-month period, another one-third (35%) lived in two different settings, one-fifth (18.4%) lived in three, and one-tenth (8.8%) lived in four placements (Needell et al., 2008). The longer a child resides in care, and the older the child, the greater likelihood they experience placement instability (Sullivan & van Zyl, 2008). This is of particular concern as placement changes are associated with an increase in children's externalizing problems and internalizing disorders (Newton, Litrownik, & Landsverk, 2000; Hussey & Guo, 2005).

In addition to out-of-home care, children whose care and custody has been transferred to the state must receive the health, mental health, and educational services they require to meet their needs. Some estimates indicate that between one-third and two-thirds of children in foster care have a chronic health condition (Takayama, Wolfe, & Coulter, 1998; Jee et al., 2006). Including children with behavioral, emotional, or developmental concerns, upwards of 80% of all children in care have a special health-related service need (Leslie et al., 2005). According to the National Survey of Child and Adolescent Well-being (NSCAW), about one-half of all school-aged children have mental health needs that require services, but less than one in five children receive such services while residing in out-of-home care (NSCAW, n.d.). Given foster children's cognitive and academic challenges, many also require additional educational supports, yet according to the NSCAW, only about one-half of children who might otherwise qualify for special educational services are actually receiving these services (NSCAW, n.d).

EXITS FROM OUT-OF-HOME CARE

Just over half of all children exit the foster care system through reunification with their birth parent (Wulczyn, 2004). The large majority of these reunifications take place within 6 months following placement (Connell et al., 2006). Unfortunately, between 15%–30% of reunifications result in reentries to care, and the more rapidly children reunify with their birth parents, the more likely a reentry will occur (Courtney, 1995; Fuller, 2005).

Children who can not reunify with birth parents are given other opportunities to develop lasting, legally permanent relationships with new families. Since 1997, the federal government has placed renewed emphasis on adoption for children who otherwise cannot go home. The Adoption and Safe Family Act of 1997 (P.L. 105–89) promoted the theme of timely permanence for foster children through the reduction of birth parent reunification time frames, the mandate of developing concurrent plans, and creation of performance-based financial incentives to reward states for increasing their adoption rates (Wulczyn & Hislop, 2002). The "Adoption 2002" goals established by the Clinton administration also set a framework for a renewed emphasis on adoption (ACF News, 2000). Based upon reports from the USDHHS (2003), the number of children adopted from foster care increased from 1998 to 2002, from 36,000 to 51,000. Since that time, the number of finalized adoptions has remained relatively stable (Barth, Wulczyn, & Crea, 2005).

More recently, a 2008 federal law has shown policy makers' continued enthusiasm for adoption as a permanency option for children who cannot reunify. Under the Fostering Connections to Success and Increasing Adoption Act of 2008 (P.L. 110–351), states were given $4,000 incentives for each child adopted over and above that state's base number of adoptions from the year 2002. For children over the age of 9, the fiscal incentive increases to $8,000 (Fostering Connections to Success, 2008). It should be noted that no fiscal incentives exist for parents who successfully reunify.

Unlike reunification, adoption is generally considered a relatively stable and lasting placement for children. Adoption disruption rates range from 6% to 11%, depending on the research study examined and the definition used (Coakley & Berrick, 2008). Disruption generally refers to a change in placement prior to legal finalization. Adoption dissolution—termination of the already finalized adoption—is generally considered a relatively rare event, although rates are difficult to track (Festinger, 2002).

Although adoption is used as one strategy to support children's permanency, it is more often used with nonrelative caregivers than with relatives. Grandparents, aunts, and uncles are sometimes reluctant to adopt the children in their care because the legal proceedings require that the birth parents' legal and custodial rights to the child are permanently severed. Instead, many relative caregivers prefer legal guardianship as a legally binding option that transfers the child's custody away from the state and to the guardian. Parental rights are left intact, and the parent can petition the court for the child's return should the parent's circumstances improve in the future.

Legal guardianship with kin was recently given significant legitimacy and federal financial support following research studies indicating its cost savings compared to long-term foster care (Testa, 2002). But little is known about the long-term stability of legal guardianship arrangements for children. Estimates of disrupted guardianships range from 4% (Testa, 2004; Webster, Magruder & Shlonsky, 2008[2]), to 33% (in press).

CURRENT POLICY AND PRACTICE CONTROVERSIES

Throughout the late 1980s and 1990s, the foster care caseload in the United States expanded very rapidly. Many suggest that this was due, in large part, to significant increases in the use of crack cocaine among women in urban areas. Concomitantly, large numbers of infants were placed in foster care, reunification rates dropped, and adoption rates stagnated (Berrick, Barth, Needell, & Jonson-Reid, 1998). Emerging from that crisis at the beginning of this century, most child welfare systems were in a state of disarray. No state passed its federally mandated Child and Family Service Review, an accountability mechanism developed by the U.S. Children's Bureau to assess child welfare system performance in the areas of safety, permanency, and stability. In addition, two-thirds of states were in litigation as a result of class-action lawsuits (Kosanovich & Joseph, 2005). Some of these lawsuits were especially noteworthy. In New York, the "Wilder" decision took over 20 years to resolve, yet it sparked a host of reforms touching almost every feature of that state's child welfare system (Bernstein, 2001). Other notable examples include Illinois where, pressed by the arm of the law, significant changes were made in kinship foster care, family assessment, and permanency (see Testa, 2010).

Using the challenging conditions of child welfare as an opportunity for change, many states and local jurisdictions initiated significant reform efforts, many of which are ongoing. Although many changes are apace in child welfare, two related areas are targeted here for discussion. They include efforts to embrace *family-centered practice,* and *cultural and community continuity.*

Family-Centered Practice

In light of the central role that biological and extended family members play in raising children, an important area for reform includes a range of practice strategies that give biological parents greater voice in decision making about their children and about their own service needs. Family Group Decision Making, imported from New Zealand and modified for the U.S. context, is used increasingly to bring parents, family members, and friends into a circle of support for the birth family (Burford, 2009). Biological parents are also used as service providers, offering peer mentoring support to other birth parents new to the child welfare system (Frame, Conley, & Berrick, 2006). And, a range of efforts are now under way to identify and locate extended family members who can play a role in assisting birth parents and children. Some of these efforts—generally referred to as Family Finding—are used as a strategy to solicit relatives as children's foster parents, and others are used as a means of diverting children away from foster care and into relatives' homes outside of the formal child welfare system (Casey Family Services, 2008).

Cultural and Community Continuity

In light of the significant overrepresentation of African American and Native American children in the child welfare system (Derezotes, Poertner, & Testa, 2004), many initiatives are in progress to better understand the causes of dispro-portionality and to address racial and ethnic disparities. One assumption under-lying racial disproportionality is that child welfare workers may unwittingly make biased decisions relating to foster care entries and exits (Drake, Lee, & Jonson-Reid, 2009), especially in light of the fact that children of color are not overrepre-sented at the first point of child welfare contact: the child abuse hotline (Ards et al., 2003). Addressing this assumption, many child welfare reforms are making greater use of community-based family support services offered by culturally con-sonant staff who are assumed to hold more strengths-oriented perspectives about vulnerable families. For those children who are ultimately placed in out-of-home care and who cannot live with extended family, the values of cultural and com-munity continuity also require that children are placed in their neighborhood of origin, close to birth parents, schools, churches, and peers (Berrick, 2006).

DISCUSSION

The changes taking place in child welfare practice have been met with great enthusiasm by social workers eager to see a broken child welfare system made whole. At first blush, the new practices appear noncontroversial, as the princi-ples upon which they are based—family-centered practice and cultural and community continuity—have obvious merit. Yet, unbridled enthusiasm for these principles can sometimes result in otherwise unrecognized hazards that a critical examination might reveal. For example, the hallmark of family-centered practice is an increasing reliance on kin as part of a natural support for birth families. In some jurisdictions, child welfare agencies have been especially aggressive in their efforts to locate relatives who might care for children in need of protection. In some cases, relatives are assessed to discern their appropriate-ness as children's caregivers and are then approved as formal foster parents. Once a formal part of the child welfare system, however, the evidence suggests they are given minimal support, no training, and only a modest degree of over-sight (Geen, 2003). In other jurisdictions, however, kin are used as a diversion from the child welfare system altogether. These kin, otherwise referred to as "voluntary kin" (Malm & Geen, 2003) are neither foster parents nor private caregivers making their own family living arrangements. Voluntary kin have been identified and solicited as children's caregivers by agents of the state, but they provide this care outside of the auspices of the state.

The obvious benefit of voluntary kinship care is that it supports children's connections to family at the same time that it has the potential to significantly reduce the foster care caseload in the U.S., thereby shrinking public expenditures dramatically. Presumably, if relatives can be identified early on, so that large numbers of children can be diverted from public care, then the children remaining in the public child welfare system will include only those without a viable extended family.

The hazard, of course, is that private arrangements relieve public agencies of oversight responsibilities regarding children's protection, lessen their obligation to support reunification efforts, and absolve child welfare from accountability for child and family outcomes. More worrisome, a close examination of children currently served through voluntary kinship care suggests that they are significantly underprivileged. These kin caregivers are more economically and socially disadvantaged than kin providing public foster care and are also more disadvantaged than kin who have made private arrangements with family members unrelated to the child welfare system (Urban Institute, 2001).[3] In addition, the children most likely diverted into voluntary kinship care are disproportionately African American and Native American, as historical trends suggest their greater reliance on kinship care compared to other ethnic groups (NSCAW, 2001). The fact that African American and Native American children are disproportionately served by this family-centered practice is intentional. Voluntary kinship care is also representative of culturally consonant practice, as children of color can thus avoid potential transracial foster care placements and their disproportionate representation in the formal child welfare system can be erased.

But the result of these voluntary diversions from the public child welfare system may be a two-tiered system, each of which will serve a different group of vulnerable children. One system will be formalized, funded, supervised, supported, and monitored by the courts. The caregivers in this system, and the system itself, while flawed, will at least offer the majority of children in its care social and economic advantages that they would not receive in their home of origin, and in the best-case scenario, rehabilitative care that will help children recover from the trauma of maltreatment. Given current trends, the first-tiered system will largely serve Caucasian children in America.

The second-tiered system will be informal, poorly funded, loosely supported, and unsupervised. Parents' and children's entitlement rights to services will be abandoned, and parents' custodial rights to their children will be become murky, at best. The caregivers, although related to the child by blood, will not generally provide therapeutic care, and the social and economic conditions of children's lives will be unchanged from their home of origin. The second-tiered system will generally serve African American and Native American children. Although the approach will be culturally consonant, it will further disadvantage children who already suffer disproportionately along a number of social indicators in the United States.

How these changing child welfare practices will be translated into policy is as yet unknown. Recent federal policy making in child welfare was not only surprising but also contradictory. In the waning days of the G.W. Bush administration, the President signed the Fostering Connections to Success and Increasing Adoptions Act. That policy showed lawmakers' endorsement of public foster care and its potential benefits for children as it allowed states to extend foster care subsidies to youth ages 18–21 with federal financial support. Such a substantial federal investment could have only occurred were lawmakers convinced of the merits of foster care for children's continued protection into emerging adulthood.

The federal law also shows policy makers' cautious support for a hybrid model of public/private kinship care. That is, states will now receive federal subsidies for kinship foster parents who exit the child welfare system to serve as children's private legal guardians. In such a model, kin enter into their relationship with the state through the front door of the public child welfare agency as kinship foster parents, yet they exit through a public/private back door, taking with them the monthly subsidy (public) but leaving behind the support, services, and supervision of the state-sponsored system (private). From federal lawmakers' standpoint, the result is reduced expenditures (as the administrative and judicial oversight costs are eliminated) for those children who would otherwise remain in long-term foster care. The result for children is that they are released into a nonsystem of supervision and support.

Finally, showing support for Family Finding activities designed to connect children in or at-risk of foster care placement with family members, the federal law supports the establishment of up to 30 Family Connection grants to assist states and local agencies as they create or enhance their capacity for intensive family-finding activities (Center for Law and Social Policy, 2009). The measure falls short of a policy proscription requiring diversion to voluntary kinship care, but suggests federal policy makers' interest in cautiously pursuing this new approach to child welfare practice.

CONCLUSION

As child welfare reform continues across the states, many questions remain unanswered about the fundamental role of the child protection system vis-à-vis children and families. U.S. policy has long shown ambivalence toward offering substantial family support programs that might alleviate family stress and reduce the need for protective interventions (Berrick, 2008). As a result, when family crises are acute, the hand of the state has always been fairly heavy and swift in its response. Now, in an effort to wrap the hand of the state in softer material, we risk withdrawing a hand of support altogether. It is challenging to predict the direction of future child welfare policy, but difficult dialogues about the responsibility of the state, the role of the family, and the place of the community in protecting children and supporting families are likely in the years ahead.

NOTES

1   The remaining 18% of children's maltreatment was categorized into smaller categories, such as "medical neglect," or "abandonment." Approximately 13% of children were victims of multiple types of maltreatment.

2   Webster, Magruder, and Shlonsky found that 13% of children were reported for maltreatment within 6 years of placement in legal guardianship arrangements with kin and 6% ultimately reentered foster care.

3   According to Urban Institute researchers, about 20% of children residing in kinship foster care face three or more documented risk factors in their kinship home environments. This compares unfavorably with the 8% of children in the general population facing such a high degree of disadvantage. Among children in voluntary kinship placements, 30% face three or more risk factors in their caregiving environment. For more information see: Ehrle, J., Geen, R., & Clark, J. (2001). *Children cared for by relatives: Who are they and how are they faring?* Washington, D.C.: Urban Institute.

REFERENCES

ACF News. (2000). HHS awards adoption bonuses and grants. Washington, D.C.: Administration for Children and Families. Retrieved March 6, 2006 from http://www.acf.hhs.gov/news/press/2000/adopt00.htm.

Ards, S., Myers, S.L., Chung, C., Malkis, A., & Hagerty, B. (2003). Decomposing black-white differences in child maltreatment. *Child Maltreatment, 8*, 112–121.

Barth, R.P., Wulczyn, F., & and Crea, T. (2005). From anticipation to evidence: Research on the Adoption and Safe Families Act. *Virginia Journal of Law and Social Policy, 12*, 371–399.

Bernstein, N. (2001). *The lost children of Wilder*. New York: Vintage books.

Berrick, J.D. (2008). *Take me home: Protecting America's vulnerable children and families*. New York: Oxford University Press.

Berrick, J.D. (2006). Neighborhood-based foster care: A critical examination of location-based placement criteria. *Social Service Review, 80*: 569–583.

Berrick, J.D., Barth, R.P., Needell, B., & Jonson-Reid, M. (1998). *The tender years*. New York: Oxford University Press.

Burford, G. (2009). Family group decision making: Introduction, principles and processes. American Human Association. Retrieved from http://www.americanhumane.org/protecting-children/programs/family-group-decision-making/re_annotated_bibliography/introduction.html.

Casey Family Services. (2008). Kevin Campbell, Pioneer in finding families for children. *Voice magazine*.

Center for Law and Social Policy. (2009). *New help for children raised by grand-parents and other relatives: Questions and answers about the Fostering Connections to Success and Increasing Adoptions Act of 2009*. Washington, D.C.

Child Abuse Prevention and Treatment Act. (1974). (42 U.S.C.A. 5106g) amended by Keeping Children and Families Safe Act, 2003.

Child Welfare Information Gateway. (2008)Mandatory reporters of child abuse and neglectRetrieved fromhttp://www.childwelfare.gov/systemwide/laws_policies/statutes/manda.cfm#backfn1

Coakley, J.F., & Duerr-Berrick, J. (2008). Research review: In a rush to permanency: Preventing adoption disruption. *Journal of Child and Family Social Work, 13*, 101.

Conley, A., & Berrick, J.D. (2008). Implementing differential response in ethnically diverse neighborhoods. *Protecting Children.*

Connell, C.M., Katz, K.H., Saunders, L., & Tebes, J.K. (2006). Leaving foster care: The influence of child and case characteristics on foster care exit rates. *Children and Youth Services Review, 28*, 780–798.

Courtney, M. (1995). Reentry to foster care of children returned to their families. *Social Service Review, 69*, 226–241.

Cross, T.P., Finkelhor, D., & Ormrod, R. (2005). Analysis police involvement in child protective services investigations: Literature review and secondary data. *Child Maltreatment, 10*, 224–244.

Derezotes, D.M., Poertner, J., & Testa, M. (2004). *Race matters*. Washington, D.C.: Child Welfare League of America.

Drake, B., Lee, S.M., & Jonson-Reid, M. (2009). Race and child maltreatment reporting: Are blacks overrepresented? *Children and Youth Services Review, 31*, 309–316.

Festinger, T. (2002). After adoption: Dissolution or permanence? *Child Welfare, 81*, 515–533.

Finkelhor, D., & Jones, L. (2006). Why have child maltreatment and child victimization declined? *Journal of Social Issues, 62*, 685–716.

Fostering Connections to Success and Increasing Adoptions Act of 2008 (H.R. 6893), Social Security Act Title IV, Part E, Sec. 473A. Retrieved from http://www.ssa.gov/OP_Home/ssact/title04/0473A.htm#ft258.

Frame, L.C., Conley, A., & Berrick, J.D. (2006). "The real work is what they do together:" Peer support and child welfare services. *Families in Society, 87*, 509–520.

Fuller, T.L. (2005). Child safety at reunification: A case-control study of maltreatment recurrence following return home from substitute care. *Children and Youth Services Review, 27*, 1293–1306.

Gambrill, E., & Shlonsky, A. (2000). Risk assessment in context. *Children and Youth Services Review, 22*, 813–837.

Geen, R. (2003). *Kinship care: Making the most of a valuable resource*. Washington, D.C.: Urban Institute.

Hussey, D.L, & Guo, S. (2005). Characteristics and trajectories of treatment foster care youth. *Child Welfare, 84*, 485–506.

Jee, S.H., Barth, R.P., Szilagzyi, M.A., Szilagyi, P.G., Aida, M., & Davis, M.M. (2006). Factors associated with chronic conditions among children in foster care. *Journal of Health Care for the Poor and Underserved, 17,* 328–341.

Kaplan, C., & Merkel-Holguin, L. (2008). Another look at the National Study on Differential Response in Child Welfare. *Protecting Children, 23,* 5–21.

Kosanovich, A., & Joseph, R.M. (October 2005). *Child welfare consent decrees: Analysis of 35 court actions from 1995–2005.* Washington, D.C.: Child Welfare League of America.

Leathers, S. J., Falconnier, L., & Spielfogel, J. E. (2010). Predicting family reunification, adoption, and subsidized guardianship among adolescents in foster care. *American Journal of Orthopsychiatry, 80*(3), 422–431.

Leslie, L.K., Gordon, J.N., Meneken, L., Premji, K., Michelmore, K.L., & Ganger, W. (2005). The physical, developmental and mental health needs of young children in child welfare by initial placement type. *Journal of Developmental and Behavioral Pediatrics, 26,* 177–179.

Lino, M. (2006). *Expenditures on children by families, 2005.* Misc. publication no. 1528–2005. Washington, D.C.: U.S. Department of Agriculture, Center for Nutrition Policy and Promotion.

Malm, K., & Geen, R. (2003). *When child welfare agencies rely on voluntary kinship placements.* No. A-61. Washington, D.C.: Urban Institute.

Needell, B. et al. (2008). *Child welfare dynamic report system.* Berkeley: University of California at Berkeley, Center for Social Services Research. Retrieved from http://cssr.berkeley.edu/ucb_childwelfare/Ccfsr.aspx.

Needell, B., & Barth, R.P. (1998). Infants entering foster care compared to other infants using birth status indicators. *Child Abuse & Neglect, 12,* 1179–1187.

Newton, R.R., Litrownik, A.J., & Landsverk, J.A. (2000). Children and youth in foster care: Disentangling the relationship between problem behaviors and number of placements. *Child Abuse and Neglect, 24,* 1363–1374.

NSCAW (National Survey of Child and Adolescent Well-being). (n.d.). Children's cognitive and socioemotional development and their receipt of special educational and mental health services. Research brief No. 3. Retrieved from http://www.acf.hhs.gov/programs/opre/abuse_neglect/nscaw/reports/spec_education/spec_edu.pdf.

NSCAW (National Survey of Child and Adolescent Well-Being). 2005. CPS Sample Component Wave 1: Data Analysis Report. Retrieved from http://www.acf.hhs.gov/programs/opre/abuse_neglect/nscaw/reports/cps_sample/cps_toc.html.

NSCAW (National Survey of Child and Adolescent Well-Being). (2001). *National survey of child and adolescent well-being: One year in foster care report.* Washington, D.C.: U.S. Department of Health and Human Services, Administration for Children, Youth, and Families.

Reed, D., & Karpilow, K. (2002). *Understanding the child welfare system in California: A primer for service providers and policymakers.* Berkeley: California Center for Research on Women and Families. Public Health Institute.

Sedlak, A., Mettenburg, J. Basena, M., Petta, I., McPherson, K., Greene, A., & Li, S. (2010). *The fourth national incidence study of child abuse and neglect.* Washington, D.C.: Department of Health and Human Services, Administration for Children and Families.

Shook, K. (1999). Does the loss of welfare income increase the risk of involvement with the child welfare service system? *Children and Youth Services Review, 21,* 781–814.

Sullivan, D.J., & van Zyl, M. (2008). The well-being of children in foster care: Exploring physical and mental health needs. *Children and Youth Services Review, 30,* 774–786.

Takayama, J.I., Wolfe, E., & Coulter, K.P. (1998). Relationship between reason for placement and medical findings among children in foster care. *Pediatrics, 101,* 201–207.

Testa, M. (2010). *Fostering accountability.* New York: Oxford University Press

Testa, M. (2002). Subsidized guardianship: Testing an idea whose time has finally come. *Social Work Research, 26,* 145–158.

Testa, M. (2004). When children cannot return home. *The Future of Children, 14,* 115–119.

Urban Institute. (2001). *Kinship care: When parents can't parent.* Retrieved November 20, 2007 from http://www.urban.orgurl.cfm?ID+900378&render forprint=1.

U.S. Department of Health and Human Services. (2009). Major federal legislation concerned with child protection, child welfare, and adoption. Child Welfare Information Gateway. Retrieved from www.childwelfare.gov.

U.S. Department of Health and Human Services. (2008). Trends in foster care and adoption. AFCARS Report #14. Washington, D.C.: U.S. DHHS Administration for Children and Families. Retrieved from http://www.acf. hhs.gov/programs/cb/stats_research/afcars/tar/report14.htm.

U.S. Department of Health and Human Services. (2007). Child Maltreatment: 2007. U.S. DHHS Administration for Children and Families. Retrieved from http://www.acf.hhs.gov/programs/cb/pubs/cm07/index.htm.

U.S. House and Ways committee. (2004). *Government Green Book.* Washington D.C.: U.S. Government Printing Office.

Webster, D., Magruder, J., & Shlonsky, A. (2008). *Increasing permanency options in child welfare: The Kinship Guardianship Assistance Payment (Kin-GAP) Program.* Presentation at the National Child Welfare Data and Technology Conference. Washington, D.C.

Winokur, M., Holtan, A., & Valentine, D. (2009). *Kinship care for the safety, permanency, and well-being of children removed from the home for maltreatment.* Campbell Systematic Reviews.

Wulczyn, F., & Hislop, K. (2002). *Growth in the adoption population.* Chicago, IL: Chapin Hall Center for Children.

Wulczyn, F. (2004). Family reunification. *The Future of Children, 14,* 95–112.

3

CANADIAN CHILD WELFARE: CHILD PROTECTION AND THE STATUS QUO[1]

KAREN J. SWIFT

anadian child welfare was cast in *Combatting Child Abuse* (Gilbert,1997) as a system focused on child protection, along with the United States and England, rather than on family services. Although family service is not absent, it remains, in 2009, as a lesser and sometimes invisible goal in the Canadian "system," which is made up of 13 separate jurisdictions. In this chapter, I examine the intensification of protection concerns since 1994, resulting in a "child protection" model entrenched, at least for the time being, as the status quo of Canadian child welfare. I also point out the close association between low-income families and those involved with child protection authorities. In the following pages, some relevant features of Canadian social welfare conditions are introduced, specific features of child welfare in Canada are discussed, and relevant trends affecting the direction of Canadian child welfare practice are examined.

CANADA AND ITS "SOCIAL SAFETY NET"

Canada is a country of spacious and varied geography, a highly diverse population of just over 33 million, about 7 million of whom are aged 17 or under, and a complex governing structure. It is a safe haven for a steady stream of immigrants and refugees, and a country with a reasonably effective social welfare system. Canada is a bilingual country, with French and English as its official languages. About three-quarters of Canada's population live within 100 miles of the American border, and most are urban dwellers. The country's three largest cities,

Vancouver, Toronto, and Montreal, are magnets for people from many different countries, circumstances, and cultures. In Toronto, the majority of the population is now constituted of people of color, and more than 100 different languages are spoken. Further north, the smaller cities are less diverse. The northern parts of most provinces and the far north are thinly populated, mainly by Aboriginal peoples of many different languages and traditions. These features help to shape and explain Canada's contemporary child welfare laws, institutions, and practices.

The country consists of ten provinces of varying size and population and three northern territories that are geographically large and sparsely populated. As a matter of law (British North America Act [BNA], 1867, now the Constitution Act), Canada has separated its powers of governing between the federal and provincial/territorial governments,[2] with the provinces and territories retaining jurisdiction over most matters related to health, education, and welfare, including child welfare. Naturally, there are ongoing disputes about how these provincial and territorial responsibilities are to be funded and implemented, and there is an ever-shifting boundary between the two authorities.

For historically specific reasons, the federal government has responsibility for certain social programs, including Employment Insurance, Old Age Security, the Canada Pension Plan, and the Canada Child Tax Benefit. Up until 1995, provinces and territories received funding for their social programs through the Canada Assistance Plan (CAP), a policy introduced in 1966 that enshrined national standards for welfare policies and guaranteed matching federal funds for every dollar spent by provinces on social welfare programs, based on a core concept of "need."

In 1995, as part of a debt reduction strategy, the federal government changed its formula to a block funding model, called the Canada Health and Social Transfer (CHST), which combined funding for health, education, and social welfare into one block transfer to each province and at the same time reduced national standards and the amount of funding that each province would receive. In fact, the CHST[3] left provinces virtually on their own to fund programs as they saw fit, and many of them lowered social spending considerably in response. Figures published by the Organization for Economic Cooperation and Development (OECD, 2005), which include a broad range of social expenditures, show Canada's social spending at about 16% of the gross domestic product (GDP) as of 2005, ranking just above the United States but well below most European countries. The federal budget of 2007–2008 shows that only $850 million was to be allocated to children's programs out of a total $9.5 billion budgeted for federal transfers overall (Graham et al., 2008).

The change to the CHST reduced the size and scope of welfare state provision, which was one of its objectives. Over the past decade, the number of people in receipt of income assistance has been drastically reduced across Canada, and the benefits, always inadequate, have declined considerably, the result of stringent eligibility restrictions enacted by most provinces. The overall number of people receiving social assistance fell from just over 3 million in 1993 to 1.75 million in 2003 (National Council of Welfare, 2006) in spite of a growing population.

For many years, Canada has had a universal health care system that provides broad access to basic health care for all Canadians and other eligible groups living in Canada. Although the system has been criticized for overly long wait times and some accessibility issues, low-income groups are generally able to access health care when needed. However, this population is disproportionately affected by a severe shortage of affordable housing, a problem that has steadily worsened since 1993, when the federal government eliminated funding for new social housing. Instead, provinces, territories, and private markets were expected to meet the increasing need for low-cost housing, particularly in urban areas (Shapcott, 2001; Hulchanski & Shapcott, 2004). As a result, Canada "now has the most private-sector-dominated, market based housing system and the smallest social housing sector of any Western nation, with the exception of the United States" (Bryant, 2004, p. 218). This means that socially supported housing is in short supply, in both urban and rural areas. The Calgary-based Sheldon Chumir Foundation for Ethics in Leadership released a report, based on statistics from a range of organizations, estimating Canada's homeless population at somewhere between 200,000 and 300,000 people, with another 1.7 million struggling with "housing affordability issues" (Laird, 2007). Laird cites poverty—not substance abuse or mental illness—as the leading cause of homelessness in Canada and identifies specific populations that continue to be overrepresented in homeless counts across Canada, including children, Aboriginal people, and new immigrants.

All Canadian jurisdictions have legislated provisions allowing for maternity leave benefits. Expectant mothers must meet a number of conditions, varying by jurisdiction, such as a specified amount of employment, specified notice time, and maximum length of leave. Canada has no universal child care system, although such a program has often been proposed. Barriers to a national program include the fragmentation of responsibilities between the provinces and the federal government and the substantial involvement of the private sector in the delivery of early childhood programs (Friendly & Ferns, 2005). Quebec is the only province in Canada that has made universal child care a priority, with its plan of charging $7.00 a day for all programs. Somewhat surprisingly, it has been the ruling federal Conservatives who recently put in place a universal child care benefit of $100 per month for every child under 6, the first universal program to be instituted in the country for quite some time. Clearly, this benefit does not even begin to cover the cost of child care, and certainly not any kind of organized care, but it is in keeping with neo-liberal principles of "choice" as opposed to tying the benefit to any particular kind of care or cost.

To summarize, Canada has a social safety net in place that helps to cushion the "social risks" of its capitalist economy and current neo-liberal approach to governing. However, significant holes in the net affect families, for instance the absence of a real child care program. Moreover, the existing programs exclude many people and have reduced benefits to recipients. How do the health and welfare of Canada's children fare in these circumstances? In 1989, Canada's House of Commons unanimously resolved to end child poverty by the year 2000. According to the watchdog group overseeing this promise, almost one in nine Canadian children now live in poverty (Campaign 2000, 2008). This is an improvement from the late 1990s and early years of the 21st century, when approximately one in five children were living below the poverty line, but is about the same as in 1989, when promises of ending child poverty were made. UNICEF ranks Canada 12th of 21 OECD countries in terms of child well-being. Although rated sixth for "material well being" in the 2007 survey, the country ranks only 13th for child health and safety (UNICEF, 2007). Of course, poor children live in poor families, and the family type with the highest incidence of poverty in Canada is the single mother-led family, at 38.4% (Hunter, 2006, p. 186). Aboriginal and children of color are also much more likely than others to be poor. The poverty rate for Aboriginal children in 2000 was 41.1%, whereas the total child poverty rate in that year was 19.1%. The poverty rate for children of color aged 15–17 in that same year was 30.1% compared with 10.9% for children in that age group overall (Hunter, 2006, pp. 186–7). All of these groups are well represented in child protection populations.

Inadequate resources for child health and well-being, especially income support, housing, and child care, are among the reasons why children may be brought into state care (Thoburn, 2007). In a Toronto study conducted in 1992 and repeated in 2000, inadequate housing was identified as a factor in 18.6% (1992) and 20.7% (2000) of cases in which decisions were made to place or keep children in care (Chau et al., 2001). Other studies (e.g., Leschied et al., 2003; Trocmé et al., 2001) show the close association between poverty and child welfare involvement, especially for child neglect. Hence, we might anticipate increases in child protection activity as the economic downturn of 2008 further impacts low-income groups.

THE CANADIAN CHILD PROTECTION SYSTEM

In Canada, each of the 13 provincial and territorial jurisdictions has its own child welfare legislation. This arrangement complicates Canadian research on the topic, since no official, nationally collected statistics exist and there are no universal categories of data. Two national reports on child welfare (Federal Provincial Working Group, 1994, 2001) provide detailed provincial information up to 2001, but no further reports have been issued. In 1998, and again in 2003, the Canadian Incidence Study (CIS), carried out under auspices of the Canadian Centre of Excellence for Child Welfare (CECW), produced our first national examinations of child protection activities, focusing primarily on investigations and substantiated cases of abuse or neglect[4] (Trocmé et al., 2001, 2005). In 2003, the CIS tracked 14,200 maltreatment investigations in 63 of 400 sites across the country. Composite knowledge of activities and trends in the sector relies heavily on information from these studies.[5]

Child welfare as an organized activity originated in Toronto, Ontario, in response to economic conditions producing many homeless and neglected children visible on city streets. The first child protection organization, which still exists, opened in Toronto in 1891, and the first protection law in Canada was passed in 1893. In general, other jurisdictions followed the Ontario initiative, basing their laws and practices on the Toronto model, which used the British doctrine of *parens patriae* (parent of the nation) as its legal basis for intervention into the lives of children and families. The approach from the outset was based on investigation, meager support for "deserving parents," and foster care for children whose parents were deemed unfit to care for them. There were exceptions to this history. In Quebec, the influence of the Catholic Church meant that often the Church was relied upon to step in when parents could not care for their children. Their model focused on institutional care. In recent years, numerous lawsuits have been launched by people who were in these residential facilities as children and who claimed considerable abuse and neglect while in care, and many settlements have been awarded. There have also been settlements in other provinces that used residential facilities to house children.

Another alternative to the Toronto model involves the approach to Aboriginal peoples. Standing as an exception to the usual separation of powers, the federal government is responsible, via the Indian Act, for Canada's Aboriginal population, including housing, health, education and, until the 1950s, child protection. Before the 1950s, the primary form of "child protection" for this population was forced attendance in residential schools for Aboriginal children aged 7 and above for most months of the year.[6] Schools were often run by religious authorities and are now known to have been extremely harsh and often abusive to the children, who were required to shed their cultural practices and languages, based on an official government effort to assimilate them into the general population. Instances of physical and sexual abuse were rampant in these schools, and in 2007, Prime Minister Stephen Harper finally issued a formal apology on behalf of Canada to Aboriginal people affected by this policy. The ongoing effects of this longstanding practice include generations of parents unable to actually know and rear their own children, the total destruction of many families and communities, and continuing overrepresentation of Aboriginal children in the child welfare population.

Beginning in the 1950s, provinces were increasingly authorized to intervene in child protection matters on the lands, known as *reserves*, set aside for status Indians as defined by the Indian Act. At this time, the residential school policy began to soften. However, these new provincial powers resulted in the apprehension of thousands of Aboriginal children, an effect popularly known as the "Sixties Scoop" (Johnston, 1983). Following this, individual bands began to agitate for more control in matters of child protection. There now exist dozens of bands across the country that manage and run their own mandated services. All but one, however, must carry out their activities in accordance with provincial/territorial policy and law.[7] Even so, the number of Aboriginal children in care, and the percentage of them relative to their population numbers, is considered to be a matter of national shame.

In general, Canada takes a residual approach to child welfare, perhaps even more so at this time, since the neo-liberal economic policies currently entrenched in the political system at both federal and provincial levels focus on reducing the cost and scope of the welfare state while encouraging individuals to take responsibility for their own fate. Each province takes account of its own size, resources, and population mix in determining its child welfare policies. In a number of ways, provinces/territories show similarities in law and policy, no doubt because they regularly draw ideas from one another. At the same time, some significant differences exist among jurisdictions with respect to child protection law and practice. One such difference is the definition of a "child" provided in law. Four provinces, Ontario, Saskatchewan, Nova Scotia, and Newfoundland and Labrador, define a child as a person less than 16 years of age, which is in contravention of the definition of a child in the United Nations (UN) Convention on the Rights of the Child (UNCRC). Two provinces, British Columbia and New Brunswick, legislate under 19 as the age of a child, whereas all others are in keeping with the UN definition of 0–17.

Defining Child Maltreatment

The legislation of each jurisdiction is guided by a set of principles, generally focused first on the "best interests of the child," directing authorities to intervene in the "least intrusive" ways, in keeping with the best interests of the child. It is the variable balance between these two principles that determines whether parents' rights or children's rights are weighed more heavily at any given moment. This balance shifts with policy changes, including amendments to legislation, which occur at regular intervals, often spurred by death reviews and media attention to them, or by cost containment motives.

Considerable consistency is seen among the laws of the 13 jurisdictions related to defining a "child in need of protection." All refer in some way to physical and sexual abuse and to various forms of neglect, particularly deprivation, failure to provide medical care, and abandonment. Ontario's law includes the idea of "pattern of neglect" in order to distinguish the isolated incident from longstanding conditions affecting a child. All make some reference also to emotional or psychological harm to children. Most make special reference to children under 12 who engage in dangerous or "criminal" behaviors. This wording relates to Canada's Youth Criminal Justice Act, which has jurisdiction only over criminal behavior by children between the ages of 12 and 18.

Some differences among jurisdictional legislation have a bearing on the balance between parents' and children's rights. For instance, some address the child's needs as the major focus, while others attend primarily to the behaviors of the person in charge, variously named as the "parent," the "guardian," "another person," or "the person having custody, control, or charge" of the child, wordings that influence the attention of workers and the capacity of authorities to intervene.

Although risk and risk technologies have been major factors in child protection over the past decade, only eight of the 13 Canadian jurisdictions include risk in legal definitions of a child in need of protection, and these vary from occasional mentions to an intense focus on risk. Some jurisdictions qualify and expand clauses outlining forms of abuse and neglect, as in Nova Scotia's phrase "there is a substantial risk that the child will suffer physical harm"... (Nova Scotia CFSA, 1990, Ss 22[2]). Ontario's law, which contains by far the most detailed description of a child in need of protection, also has the lowest threshold of intervention, using "risk" rather than substantial risk as its criterion in relation to most of the many clauses in its definition. Several jurisdictions have recently added wording about "severe" or "repeated" domestic violence to the relevant legislation, reflecting concern appearing in recent literature (e.g., Dauvergne & Johnson, n.d.) about the effects on children of witnessing violence in the home.

Most jurisdictions now include some form of "failure to protect" in their child protection laws, a phrase suggesting that a parent, virtually always the mother (Strega et al., 2008), could have or should have known about harm to a child yet failed to act. Generally, failure to protect relates to physical and especially to sexual abuse. These clauses have had a significant impact on mothers and their rights, and have been severely criticized by feminists, who argue that this approach revictimizes the mother by requiring her to protect the child from witnessing beatings inflicted on herself. These clauses also can and have been used to punish the mother for the father's sexual abuse of a child (Krane, 2003).

A few jurisdictions have interesting wording not repeated widely across the country. Quebec's legislation, which is more child focused, defines a child needing protection as one "deprived of the material conditions of life appropriate to his needs and to the resources of his parents or of the person having custody of him" (Youth Protection Act, Quebec, R.S.Q., Section 38[b]). Aligning material conditions with the actual means of the providers can assist in distinguishing neglect from poverty. Legislation in both Prince Edward Island (PEI) and Quebec contains clauses prohibiting a child from being "forced or induced" to do work inappropriate to capacity or to "perform for the public in a manner that is unacceptable for his age" (PEI Child Protection Act, 2003; Youth Protection Act, Quebec, R.S.Q., Section 38 [b]). Two of the territories, Northwest Territories and Nunavut, whose legislation is very similar, refer to specific problems faced by the children they must deal with. Their legislation speaks of substantial risk that a child's health is being harmed by the child's use of "alcohol, drugs, solvents, or similar substances" that the parent is not attending to. Their laws also have clauses addressing "malnutrition" suffered by a child (NWT Child and Family Services Act, Section 7[3]; Nunavut Child and Family Services Act, Section 7[3]).

Mandatory Reporting

All the jurisdictions include mandatory reporting of harm to children in the legislation, and all require "everyone," including those with confidential information, to report. Three jurisdictions, however, exempt lawyer–client privileged information from this requirement. Some laws specify particular professionals who must report, but still emphasize that everyone has this responsibility. Grounds for reporting are usually worded as "belief" or "reasonable belief" of a child's need for protection, "information or suspicion of abuse or neglect" or "knowledge of or probable cause to suspect" that a child has been abandoned or abused. Quebec distinguishes between professionals, who must report based on "reasonable grounds" of a need for protection, and members of the general public, who are required to report suspected cases of abuse or neglect, but are "not bound" to report other situations in which a child may be in danger. Fines ranging from $250 to $25,000 and jail terms of up to 2 years may also be imposed, depending on the jurisdiction, but this rarely occurs.

Investigations

Mandated authorities in the various jurisdictions are under a variety of legislated instructions as to when and how to respond to reports. Some jurisdictions such as Ontario, British Columbia (BC), Alberta, and Nova Scotia, outline very specific methods, time frames, and steps that must be followed when a report is received. Alberta has led the way in the "differential response" approach, which discriminates between those reports requiring a protection response and those that either require no response or that can be referred elsewhere. If referred, the organization receiving the referral must report back to child protection services. Most jurisdictions specify time frames for investigation and decision-making based on the presumed severity of danger to the child. In Nova Scotia, high-risk cases must be investigated within 1 hour, and low-risk can wait for 21 days. Quebec specifies four stages in dealing with reports: risk assessment, safety assessment, evaluation (investigation), and determination of required intervention. Other jurisdictions, especially the territories, have less infrastructure to support such detailed plans and larger geographic areas to cover. Nevertheless, all three territories require a 24-hour response time for investigations of suspected abuse or neglect.

Most jurisdictions now have specific protocols in place for contacting and working with the police if investigations involve allegations of physical or sexual abuse. Only Newfoundland and Labrador seems not to mention police in its policy statements about investigation. Saskatchewan has developed an interesting model for investigations of physical and sexual abuse. They have established two Children's Justice Centres, one in each of its major cities, where there are significant populations of off-reserve Aboriginal people who often suffer from poverty, poor housing conditions, and various kinds of substance abuse problems. The approach is one of joint investigations involving child protection workers and police from the Centres. These staff are specially trained in "nonthreatening" approaches and supportive measures, and the Centres are designed with "soft" interviewing rooms designed to reduce the anxiety of families fearful of losing their children.

The 2003 CIS survey (Trocmé et al., 2005) estimated that 235,315 child protection investigations were conducted in the country in that year (excluding Quebec), with 49% resulting in substantiated cases of child maltreatment (Table 3.1). The largest category, as in 1997, was neglect.

One of the most interesting features of the CIS studies in both 1998 and 2003 is the very small percentage of substantiated cases involving serious physical harm to a child. The 2003 data advise that 71% of substantiated physical abuse cases involved no harm at all to the child, and only 4% involved injuries requiring treatment.[8] The most common kinds of physical harm entailed bruises, cuts, and scrapes (25% of physical abuse cases). Criminal charges were laid in only about 5% of cases.

The data from the 2003 survey were later used in an attempt to estimate whether Aboriginal and children of color were "selected" for investigation more often than Caucasian children (Lavergne et al., 2008). This estimate is treated with caution, since there is no systematic way of recording the ethno-racial backgrounds of children or families in the child protection system, with the exception of Aboriginal children, who are treated in law and practice differently than others.[9] Findings from this study suggest that minority and Aboriginal children are overrepresented, being investigated by child protective services 1.77 times more often than children in the general population. As Table 3.2 shows, the categories examined contain a mix of racial and ethnic groupings.

Table 3.1: Substantiated Child Maltreatment Types and Percentages for 2003 in Canada

Child Maltreatment Type	Percentage of Total
Neglect	34%
Exposure to domestic violence	26%
Physical abuse	23%
Emotional abuse	14%
Sexual abuse	3%
Total	**100%***

Source: Canadian Incidence Study of Reported Child Abuse and Neglect–2003. *Based on a sample of 7,328 substantiated child maltreatment investigations.

Table 3.2: Representation of Ethno-Cultural Groups at System Intake of Canadian Child Protective Services

Ethno Cultural Groups	Percentage in the Canadian Population	Percentage of Reports
Caucasian	82%	67%
Aboriginal	5%	18%
Black	3%	5%
Asian	9%	7%
Latino	0.5%	2%
Arabic	1%	1%

Adopted from Lavergne, C., Dufour, S., Trocmé, N., & Larrivee, M.-C. (2008). Racial disproportionality in child welfare: Visible minority, Aboriginal and caucasian children investigated by Canadian Protective Services. *Child Welfare League of America, 82*(2), 59–76. Study of Canadian Protective Services. Quebec figures not included.

Another CIS survey finding of interest was that atleast two-thirds of open cases had at least one previous case opening, suggesting that whatever action was taken had not been sufficient. A comparison of the 1998 data to the 2003 survey demonstrated a striking 78% increase in the rate of investigations over the period—21.52/1,000 children investigated in 1998 as compared with 38.33/1,000 children in 2003, demonstrating the increasing focus on investigation in that time period.

Substantiations and Responses

All jurisdictions allow for closing a case if it is determined that a child is not in need of protection; some retain records of all reports, including those not verified, and some do not. In Ontario, for instance, all reports received will remain in records for "99 years," a fact many find troubling. Data collected for the CIS demonstrate that rates of case substantiation vary considerably by type of maltreatment, ranging from 20% for sexual abuse to 75.9% in cases of witnessing domestic violence (Trocmé et al., 2006). These researchers identified certain features of a case that are predictive of substantiation. For instance, cases with two or more housing risk factors are almost four times more likely to be substantiated as other cases, as are police referrals and situations involving three or more major risk factors of caregivers. Over one-third of substantiated investigations involve exposure of children to domestic violence, according to Black et al. (2006), but only 36% of these cases remained open for ongoing service. Data from 1998 show that children with developmental delays are more likely than others to have substantiated reports of maltreatment. At that time, these children constituted about 2.25% of the population of children but 9.9% of substantiated cases, which is 4.4 times more often than their population representation would suggest (Brown & Schormans, 2004). Interestingly, child age was not found to be related to case substantiation.

When a report is substantiated, there are several options for response. In fact, nothing at all may happen. According to 2003 CIS data, only 45% of substantiated cases remain open for ongoing service. Cases may be closed at this point for a number of reasons. For instance, the perpetrator might be removed from the home or barred from visits with the child, or the child might move with the family to another jurisdiction. For those cases that remain open, staff in most jurisdictions may recommend various kinds of support services, which are often in limited supply, especially in rural areas (Budau & Barniuk, 2009). Plans may also include court ordered in-home supervision of children in cases where care may be inadequate and/or parents are not cooperating with the protection worker; voluntary out-of-home care of a child while parents prepare to provide better care; and taking the child into court-ordered out-of-home care. An exception to this typical Canadian model is Prince Edward Island (PEI), which operates under a broader mandate than child protection. Within this mandate, staff can assess and investigate cases that require support for families rather than protection intervention, a model intended to offer preventive services to families that might otherwise become child protection cases.

Between 1998 and 2003, the rate of substantiation increased dramatically, by 125%. The kinds of injuries children experience in substantiated cases, previously cited, demonstrate that in the majority of cases, physical harm is below the level requiring medical intervention, even as investigation activities increase. Over the past 30 years, an average of 35 children in Canada under the age of 13 have been killed each year by a parent (Trocmé et al., 2007), and this number has remained fairly constant in spite of significant increases in protection activity and in budget allocations. Given the low percentage of cases involving serious physical harm to a child, it appears that the increasing number of substantiated cases was driven by other factors. Although the CIS survey authors do not speculate on reasons for this trend, it is clear that the introduction of required risk assessments in larger provinces played a significant role (Swift & Callahan, 2009). (As suggested in the introduction to this volume, there is some evidence that infant maltreatment deaths may represent a special category of parental pathology that does not mirror the overall level of abuse in society.)

Out-of-Home Care

Historically, the main type of out-of-home care for child welfare has been foster home care. In the last national survey of placement types (Federal Provincial Working Group, 2001) most provinces reported at least 50% of all types as foster care, with some reporting 70% or more. However, these figures must be treated with caution as they may include kinship and other kinds of care. Over the years, other types of facilities and practices have emerged. Among these are treatment foster homes, involving specially trained caregivers; group care, usually for small numbers of adolescents in a setting with staff; institutional care for children with significant health or mental health issues; and recently, kinship care involving care by extended family members, either sanctioned or not, by child protection authorities, a form of care gaining in popularity and encouraged in many jurisdictions. A relatively new form of care in Canada is "guardianship," intended to be a more permanent form of care by relatives or a specified family friend, but with the provincial authority retaining legal guardian status in order to avoid legal termination of the parents' rights (Farris-Manning & Zandstra, 2003). For youth who are over the legislated age of a child but who still require some form of support, independent living plans and extended foster care are available for small numbers of young adults. All these forms of care have variations in form and function and therefore cannot easily be compared across jurisdictions. It is safe to say that foster care remains the most prominent form across the country, with kin care apparently increasing.

Adoption of children from out-of-home care has decreased substantially over the past several decades. In past times, many young, single mothers "gave up" their babies for adoption through the auspices of child welfare agencies. As this trend has decreased, the children becoming available for adoption in Canada have tended to be older, often with troubled pasts and/or significant disabilities, creating difficulties in finding suitable, willing parents for them. The larger provinces now show quite small numbers of adoptions concluded in recent years, with British Columbia reporting 294 adoptions in 2008 (BC Ministry of Children and Family Development, 2008–09, p. 18); Alberta reporting 298 in 2007–08 (Alberta Children's Services, 2007–08, p. 47), and Ontario reporting 819 in 2008–09. These numbers are a tiny fraction of the total numbers of children in care in these provinces, but of course a larger percentage of those actually available for adoption. In British Columbia, for instance, adoption in 2008–09 represented 16.6% of those eligible to be adopted, and Ontario reported adoptions for about one-third of the estimated 2,500 children available for adoption in 2009–10 (OACAS, 2010, p. 28).

Data on out-of-home care numbers and types are difficult to access and hard to compare across jurisdictions because no standardized information is required on a national level and because jurisdictions do not regularly publish reports. The population of children aged 0–17 has remained relatively stable over the past two decades, hovering at around 7 million since 1991. However, trend studies carried out within these two decades all show substantial increases in the numbers and percentages of children per thousand being placed in out-of-home care. Two studies reported on out-of-home care numbers and trends over the period from 1996 to 2001. One of these indicated that, between 1996 and 2001–2, the number of children in care almost doubled, from 40,000 to 76,000 (Farris-Manning & Zandstra, 2003). The other study focused on increases in several large provinces, with Alberta increasing 43.4% in the same period and British Columbia increasing 20.9% (Swift & Callahan, 2006).

A more detailed comparison among jurisdictions over a longer period of time compares figures of children in care collected by the Federal Provincial Working

Group (1994, 2001) for 1991 and 1999. Table 3.3 shows numbers of children in care per thousand for those 2 years and the percentage increases over the period, which are substantial.

Table 3.4 continues the comparison, showing the trends between 2004 and 2007. Calculation of the in-care rates per thousand children 0–17, shown in the last line, are based on total child populations 0–17 for 2004 and 2007.

The chart shows a slight downward trend of children in care per thousand over the period, much of which can be explained by the significantly lower number of children in care counted as such by Quebec for 2007. It should be noted that the jurisdictions shown vary considerably along many dimensions. The child population 0–17, for instance, varies from 7,220 children in the Yukon to 2,763,951 in Ontario in 2007. Most jurisdictions, except Quebec, demonstrated modest changes in numbers of children in out-of-home care over the period. Jurisdictions showing dramatic increases in rates per thousand are generally those with small in-care populations. Jurisdictions such as the three Territories that show high rates per thousand also include a very high percentage of Aboriginal children in the general population. The significant differences among jurisdictions demonstrate that policies and practices in each jurisdiction need to be examined over time in order to develop a national picture of children in care. What we can clearly see in examining rates of children in out-of-home care, however, is a significant increase over the past two decades, going from 4/1,000 in 1991 to 9.7/1,000 in 2007, an increase of 143% and a long-term trend that surely demands further attention.

The ages of children in care have tended toward higher representation of older age groups. Children over 12 years of age in care in 1992 averaged well over 50%, with Nova Scotia showing those over 12 years old accounting for 82.1% of the care population (Swift, 1997, p. 59) As illustrated in Table 3.5, figures from 2001 show a similar trend (Swift & Callahan, 2006, p. 130).

Table 3.3: Children in Care as a Percentage of Children Aged 0–17 Years in Canada in 1991 and 1999

Year	Number of Children in Care	Total Population of Children (0 to 17)	Approx. % of Children in Care	Number of Children in Care Per 1,000
1991	27,567*	6,912,479	0.4/%	4/1,000
1999	62,123*	7,157,153	0.87%	8.7/1,000
Percent Increase	125%	3.5%		117%

Sources: Federal Provincial Working Group, 1994 and 2001.
Number of children 0 to 17 data were obtained from Statistics Canada (1991, 1999, 051–0001)
*Number of children in care in 1991 for provinces only.
**Number of children in care in 1999 in all Canadian provincial and territorial jurisdictions except Nunavut.

Table 3.4: Children in Care as a Number Per Thousand of Children Aged 0–17 Years, by Jurisdiction, 2004 and 2007, and Percentage Change

Provinces and Territories	Number of Children in Care		Number of Children in Care Per 1,000		Number of Children in Care		Number of Children in Care Per 1,000		Percentage Change of Children in Care Per 1,000
	2004		2004		2007		2007		2004–2007
Provinces									
Alberta	8,561		11.1		8,891		11		-0.9
British Columbia	9,086		10.5		9,271		11		4.8
Manitoba	5,782		20.3		7,241		26		28
New Brunswick	1,502		9.8		1,388		9.5		-3.1
Newfoundland and Labrador	602		6		1,329		13.8		130
Nova Scotia	2,079		10.7		1,706		9.3		-13.1
Ontario	18,490		6.6		18,763		6.8		3
Prince Edward Island	240		7.7		166		5.6		-27
Quebec*	23,242		15		12,750*		8.3		-45
Saskatchewan	2,798		11.4		5,447		23		102
Territories									
Northwest Territories	527		41.4		395		32		-23
Nunavut	299		24.6		197		16		-35
Yukon	189		25.3		178		25		-1.2
Totals	**73,397**		**10.4**		**67,722**		**9.7**		

These comparisons are to be viewed with caution, since the methods of calculating the in-care population vary among provinces and territories. Most jurisdictions shown, however, are reporting numbers of children in care as of March 31, 2004 and 2007.

Source: Centre of Excellence for Child Welfare. http://www.cecw-cepb.ca/statistics,

Total rate per thousand child population is based on 7,023,932 in 2004 and 6,966,317 in 2007. Number of children 0– 17 data was obtained from Statistics Canada (E-STAT, 2007. Table 051-0001, 6210 Series. http://estat.statcan.gc.ca/cgi-win/cnsmcgi.pgm?LANG=E&C2DB=EST&ROOTDIR=EST&ResultTemplate=ESTAT/CII_FLst&SrchVer=2&ChunkSize=50&CIITables=3433).

*Figures from Quebec are considerably lower in 2007 because of a shift in the way cases were counted (Trocmé, 2010).

Table 3.5: Age Group Percentages of Children in Care in Canada, 2001

Age Group	Percentage
0–3	27%
4–7	12%
8–11	20%
12–15	42%
Total	**101%***

Source: Thoburn, J. (2007). Globalisation and child welfare: Some lessons from a cross national study of children in out-of-home care. School of Social Work and Psychosocial Sciences. Norwich: University of East Anglia.
*The percentage number of children in care by age group is slightly above 100% as presented in the Thoburn report.

One stable feature of out-of-home care in Canada is the continuing overrepresentation of Aboriginal children in the system. Available data suggest that from 30% to 40% of all children in care in Canada are Aboriginal (Blackstock et al., 2004), although census figures show these children make up only 5.6% of all children in Canada (Statistics Canada, 2001). CIS data from 2003 showed 17% of Aboriginal children substantiated as maltreated were placed in out-of-home care, compared with 6% of non-Aboriginal children (Trocmé et al., 2005). In individual jurisdictions, especially in the western provinces, the picture is alarming. In Manitoba, up to 68% of children in care are Aboriginal (Foster, 2007), and by 2006–07, 50% of all children in care in British Columbia were Aboriginal, up from 38% in 2000–01 (British Columbia Ministry of Children and Family Development, 2007). Although these numbers are widely recognized to be unacceptable, there appear to be no viable plans in place leading to a change in this trend.

Because data and provincial reports are difficult to access, it is impossible to report with any accuracy the cost of child protection in general across the country, and more specifically the costs of keeping children in care. Of the 13 jurisdictions, Ontario has the most accessible information on this and other topics. The overall Ontario budget for child welfare increased over 200% between 1998 and 2006, going from approximately $381 million to $1.221 billion. Others among the larger provinces likely did not increase so dramatically. British Columbia, for instance, increased its child welfare budget about 48% during the same period (Swift, 2010). Ontario's information on costs of out-of-home care for 2007–08 shows 6,679,819 total care days and an annual care budget of $537 million. Based on these figures, the average daily cost for 2007–08 was $80.38. These figures represent a 2.7% decline in total care days since 2003–04, but a total cost increase of 9.3% during the same period (CAS Facts, 2008).

TRENDS IN CANADIAN CHILD PROTECTION

In the following section, two significant trends in the policy and practice of child welfare are examined. The first, related to the definition of physical abuse, follows directly from a Supreme Court decision, whereas the second, involving risk and its assessment, has evolved over the past decade.

The "Spanking Law"

An event related directly to child welfare policy and practice is the movement in the late 1990s to eliminate Section 43 of Canada's Criminal Code. This section, frequently referred to as the "spanking law," allows caregivers, including parents and teachers, to use "reasonable force" in correcting a child in his or her care:

> Every schoolteacher, parent, or person standing in the place of a parent is justified in using force by way of correction toward a pupil or child, as the case may be, who is under his care, if the force does not exceed what is reasonable under the circumstances.

Social workers played a large part in bringing this issue forward, on the basis that it contravened the Canadian Charter of Rights and Freedoms and conflicted with the UN Convention on the Rights of the Child concerning violence against children. Among the concerns of those who opposed this proposal was the realization that removing the section could result in the criminalization of parents who spank their children as a disciplinary measure, since spanking would then be considered assault and therefore chargeable under other sections of the Code. In particular, some of Canada's immigrant communities claimed that physical discipline was part of their culture and could not easily be abandoned.

The case was tried before the Supreme Court of Canada, which determined in 2004 that Section 43 did not contravene Canada's Charter of Rights and would therefore stand. However, the decision included substantial restrictions on the kinds and force of physical discipline that could be considered within the law. The age of the child, degree of force, and behavior to be corrected are among the considerations now required. What has been taken up in child protection and may play a role in other situations as well, for instance domestic assault cases, is that if any mark remains as the result of physical force, police can be called and charges can be laid. Thus, the bruise has, in effect, become the minimum standard of abuse in Canada. This does not mean every bruise or mark on a child will result in arrest of the parents, but such evidence can bring about an investigation if parents appear culpable. Thus, even though Section 43 remains in the Code, the current solution is leading to increased investigation and potential criminalization of parents whose disciplinary measures leave any sort of mark on a child, a trend reflected in CIS findings of increased investigations of cases without significant physical harm to the child demonstrated. Several media-worthy stories of children "ripped" from the arms of parents over their alleged disciplinary measures have produced considerable public debate over this issue (http://www.canadianchristianity.com/cgi-bin/bc.cgi?bc/bccn/0901/courts).

Risk and Security

Risk and technologies of risk have been another important new development in child protection in Canada since the mid-1990s. As in other Western, English-speaking countries, the 1990s saw a number of high-profile media stories about the deaths of children known to protection authorities. The most prominent review of child deaths in this period was in British Columbia, resulting in the Gove Commission Report of 1995, which examined the provincial child welfare system in the wake of the death of a child well known to protection authorities. Unsurprisingly, Judge Gove's report emphasized the safety of children over family support. Two recommendations in the report specifically called for a "comprehensive risk assessment" approach to be instigated. Substantial changes in the training and practice of child protection soon followed (Callahan & Swift, 2007).

Across Canada during this period, numerous inquests and reviews of child deaths occurred (Swift, 2001). Workers and supervisors involved in such cases were called to testify, and media coverage of this testimony frequently resulted in news items excoriating the workers in particular and protection services in general. Research on the effects of negative media attention points out the high levels of stress for protection staff, as well as high levels of staff turnover in protection services during this period (Regehr et al., 2002). In addition, in the late 1990s, a worker in one Ontario agency was arrested in connection with the death of a child on her caseload. She was charged, along with the mother, with negligent homicide. Although these charges were eventually dropped, workers still routinely mention this event and their reactions to it when speaking of their experiences in child welfare practice.

The various inquests and death reviews following on child deaths in the 1990s typically involved recommendations for the introduction of "comprehensive risk assessment tools," training in the use of these tools, and significant administrative efforts to standardize and manage the work practices of child welfare staff. As of 2002, eight Canadian provinces had adopted some type of risk assessment tool (Swift & Callahan, 2009). A number of provinces adopted the 23-item, consensual New York model in its entirety, and some added other complex processes of screening and evaluating cases to create "systems" of risk estimated through computer programs, which staff are required to conduct for all reports received. Consistency and accountability were the watchwords of the new system, enforced more in some provinces than in others. The frequency of audits and the range of issues subject to audit were also increased (Regehr et al., 2001). Requirements for computer-based reporting meant a very substantial increase in the workload for workers in some jurisdictions and a concomitant reduction in time spent with families, both sources of considerable complaint by social workers. Standards of practice were revised to support this new regime. Taken together, these measures created the potential for workers' every action to be documented and tracked and, in fact, for every decision taken at the supervisory level and above to be subject to review. In some jurisdictions, budgets became closely tied to risk activities, including time limits for specific investigatory tasks. In this way, an instrument designed to guide practice also, in effect, assigned budget responsibilities to workers because they were required to calculate and translate their professional interventions into monetary terms (Swift & Parada, 2004). Some child protection laws were also revised to reflect the significant focus on the safety of the child, with support for the family as a secondary concern, and the associated lowering of the thresholds for protection intervention. Although not every jurisdiction went to these extremes, most went in a much more managed direction, and came to focus more than before on child safety rather than on family support.

These risk assessment systems characterized child protection efforts especially in the larger provinces for several years. However, it has become apparent that escalating costs and increased numbers of children in care produced by this intensive risk approach were becoming politically unacceptable. With the new "interventionist" regime came substantial increases in reports, investigations, and apprehensions of children, noted by Trocmé et al. as early as 2003. Workers' fears of making "mistakes" in scoring risk led to higher risk scores, determined at least in part by a felt need for self-protection, and leading inevitably to increasing numbers of children in care (Swift & Callahan, 2009).

The standardized risk model was not applicable in many Canadian settings. In the North, short investigation times were often not feasible, as many referrals required workers to fly in or use all-terrain vehicles to reach communities. Many rural and Northern workers found the tools inappropriate for their communities—for instance, how would they rate a risk item measuring inadequate support networks for a family living on an isolated reserve? Indeed, standardization was seen by many as forcing Aboriginal people to conform to mainstream ways: "standardization is assimilation" (Swift & Callahan, 2009), and assimilation is something Aboriginal peoples in Canada have resisted for at least 400 years, with some success.

Another problem with the intensive risk systems is that they were "front end loaded," requiring such significant resources in the investigation phase that little money remained to fund resources. In addition, little attention was paid to risk management efforts that were supposed to be matched to the assessment results. Workers continued to prescribe the traditional standardized programs, such as parenting education, even though there is scant evidence of their effectiveness in increasing child safety (Gambrill & Shlonsky, 2001; Swift, 2010). And, as longitudinal research shows, the number of children actually killed by a parent has remained constant in Canada over many years, regardless of child protection systems in place (Trocmé et al., 2007).

Given these issues, jurisdictions heavily invested in risk assessment are now turning to assessment forms that are less onerous to complete. The differential response approach, which actually seems very familiar to those with several decades of experience in Canadian child welfare, involves a swing of the pendulum at least somewhat in the direction of supporting families (Dumbrill, 2005). It entails more emphasis on kin care in instances when the children cannot stay at home, and more "community partnerships" with other agencies and services, partnerships that involve more referrals and contracting out of services. The new model also recommends the use of customary care, which refers to the traditional Aboriginal practice of child rearing and care, in which all members of the nuclear family, extended family, and community are involved. Dumbrill's (2005) analysis of these directions in Ontario is that there are already some flaws in the plan. He notes, for instance, that the new plan is focused mostly on strengthening agencies rather than the families themselves. Meanwhile, the risk assessment model will still be a central component of the new plan.

CONCLUSION

In general, child welfare issues have taken a lower public and media profile over the past decade. The use of technology, together with more tightly managed systems, is now entrenched in policy and practice and will likely shape child protection for years to come. Research findings showing low and consistent numbers of children actually killed or seriously harmed by their parents stand in stark contradiction to the increasingly intensive surveillance and investigation of many families, most of them poor, raising questions about the actual purposes of much child protection activity. It would seem that as the social safety net shrinks, the focus on scrutiny and control of child welfare populations intensifies.

The difficulties faced in preparing this chapter reveal a significant need for more accessible information about the activities and resource outlays of the 13 Canadian jurisdictions responsible for child welfare. At present, information about numbers of children in care, types of out-of-home care, and costs of that care are impossible to assemble without an intensive research effort. Further, we do not know enough about the way these various kinds of data are derived. This is clearly a priority area for future research.

Based on our knowledge of the substantially increased potential for surveillance of child welfare clients (and workers), the increased number of children in care, and the intensification of investigation at the expense of resources for family support, it is clear that Canada continues to have a residual child welfare system, based on an idea of protection rather than support. There is a trend toward closer internal scrutiny of some jurisdictional systems, with performance targets established and careful reporting of activities and trends. However, the basic dynamics of the system have not changed substantively over the past decade;

rather, the focus on "security" has cemented in place the residual model. Although the Canadian "system" sometimes shifts slightly in the direction of family support, there is currently no concerted policy effort for a decisive move in that direction.

NOTES

1   My thanks to Research Assistant Daniel Kikulwe, doctoral student at York University School of Social Work, for his invaluable work in helping me prepare this chapter.
2   Provincial powers derive directly from the Constitution, whereas the powers of territories are delegated by the federal government.
3   Within a few years, the CHST was divided into the CHT, allocated to health, and the CST for social welfare.
4   Most figures reported by the CIS do not include Quebec.
5   Findings from the most recent CIS study (2008) are just beginning to emerge. See http://www.cecw-cepb.ca/cis-2008.
6   These schools originated in the 1840s; the last one closed in 1996.
7   The exception is the Spalumcheen band in British Columbia, the first native-run organization to be mandated. Its agreement was solely with the federal government.
8   Also, only 4% of sexual abuse cases involved injuries requiring treatment.
9   All jurisdictional law mentions specific activities that must be undertaken if children are of Aboriginal background, including contact with the relevant band and special emphasis on culturally appropriate treatment.

REFERENCES

Alberta Children's Services. (2007–08). Annual Report.

Alberta Child, Youth and Family Enhancement Act, R.S.A. 2000, c.C-12.

Beaumont, B. (1999). Risk assessment and prediction research. In P. Parsloe (Ed.), *Risk assessment in social care and social work*, pp. 69–106. London and Philadelphia: Jessica Kingsley.

Black, T., Trocmé, N., Fallon, B., & MacLaurin, B. (2006). *The Canadian child welfare system response to exposure to domestic violence investigations*. CECW Information Sheet #39E. Toronto, ON: University of Toronto, Faculty of Social Work.

Blackstock, C., Trocmé, N., & Bennett, M. (2004). Child welfare response to Aboriginal and non-Aboriginal child in Canada: A comparative analysis. *Violence Against Women, 10* (8), 901–916.

British Columbia Children and Family Services Act. RSBC 1996, C-46.

British Columbia Ministry of Child and Family Development. (2008–09). Annual Service Plan Report.

Brown, I., & Fudge Schormans, A. (2004). *Maltreatment rates in children with developmental delay.* CECW Information Sheet #9E. Toronto, ON, Canada: Faculty of Social Work, University of Toronto.

Bryant, T. (2004). Housing and health. In D. Raphael (Ed.), *Social determinants of health: Canadian perspectives,* pp. 217–231. Toronto: Canadian Scholar's Press.

Budau, K., & Barniuk, J. (2009). *Geographic location and short-term service dispositions in Canadian child maltreatment investigations: CIS-2003.* CECW Information Sheet #76. Toronto, ON, Canada: Faculty of Social Work, University of Toronto.

Callahan, M., & Swift, K. (2007). Great expectations and unintended consequences: Risk assessment in child welfare in B.C. In L. Foster and B. Wharf (Eds.), *People, politics and child welfare,* pp. 158–183. Vancouver: UBC Press.

Campaign 2000. (2008). Family security in insecure times: The case for a poverty reduction strategy for Canada. Retrieved July 9, 2009, from www.campaign 2000.ca.

Canadian Charter of Rights and Freedoms. (1982). Part I of the *Constitution Act, 1982.* Retrieved September 3, 2009 from http://www.efc.ca pages law charter charter.text.html.

Centre of Excellence for Children's Wellbeing (CECW). (2009). Retrieved May 5, 2009 from http://www.cecw-cepb.ca overview.

Chau, S., Fitzpatrick, A., Hulchanski, D., Leslie, B., & Schatia, D. (2001). *One in five... Housing as a factor in the admission of children to care: New survey of Children's Aid Society of Toronto updates 1992 study.* Toronto: University of Toronto, Centre for Urban and Community Studies.

Criminal Code of Canada. R.S.C. 1985, c. C-46. Retrieved May 7, 2009 from http://laws.justice.gc.ca en C-46.

Dauvergne, M., & Johnson, H. (N.d) *Children witnessing family violence.* Juristat: Canadian Centre for Justice Statistics. Statistics Canada. Catalogue no. 85–002 21, No. 6.

Drummond, D., Burleton, D., & Manning, G. (2004). Affordable housing in Canada: In Search of a new paradigm. In D. Hulchanski & M. Shapcott (Eds.), *Finding room: Policy options for a Canadian rental housing strategy,* pp. 15–68. Toronto: Centre for Urban and Community Studies, University of Toronto.

Dumbrill, G. (2005). Ontario's child welfare transformation: Another swing of the pendulum? *Canadian Social Work Review, 23*(1,2), 5–19.

Farris-Manning, C., & Zandstra, M. (2003). *Child in care in Canada: A summary of current issues and trends with recommendation for future research.* Ottawa: Child Welfare League of Canada.

Federal-Provincial Working Group on Child and Family Services Information. (1994). *The role of provincial and territorial authorities in cases of child abuse.* Ottawa, ON: Minister of Supply and Services Canada.

Federal Provincial Territorial Working Group on Child and Family Service Information. (2001). *Child and family services statistical report, 1996–97 to 1998–99.* Ottawa, ON:. Human Resouces and Skills Development Canada.

Friendly, M., & Beach, J. (2005). *Early childhood education and care in Canada 2004,* 6th ed. Toronto: Childcare Resource and Research Unit, University of Toronto.

Gambrill, E., & Shlonsky, A. (2001). The need for comprehensive risk management systems in child welfare. *Children and Youth Services Review, 23*(1): 79–107.

Graham, J., Swift, K., & Delaney, R. (2008). *Canadian social policy: An introduction,* 3rd ed. Toronto: Pearson Prentice Hall.

Hannah-Moffat, K., & Maurutto, P. (2003). *Youth risk need assessment: An overview of issues and practices.* Ottawa: Department of Justice.

Human Resource and Skills Development Canada. (2008). *Child and family services statistical report 1996–97 to 1998–March 99, 2001.* Ottawa: Government of Canada. Retrieved January 28, 2009 from http:www.hrsdc.gc.ca eng cs sp sdc socpol publications reports 2001–001347 page08.shtml.

Hunter, G. (2006). Child Poverty and the Canadian Welfare State. In A. Westhughes, Ed., *Canadian social policy: Issues and perspectives,* 4th ed. Waterloo, ON: Wilfrid Laurier University Press.

Indian Act. R.S., c. I-6. Retrieved September 3, 2009 from http://www.canlii.org en ca laws stat rsc-1985-c-i-5 latest.

Johnston, P. (1983). *Native children and the child welfare system.* Toronto: Canadian Council on Social Development, in association with James Lorimer Publishers.

Kemshall, H., & Maguire, M. (2001). Public protection, partnership and risk penalty: The multi-agency risk management of sexual and violent offenders. *Punishment and Society, 3*(2), 237–264.

Krane, J. (2003). *What's mother got to do with it.* Toronto: University of Toronto Press.

Laird, G. (2007). *Shelter: Homelessness in a growth economy–Canada's 21st century paradox.* Calgary: Sheldon Chumir Foundation for Ethics in Leadership.

Lavergne, C., Dufour, S., Trocmé, N., & Larrivee, M.-C. (2008). Racial disproportionality in child welfare: Visible minority, Aboriginal and Caucasian children investigated by Canadian Protective Services. *Child Welfare League of America, 82*(2), 59–76.

Leschied, A., Chiodo, D., Whitehead, P., & Hurley, D. *The association of poverty with child welfare service and child and family clinical outcomes.* London, ON: The University of Western Ontario.

Manitoba Child and Family Services Act, C.C.S.M. c. C-80.

National Council of Welfare. (2006). *Welfare Incomes 2005.* Ottawa, ON: National Council of Welfare (Canada).

New Brunswick Family Services Act, S.N.B.1980, c. F-2.2.

Newfoundland and Labrador Child, Youth and Family Services Act, S.N.L. 1998 c. C-21.1.

Northwest Territories Child and Family Services Act, R.S.O., 1997, c. C. 13, s. 7 (3), p. 6–9.

Nova Scotia Child and Family Services Act, R.S.O., 1990, c. C. 5, s. 22 (2).

Nunavut Child and Family Services Act, R.S.O., 1997, c. C. 13, s. 7 (3), p. 7–8.

Ontario Association of Children's Aid Societies. (2008). CAS Facts, April 1, 2007–March 31, 2008.

Ontario Association of Children's Aid Societies. (2000). Eligibility Spectrum. Toronto.

Ontario Association of Children's Aid Societies. (2010). Your Children's Aid: Child Welfare Report, 2009–10. Retrieved May 11, 2010 from www. oacas.org.

Ontario Child and Family Services Act, R.S.O. 1990, c.C-111.

Organization for Economic Co-operation and Development (OECD). (2005). Retrieved July 10, 2009 from http://stats.oecd.org brandedviewpilot default. aspx?datasetcode=socx_agg.

Prince Edward Island Child Protection Act, R.S.O., 2003, c. C. C-5.1, s. 3, p. 5.

Quebec Youth Protection Act, R.S.Q., 1979, c. C. 4, s. 38 (b), p. 20.

Regehr, C., Chau, S., Leslie, B., & Howe, P. (2002). An exploration of supervisors' and managers' responses to child welfare reform. *Administration in Social Work, 26*(3), 17–36.

Saskatchewan Child and Family Services Act, S.S. 1989–90, c. C-7.2.

Shapcott, M. (2001). *The Ontario alternative budget 2001. Technical Paper 12.* Ottawa: Canadian Centre for Policy Alternatives.

Smith, B., & Donovan, S. (2003). Child welfare practice in organizational and institutional context. *Social Service Review, 77*(4), 541–5 63.

Statistics Canada. (2001). *Aboriginal Peoples of Canada.* Ottawa: www.statscan. gc.ca.

Statistics Canada. *The Daily.* Retrieved May 16, 2008 from http://www.statcan. gc.ca.daily-quotidien 080516a-eng.htm.

Strega, S., & Carriere, J. (2009). *Walking this path together: Anti-racist and anti-oppressive child welfare practice.* Halifax: Fernwood.

Strega, S., Fleet, C., Brown, L., Dominelli, L., Callahan, M., & Walmsley, C. (2008). Connecting father absence and mother blame in child welfare policies and practice. *Children and Youth Services Review, 30,* 705–716.

Swift, K. (1997). Canada: Trends and Issues in Child Welfare. In Gilbert, N. (Ed.), *Combatting child abuse: International perspectives and trends.* New York: Oxford University Press.

Swift, K. (2001). The case for opposition: An examination of contemporary child welfare policy directions. *Canadian Review of Social Policy, 47*(Spring), 59–76.

Swift, K. (2010). Risky Women: The Role of "Risk" in the Construction of the Single Mother. In S. Gavigan & D. Chunn (Eds.), *The legal tender of gender: Historical and contemporary perspectives on welfare law, state policies and the regulation of women's poverty.* Portland, Oregon: Hart Publishing.

Swift, K., & Callahan, M. (2009). *At risk: Social justice in child welfare and other human services.* Toronto: University of Toronto Press.

Swift, K., & Callahan, M. (2006). Problems and Potential of Canadian Child Welfare. In N. Freymond & G. Cameron (Eds.), *Toward positive systems of child and family welfare.* Toronto: University of Toronto Press.

Swift, K., & Parada, H. (2004). Child welfare reform: Protecting children or policing the poor? *Journal of Law and Social Policy, 19,* 1–17.

Thoburn, J. (2007). *Globalisation and child welfare: Some lessons from a cross national study of children in out-of-home care.* School of Social Work and Psychosocial Sciences. Norwich: University of East Anglia.

Trocmé, N. January 18, 2010. Personal communication.

Trocmé, N., Fallon, B., MacLaurin, B., Daciuk, J., Felstiner, C., Black, T., et al. (2005). *Canadian incidence study of reported child abuse and neglect–2003.* Public Health Agency of Canada.

Trocmé, N., Knoke, D., Fallon, B., & MacLaurin, B. (2006). *Substantiating child maltreatment: CIS-2003.* CECW Information Sheet #40E. Toronto, ON: University of Toronto, Faculty of Social Work.

Trocmé, N., Lajoie, J., Fallon, B., and Felstiner, C. (2007). *Injuries and deaths of children at the hands of their parents.* CECW Information Sheet #57E. Toronto, ON: University of Toronto Faculty of Social Work.

Trocmé, N., & Wolfe, D.A. (2001). *Child maltreatment in Canada: Canadian incidence study of reported child abuse and neglect selected results.* Ottawa, ON: Health Canada.

UN Convention on the Rights of the Child. Retrieved September 9, 2009 from http://www.unicef.org/crc/.

UNICEF. (2007). Child Poverty in Perspective: An Overview of Child Well-being in Rich Countries. Innocenti Report Card 7. Innocenti Research Centre, Florence, Italy. Retrieved July 10, 2009 from http://www.unicef-irc.org/publications/pdf/rc7_eng.pdf.

Youth Criminal Justice Act of Canada. Retrieved September 3, 2009 from http://laws.justice.gc.ca/en/Y-1.5/index.html.

Yukon Children's Act, R.S.Y. 2002, c. 31.

4

CHILD PROTECTION IN ENGLAND

NIGEL PARTON AND DAVID BERRIDGE[1]

The focus for this chapter is the development of child protection policy and practice in England. England is the largest nation in the United Kingdom (U.K.) with a population of just under 50 million out of a total of 59 million in the U.K. as a whole. There are about 11 million children in England (under 18 years). The last 12 years have seen an important process of devolution, so that Scotland, Northern Ireland, and Wales each now have their own Parliament or Assembly and Executive with increased legislative and expenditure powers in relation to a wide range of devolved matters, and these include child protection and child welfare. Although the nations continue to have many similarities in relation to the challenges and policy responses to child abuse, increasingly, each is developing its own distinctive approach (Stafford, Vincent, & Parton, 2010).

In England, the legal and policy framework is determined centrally and includes the production of an increasing amount of detailed guidance and procedures. However, the responsibility for the provision of services and the implementation of child protection law policy remains with the 152 local authorities. These range in size from large, primarily rural, counties to densely populated metropolitan councils and London boroughs. The largest authority has a population of over 1.5 million people, whereas the smallest is under 50,000, and the majority are between 200,000 and 600,000 population. Until 2006, statutory child protection services were the responsibility of the local authority social services department, but following the *Every Child Matters* reforms (DfES, 2004a), which we discuss later, this has moved to the new departments of children's services.

Ever since the tragic death of Maria Colwell at the hands of her stepfather in 1973, and while under the supervision of social workers (Secretary of State, 1974), a major determinant of policy change in child welfare in England has been public, media, and political concerns about failures in professional responses to cases of child abuse. Usually, these have been orchestrated by high-profile public inquiries into the failures of health and welfare professionals to protect certain children from death or serious injury; other public inquiries have been concerned with possible cases of over-intervention, in which children have been removed from parents inappropriately (Parton, 2006). In addition, public inquiries have also been established to investigate abuse in residential and day care settings (Corby, Doig, & Roberts, 2001).

The past 15 years have been no exception, and since November 2008, the country has been gripped by major concerns about the death of "Baby Peter," and the failures of a variety of health and welfare professionals to protect him. As a result, England has been living through a period of exceptionally high-profile, intense, and often rancorous debate and criticism of professional practice, current policies, and child protection systems. It has seemed more hostile and angry than anything seen before, certainly a moral panic if not a witch-hunt, and will almost certainly have considerable implications for the direction, focus, and philosophy of future policy and practice.

In this chapter, we begin by outlining the most significant developments in law and policy since the mid-1990s, together with discussing the most significant changes in the wider political and policy contexts during the period. We then identify the key criteria that define child maltreatment; who is responsible for reporting suspected cases; the processes for enquiring into these reports and how allegations of maltreatment are substantiated; and the recent patterns and make-up of services and out-of-home placements. Throughout, we will attempt to analyze what the key changes have been and, in particular, assess how far and in what ways the overall model can be characterized primarily in terms of a child protection or family service orientation. We will return to these issues at the end, when we also consider how far this might be subject to further change in the light of the policy and practice reactions to the death of "Baby Peter."

LEGAL, POLICY AND POLITICAL CHANGES 1995–2009

For the purposes for this discussion, we are going to split the period into three, interrelated, but separate phases: 1995–1997; 1997–2004; and 2004 onward.

In the first edition of this book, England was clearly categorized, along with the United States and Canada, as fitting primarily within a "child protection orientation." It was also noted, however, that in 1995 a major government commissioned program of research was published that raised a series of fundamental questions about the operation of the child protection system in England

(Berridge, 1997). In particular, it was noted that the system seemed preoccupied with protection rather than the overall welfare of the child and that the "investigation" had become an end in itself.

1995–1997: *Messages from Research* and the "Refocusing Debate"

The publication of *Child Protection: Messages from Research* (Department of Health, 1995), which summarized the key findings from the research program, was to prove crucial in opening up a major debate about the future shape of child protection policy and practice (Parton, 1997). It demonstrated that only around one in seven of those referred to the statutory child welfare service as children at risk of abuse was ever subject to a child protection plan and named on a child protection register, and fewer than one in 25 was ever removed from home as a result.

The key recommendation from the research was that policy and practice should be "refocused" and should prioritize Section 17 and Part III of the Children Act 1989, in terms of supporting families with "children in need," rather than simply concentrating on investigating incidents of abuse in a narrow, forensically driven way. It was a serious attempt to shift practice from a child protection orientation, to one which was organized according to principles sympathetic to a family service orientation. It was argued that policy and practice should be driven by an emphasis on partnership, participation, prevention, and family support. The priority should be on *helping* parents and children in the community in a supportive way and should keep notions of policing and coercive interventions to a minimum. Subsequent government research, however, demonstrated that local authority social services departments found it very difficult to refocus their services in the ways suggested (Department of Health, 2001).

1997–2004: The New Labour Government and Social Exclusion

The New Labour government of Tony Blair was elected in May 1997. It quickly became apparent that it had a much broader view of the role of family support than simply as a counterweight to a forensically focused approach to child protection. Family support was seen as a major contributor to combat "social exclusion" (Featherstone, 2004). For New Labour, social exclusion was defined almost exclusively in terms of people being excluded or marginalized from the labor market and a key priority was placed on improved educational attainment and getting people into paid work (Byrne, 2005; Levitas, 2005). Policies were also concerned with improving behavior and social functioning, and a variety of factors were seen as putting certain people at risk of social exclusion, particularly the young, including poor parenting, not attending school, drug abuse, homelessness, unemployment, and low income. The behavior and development of children and young people was a particular concern, and it was very important that government ensured parents took their responsibilities toward their children seriously.

Policies focusing on children and young people were at the heart of the New Labour project to refashion the welfare state and tackle social exclusion, and it introduced a plethora of new policies and made significant changes to other long-established ones (Powell, 2008).

Perhaps the clearest exemplar of the New Labour strategy before 2004 was the introduction of the *Sure Start* program, modelled on the Head Start program in the United States. Sure Start was designed as a universal early education and family support service for families with children under 4 in the 20% most deprived neighborhoods in the country. It provided an administrative model for other New Labour interventions in relation to children and families, and clearly demonstrated the importance given to improving early child development, the impact of multiple disadvantages, and the extended role that the State should play in trying to combat these. In particular, it underlined the importance given by government to develop policies to aid early intervention, in order to combat problems in later life, and highlighted that children and childhood had become a prime site for State intervention of a preemptive kind. Sure Start has been extensively evaluated: compared with matched peers, parents of 3-year-olds showed less negative parenting, provided a better home learning environment, and the children had better social development (Melhuish et al., 2008).

In this context, child protection was seen as just one element in the ambitious attempts to modernize and broaden the role of children's services in the context of trying to combat social exclusion. This shift in emphasis is made clear by a comparison of the official government guidance published at the beginning and end of the 1990s. At the beginning of the decade, the priority was clearly upon forensically investigating child abuse and the guidance was entitled *Working Together Under the Children Act 1989: A Guide to the Arrangements for Inter-Agency Cooperation for the Protection of Children from Abuse* (Home Office et al., 1991). As the subtitle states, the focus was clearly upon "the protection of children from abuse," and the whole document was framed in terms of when and how to carry out an investigation in terms of Section 47 of the Children Act 1989. The key decision was whether a case (referral/report) met the criterion for formal State intervention and whether the child was "suffering or likely to suffer significant harm" (s.31(91)(9)).

By the end of the decade, the guidance had been substantially rewritten and was entitled *Working Together to Safeguard Children: A Guide to Inter-Agency Working to Safeguard and Promote the Welfare of Children* (Department of Health et al., 1999). The words "protection" and "abuse" had been dropped from the title, which was now framed in terms of the general duty placed on local authorities by Section 17(1) of the Children Act 1989 "to safeguard and promote the welfare of children in their area who are in need." The guidance underlined the fact that local authority social services departments had much wider responsibilities than simply responding to concerns about child abuse and "significant harm," and were explicitly located in the wider agenda for children's services being promulgated in the early years of the New Labour government. A whole variety of issues, apart from child abuse, were identified as "sources of stress for children and families which might have a negative impact on a child's health, either directly, or because they affected the capacity of parents to respond to their child's needs" (Department of Health et al., 1999, para.2.19), including social exclusion, domestic violence, the mental illness of a parent or carer, drug and alcohol misuse.

This shift in focus from the "risk" of child abuse to "children in need and their families" was very evident in the language used to describe the way to approach "assessments," rather than "investigations," as previously. The publication of the 1999 edition of *Working Together* was combined with the publication of the *Framework for the Assessment of Children in Need and Their Families* (Department of Health, et al., 2000), which aimed to move the focus from the investigation of child abuse and "significant harm" to one that was concerned with the possible impairment to a child's development. Both the safeguarding and the promotion of a child's welfare were seen as intimately connected aims for intervention, so that it was important that access to services was via a common assessment route. The critical task was to ascertain whether a child was in need, and how children and their parents might be helped.

There was thus an explicit attempt to try and reorient policy and practice to a more obvious family service orientation, where the emphasis was upon assessing and responding to a child's overall developmental needs in the context of his or her family and community. The concept of child protection was superseded by the much broader notion of safeguarding and promoting the welfare of the child. These ideas were further developed in the next version of *Working Together*, published in 2006 (HM Government, 2006).

Effective measures to safeguard children were seen as those that also promoted their welfare, and should not be seen in isolation from the wider range of support and services provided to meet the needs of all children and families. The 2006 *Working Together* provided the first official definition of safeguarding, which, at the same time, stated how this related to the idea of child protection. What becomes clear is that concerns to protect children from child abuse had not disappeared, but had been located in these wider concerns:

Safeguarding and promoting the welfare of children is defined for the purposes of this guidance as:

- protecting children from maltreatment;
- preventing impairment of children's health or development; and
- ensuring that children are growing up in circumstances consistent with the provision of safe and effective care;

and undertaking that role so as to enable those children to have optimum life chances and to enter adulthood successfully (HM Government, 2006, para.1.18, original emphasis).

Child protection was specifically related to attempts to assess and intervene in situations in which children were, or were likely to suffer, "significant harm," and it was local authority statutory social workers who were to play the leading and central role in identifying where there were concerns about child maltreatment and deciding whether it might be necessary to consider taking urgent action to ensure that children were safe from harm (HM Government, 2006, para.5.31).

2004–2008: The *Every Child Matters: Change for Children* Program

The 2006 *Working Together* guidance was published at a time of tremendous change in children's services in England, seen by many as the most significant change in the philosophy and delivery of children's services in England since 1948 (Hudson, 2005), when local authority child welfare departments were first established. The government had just launched its *Every Child Matters: Change for Children* (ECM) program (Department for Education and Skills, 2004a), in which the overriding vision was to bring about a "shift to prevention whilst strengthening protection" (Department for Education and Skills, 2004b, p. 3). The consultative "Green Paper," *Every Child Matters* (Chief Secretary to the Treasury, 2003) had originally been launched as the government's response to the very high-profile public inquiry into the death of Victoria Climbié[2] (Laming, 2003). However, the changes introduced were much broader than being only concerned with trying to overcome the problems with trying to identify and respond appropriately to cases of child abuse. Following the policy direction already established by the New Labour government, the priority was to intervene at a much earlier stage in children's lives, in order to prevent a range of problems in later life in relation to educational attainment, unemployment, crime, and antisocial behavior. The changes were only partially concerned with child abuse (Parton, 2006, 2008). It was to include *all children*, as it was felt that any child, at some point in his or her life, could be seen as vulnerable to some form of risk and therefore might require help. The idea was to identify problems at an early stage and before they become chronic.

The model informing the changes was derived from the public health approach to prevention and has been characterized as "the paradigm of risk and protection-focussed prevention" (France & Utting, 2005), whereby the knowledge of risk factors derived from prospective longitudinal research is drawn upon to design particular early intervention programs and to reorient mainstream services. What was particularly attractive to policy makers was that a range of generic personal and environmental risk factors seemed to have been identified, which might be able to preempt a number of social problems, including criminal behavior, violence, drug abuse, educational failure, unsafe sexual behavior, and poor mental health—all conceptualized as future negative outcomes. The Green Paper stated that:

> we have a good idea what factors shape children's life chances. Research tells us that *the risk of experiencing negative outcomes* is concentrated in children with certain characteristics (Chief Secretary to the Treasury, 2003, p. 17, emphasis added).

and these included:

- low income and parental unemployment
- homelessness
- poor parenting
- poor schooling
- postnatal depression among mothers
- low birth weight
- substance misuse
- individual characteristics, such as intelligence
- community factors, such as living in a disadvantaged community.

The more risk factors a child experienced, the more likely it was that he or she would experience negative outcomes, and it was "poor parenting" that was seen to play the key role. Identifying the risk factors and intervening early provided the major strategy for overcoming the social exclusion of children and avoiding problems in later life.

At the center of the changes was the ambition to improve the outcomes for *all* children and to narrow the gap between those who do well and those who do not. The outcomes are defined in terms of being healthy, staying safe, enjoying and achieving, making a positive contribution, and achieving economic well-being. Together, the five outcomes are seen as key to improving well-being in childhood and later life. Child protection and safeguarding, and promoting children's welfare are just some elements that contribute to the "staying safe" outcome, which also includes reducing childhood accidents and bullying and feeling safe at home, at school, and in the community more generally (HM Government, 2008).

To achieve the outcomes, the changes aimed to integrate health, social care, education, and criminal justice, and to ensure that traditional, organizational, and professional "silos" were overcome, particularly in order to share information so that risks could be identified early. This required new organizational structures both at the central and local government levels and the use of a variety of new systems of information, communication, and technology (ICT) (Parton, 2008; Frost & Parton, 2009). As a result, the rate of change since 2004 has been exceptional, and the range and complexity of computer systems designed to screen and identify those in need of attention has grown considerably. This has posed particular challenges to agencies and front-line practitioners (Frost & Parton, 2009; Peckover et al., 2009; Parton, 2010).

WHAT ARE THE CRITERIA THAT DEFINE CHILD MALTREATMENT?

In the context of these considerable changes, effective measures to safeguard children are seen primarily as those which also promote their welfare, and should not be seen in isolation from the wider range of support and services provided to meet the needs of all children and families. Although protecting children from maltreatment is seen as important, in order to prevent impairment to health and development, on its own it is not seen as sufficient to ensure that children are growing up in circumstances that ensure the provision of safe and effective care.

However, although all agencies and individuals should aim to *proactively* safeguard and promote the welfare of children, child protection continues to have a much narrower focus and is specifically related to attempts to assess and intervene in situations in which children have or are likely to suffer significant harm. It is "significant harm" that provides the key threshold criteria for compulsory state intervention in order to protect children. Under s.31(a) of the Children Act 1989, as amended by the Adoption and Children Act 2002:

"Harm" means ill-treatment or the impairment of health or development, including, for example, impairment suffered from seeing or hearing the ill-treatment of another;

"development" means physical, intellectual, emotional, social, or behavioral development;

"health" means physical or mental health; and

"ill-treatment" includes sexual abuse and forms of ill-treatment which are not physical.

Under s.31(10) of the Children Act 1989:

Where the question of whether harm suffered by a child is significant turns on the child's health and development, his health or development shall be compared with that which could reasonably be expected of a similar child.

In the most recent government guidance (HM Government, 2010) abuse and neglect are described in the following terms:

> Abuse and neglect are forms of maltreatment of a child. Somebody may abuse or neglect a child by inflicting harm, or by failing to act to prevent harm. Children may be abused in a family or in an institutional or community setting, by those known to them or, more rarely, by a stranger for example, via the internet. They may be abused by an adult or adults, or another child or children. (pp. 38–39)

And this includes physical abuse, emotional abuse, sexual abuse, and neglect (pp. 8–9).

WHO IS RESPONSIBLE FOR REPORTING SUSPECTED CASES OF MALTREATMENT?

England continues not to have a mandatory reporting system; however, as we have seen, for many years, central government has produced detailed guidance that sets out clear expectations that professionals and individual citizens should make a referral to the local authority statutory child welfare agency when there is a reasonable belief that a child is at risk of significant harm. Governments across the U.K. help fund a free, confidential, 24-hour helpline (*ChildLine*) for children in distress or danger; this is run by the largest nongovernment child protection agency (the National Society for the Prevention of Cruelty to Children). Trained, volunteer counsellors respond to around 2,500 phone calls from children each day. There is a similar free phone line for adults to report concerns about children's safety.

The current *Working Together* guidance is a long and complex document. It is 390 pages in length, which includes eight chapters (228 pages) of statutory guidance and four chapters (51 pages) of nonstatutory practice guidance, together with seven appendices (34 pages), plus an overall summary, introduction, and definition of key terms. The document has 200 "References and Internet Links" and 273 "Footnotes."

In addition, every local authority and organization that comes into contact with children has its own detailed procedures. Over the last 30 years, child protection and child welfare work more generally have become increasingly proceduralized and subject to a plethora of complex government guidance. For professionals and organizations that do not follow the guidance and procedures, the consequences, particularly when things are seen to have gone wrong, can be very severe, including being sacked from the job, being removed from the respective professional register, strong criticisms from government inspectors, and media opprobrium.

In addition, Section II of the Children Act 2004 places a statutory duty on a wide range of agencies to ensure they have regard to safeguarding and promoting the welfare of children (i.e., wider than child protection). The organizations listed include all police, probation, prison, and health bodies, although schools and general practitioners are currently excluded.

For many years, the prime strategy has been to encourage different professionals and organizations to work together when there are child protection concerns and, more recently, when there are concerns about safeguarding and promoting the welfare of the child. This was strengthened in 2006, with the establishment in all local authorities of statutory *Local Safeguarding Children's Boards* (LCSBs) for developing and coordinating safeguarding policies, practices, training, and quality control in each local authority area. It includes the responsibility for the establishment of *Serious Case Reviews*, in which a child has died and abuse or neglect are known or suspected to be a factor in the death; and *Child Death Reviews,* in which a child has died unexpectedly, notwithstanding concerns about abuse and neglect.

The membership of *LCSBs* includes the senior managers from the local authority, the police, all hospitals and health organizations, probation, education, and prisons and young offender organizations, together with representatives from nongovernment child welfare organizations operating in the area and two "lay members."

WHAT ARE THE PROCESSES FOR ENQUIRING INTO REPORTS?

Working Together (HM Government, 2010) provides the procedural framework and detailed guidance for responding to any concerns about a child's welfare, which is much broader than concerns about child maltreatment. The attempts to integrate child protection within a broader child welfare-response are clearly evident in these procedures, for responding to concerns about child maltreatment are nested within the broader child welfare-orientated *Assessment of Children in Need and their Families.*

When any professional or member of the public has concerns about a child's welfare, this should be referred to the statutory local authority child welfare agency, whose responsibility is to clarify with the referrer the nature of the concerns, how and why they have arisen, and what appear to be the needs of the child and family. The assessment process whereby the statutory agency responds is subject to the completion of a range of detailed electronic forms and clear timescales.

Following a referral, the social worker and his or her manager should decide on the next course of action within one working day, and record the decision on the "Referral and Information Record." Further action might include referral to other agencies, provision of advice or information, no further action, or whether a 10-day initial assessment, led by a "qualified and experienced social worker" (para.5.41) should be carried out.

HOW ARE ALLEGATIONS OF MALTREATMENT SUBSTANTIATED, AND WHAT IS THE STATE'S RESPONSE?

In the course of the initial assessment, the local authority has to ascertain:

- Is this a child in need? (s.17 Children Act 1989)
- Is there reasonable cause to suspect that the child is suffering, or is likely to suffer, significant harm? (s.47 Children Act 1989)

Because the guidance is very keen to promote an integrated child welfare approach, it is not good enough to consider allocating resources only where the significant harm threshold criterion is substantiated, for:

The focus of the initial assessment should be both the safety and the welfare of the child. It is important to remember that even if the reason for the referral was a concern about abuse or neglect that is not subsequently substantiated, a child and family may still benefit from support and practical help to promote a child's health and development. When services are to be provided a child in need plan should be developed based on the findings from the initial assessment. . . [however]. . . if the child's needs or circumstances are complex, a more in-depth core assessment under s.17 of the Children Act 1989 will be required in order to decide what other types of services are necessary to assist the child and family. (para. 5.46)

The core assessment should be completed within 35 days, and one of its key tasks is to establish whether significant harm or its likelihood is suspected or not. When it is not, family group conferences (FGCs), in which the responsibility for decision making is much more located with the parents and the wider family, are encouraged but still unevenly used. However, it is clear that "FGCs do not replace or remove the need for child protection conferences" (para.10.2).

Where significant harm is suspected, the local authority has a responsibility to carry out a core assessment under s.47 of the Children Act 1989. It is possible that, although the original concerns about significant harm were substantiated, because of changing circumstances—for example the departure of the alleged perpetrator from the household—the child might no longer be at continuing risk of significant harm.

However, when concerns are substantiated *and* the child is judged to be at continuing risk of significant harm, the key elements of the longstanding child protection system are drawn upon. There will be an initial multidisciplinary child protection case conference, the formal establishment of a child protection plan, a core group to provide the key day-to-day coordination and monitoring of the work, and the designation of a lead social worker to manage the plan. Not only should the lead social worker be qualified and experienced, but the responsibilities for managing and coordinating the system clearly lie with the statutory local authority child welfare agency. It may be decided that the child protection plan does not give sufficient powers to protect the child and that the case needs to be taken to court to seek a care order to the local authority, possibly leading to separation.

When there is a risk to the life of a child or a likelihood of serious immediate harm, emergency action might be necessary. An Emergency Protection Order (EPO) gives authority to remove a child from home, and places the child under the protection of the applicant (usually the local authority) for a maximum of 8 days (with a possible extension for up to another 7 days), while the police can remove a child on a Police Protection Power for up to 3 days. However, the guidance is clear that police powers should be used only in exceptional circumstances, when there is insufficient time to seek a court approved EPO or for reasons relating to the immediate safety of the child.

Although new systems have been set in place to safeguard and promote the welfare of children, which are far more complex and wide-ranging than the much narrower and forensically focused system of the early 1990s, concerns about child protection very much lie at the center of the arrangements. In a country of some 11 million children, it is reported that every 10 days in England and Wales one child is killed by his or her parents (1 in 301,370 per annum) (Home Office, 2007). In half of all cases of children killed at the hands of another person, a parent is the principal suspect. In 2008, Local Children's Safeguarding Boards considered that 110 child deaths were thought to have been preventable (5%) (DCSF, 2009b).

Figure 4.1 provides a schematic summary of the nature and distribution of the work of local authority child welfare departments in England over a year and the key components of the different processes involved. What is demonstrated is that a major system has been established that aims to filter and categories cases, but which is much broader than child protection. From a starting point of 547,000 referrals to children's social care during 2009, just 37,900 ceased to be subject with a child protection plan (6% of the total referrals); 32,600 ceased to be subject to a child protection plan in the same year. A considerable amount of time, resources, and professional judgement are invested in trying to manage such a complex and demanding series of decision-making processes and to ensure that children are protected and their needs met.

Furthermore, when we look at the national statistics on the distribution between the categories of abuse for cases registered each year with child protection plans since 1994, a very interesting trend emerges (see Table 4.1).

Figure 4.1: Children in each stage of the referral and assessment procedure, year ending March 31, 2009

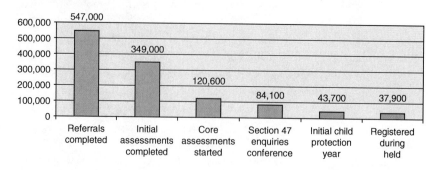

Source: Referrals, Assessments and Children and Young People who are subject of a Child Protection Plan or on Child Protection Registers, England. Year ending 31 March 2009.

The total has increased from 30,700 in 1994 to 37,900 in 2009: from 26 to 31/10,000 of the child population. In addition, the distributions between the different categories of abuse have changed significantly:

- The absolute and percentage increase in registrations for neglect from 7,800 (27%) in 1994 to 16,900 (45%) in 2009
- An increase in emotional abuse from 3,500 (12%) in 1994 to 9,700 (25%) in 2009
- A decline in physical abuse from 11,400 (40%) in 1994 to 5,800 (15%) in 2009
- A decline in sexual abuse registrations from 7,500 (26%) in 1994 to 2,200 (6%) in 2009.

Putting these figures together, child protection plan registrations for neglect and emotional abuse accounted for 11,300 cases (39% of total) in 1994, but 26,600 cases (70%) in 2009; whereas child protection plans categorized as physical and sexual abuse accounted for 18,900 (66% of total) in 1994, but just 8,000 (22%) in 2009. These figures provide an interesting insight into the changing professional and organizational responses to child abuse over the last 15 years and the way in which cases are categorized.

OUT-OF-HOME PLACEMENTS

So, given these patterns of child abuse and neglect in England, what services do children and families receive, and where do they live? Initially, it is interesting to consider to what extent government prioritizes families in its overall expenditure patterns. Public expenditure is complex to analyze, and international comparisons

Table 4.1: Numbers and Percentages of Children With Child Protection Plans Registered During the Period March 31, 1994–March 31, 2009, By Category of Abuse, in England (Alternate Years Before 2009)

Category of Abuse	Numbers (%)							
	1994	1996	1998	2000	2002	2004	2006	2009
Neglect	7,800	9,400	11,600	14,000	10,800	12,600	13,700	16,900
	(27%)	(33%)	(39%)	(46%)	(39%)	(41%)	(43%)	(45%)
Physical Abuse	11,400	10,700	9,900	8,700	5,300	5,700	5,100	5,800
	(40%)	(38%)	(33%)	(29%)	(19%)	(19%)	(16%)	(15%)
Sexual Abuse	7,500	6,200	6,100	5,600	2,800	2,800	2,600	2,200
	(26%)	(22%)	(20%)	(18%)	(10%)	(9%)	(8%)	(6%)
Emotional Abuse	3,500	4,000	4,800	5,500	4,700	5,600	6,700	9,700
	(12%)	(14%)	(16%)	(18%)	(17%)	(18%)	(21%)	(25%)
Mixed (not recommended by Working Together)	500	400	700	310	4,100	4,300	3,300	3,300
	(2%)	(1%)	(3%)	(1%)	(15%)	(14%)	(11%)	(9%)
Total	30,700	30,700	33,100	34,110	27,700	31,000	31,400	37,900

especially so. However, the Organization for Economic Cooperation and Development (OECD) (2009) publishes annual statistics on family expenditure: this includes family allowances, maternity or paternal leave, day care/home help services, and other benefits in kind. The data cover the U.K. as a whole (England, Scotland, Wales, and Northern Ireland). Of the 30 countries listed, U.K. government family expenditure is one of the highest. The latest statistics are for 2005, and in this year, the U.K. government allocated 3.2% of total gross domestic product (GDP) on family expenditure. This compared with 2% for the OECD countries overall. Furthermore, over the previous decade, the proportion of U.K. GDP allocated to family expenditure had risen noticeably from 2.3%. As noted in the introduction to this volume, of the 10 countries covered here, U.K. spending is on a par with Scandinavian countries—second only to Denmark and level with Sweden. Of the 15 million or so children in the U.K., at current prices, this equates to approximately £2,670 per child per annum.

Expenditure on preschool services is arguably a good indicator of how a society values its children. This has been a contentious subject in the U.K., going to the heart of the debate about family and State responsibilities for young children. Services should be high quality and aim to benefit children's social and educational development, not just to provide child care to encourage mothers to gain paid employment. We saw earlier how the government has made a major investment in the *Sure Start* initiative. Almost all four year-olds in England now access free early education as do 89% of three year-olds (DCSF, 2009c). Total U.K. government spending on under fives education is 5.7% of all education spending, which equates to approximately £3,700 per annum for each three- and four year-old (HM Treasury, 2009).

A national survey undertaken in 2005 indicated that, during a one-week period, approximately 385,000 children ("children in need") and/or their families were receiving a social work service of some form (DfES, 2006). This was about 1 in 50 of the total 0–17 child population but higher in some areas, including London (where the figure was 1 in 36), and between double and triple the national rate for some inner city boroughs. Overall, there were slightly more males "in need" than females and four in five were living at home (or independently). Average cost per child *per week* for local authorities in providing these services was calculated at £140 for children living at home and £675 for those living away in foster or residential care (DFES, 2006).

Child protection concerns were stated as the most common reason for children receiving a service: 30% of those remaining at home, rising to 55% of children who are "looked after" (or "in care"), mainly living in foster families[3] and residential homes. Of those for whom neglect or abuse were identified as the main factors in receiving a service, the majority (59%) remained with parents, although as ever this would have varied.

Comparing child care trends historically is complex. At the time of the previous section in 1994, some 49,300 children in England were being looked

after (DCSF, 1999). (This excludes children looked after under an agreed series of short-term placements ["respite care"], often disabled children.) The total annual cost of services for looked-after children in England is currently reported as approximately £2.19 billion—on average, £190 for each child in the country (House of Commons, 2009). The looked-after population had fallen markedly over the previous decade but has risen again and now stands at 60,900 (DCSF, 2009a) (see Table 4.2). Unaccompanied asylum seeking children account for 3,700. The looked-after population has increased steadily from 45/10,000 in 1994 to 55 in 2009. But interestingly, this does not reflect an increase in admissions, which had dropped by a quarter to 25,400 in 2009; instead, children are being looked after for longer. The rate has now remained broadly stable for the past 5 years. A third of all care leavers now are over 16 years old, compared with 27% in the mid-1990s. Several reasons could account for this pattern. The greater emphasis on family support highlighted in the 1989 legislation may have resulted in fewer avoidable, short-term separations but a greater realization of the more entrenched family problems of those who cannot return. There is also now

Table 4.2: Selected Looked-After Children Statistics 1994 and 2009, England

	Numbers (%)	
	1994	**2009**
All looked-after children	49,300	60,900
Rate per 1,000 under 18 years	4.5	5.5
Admissions	31,100	24,400
Number fostered	31,300 (65%)	44,200 (73%)
% fostered with unrelated	[not known]	(85%)
% fostered with related		(15%)
Number in residential care[1]	8,100 (16%)	7,920 (13%)

[1] Includes homes and hostels, residential special schools for pupils with special educational needs, and secure units.

greater recognition of the dangers of discharging prematurely vulnerable older adolescents from the care system into independence (Stein & Munro, 2008).

The average age of looked-after children in England is currently about 12 years. A fifth are 16 years and older. However, linked with the previous point, the average age of those *entering* the care system is nearer 8 years. Only 2,600 children (4%) of looked-after children are placed with consent for adoption, and 3,300 were adopted from care in 2009. As adoption numbers have declined in recent years, questions have been raised about the future of adoption in England (Simmonds, 2009). Doubts exist due to the human rights issues of contested adoptions (intercountry adoption is not encouraged in England), the often negative public depiction of adoption, the growing age profile of children, and legal barriers, including delay.

International comparisons are interesting, for example of different outcomes from care, but we need to be cautious as different care systems may be doing quite different things with contrasting populations. This is best exemplified in Thoburn's (2007) comparative study of out-of-home care services. Her research spanned 14 countries, including six of the 10 represented in this book. She concluded that countries have very different patterns of out-of-home care, including living-away rates. Compared with many countries, England and other U.K. nations tend to have comparatively low numbers in care with high thresholds for entry, high early exit rates with fewer children growing up in long-term placements, and a large number of teenage admissions. These factors would affect comparative outcomes, such as the educational achievements of care leavers.

The same authors, Thoburn et al. (2005), also explored patterns of child welfare service use of minority ethnic families. In England, in 2008, three-quarters of looked-after children were white, and minority ethnic groups overall were therefore over-represented. But this masks important differences. (Information on ethnicity of looked-after children was not gathered in the 1990s.) The largest single minority grouping is actually children of mixed ethnicity, which is a very diverse category but mostly constitutes those of African-Caribbean/white parentage. Alongside this mixed ethnicity group, those of African and also Caribbean descent are over-represented by a factor of more than 2:1. In contrast, those of South Asian origin—Pakistani, Indian, and Bangladeshi—are very small in number and greatly under-represented. The authors argue for further research that disaggregates ethnic groups, including local studies that focus on particular populations, histories, and dynamics. This would include the particular barriers to service use, including racism and discrimination; experiences of caring for disabled children; and the impact of domestic violence.

Better evidence is available of the experiences of minority ethnic children in the care system in England (Selwyn et al., 2010). It is unwise to make broad generalizations about minority ethnic children as a homogeneous group, as quite specific factors apply to different ethnic groups. The practice has been questioned of social workers who mainly perceive mixed-ethnicity children as "black" and often, therefore, priorities the ethnicity of the birth father in seeking care placements. This could limit permanency options. Particular barriers have been found to the adoption of Asian, African-Caribbean, and African children due to delay, poor assessments, and social workers being unduly pessimistic about the likelihood of finding a permanent family (Selwyn et al., 2010).

Foster Family and Residential Care

Table 4.2 shows the placement patterns of looked-after children in England. Over 70% of all looked-after children on any one day are living with foster families, and only 13% are based in residential homes. (Most of the remainder live with birth parents or independently in the community.) Five in every six of the fostered group live with unrelated carers, and one in six are with relatives (or friends). Foster family care has continued to grow over the past decade, and residential care has diminished in scale, which appears part of a broader international trend (Bullock et al., 2006).

Foster family care in England has witnessed a major transformation over the last 10 years. Around the time of the previous publication, it was argued that foster care was professionally underdeveloped, had low status, and attracted little research interest (Berridge, 1997). Some questioned at the time whether there was a finite number of foster carers in society who were prepared to undertake their challenging role; yet, as the table shows, the number being fostered has grown by over a third. About a quarter of placements are now provided by private and voluntary agencies. Foster care has achieved greater professional parity with other placement options, partly perhaps for this reason. Remuneration, support, and training have improved to some degree, but many would argue are still insufficient. For example, in recent years, government has set recommended minimum allowances for foster carers: these concern meeting the costs of accommodating children rather than any reward element. These are age-related and currently stand at £108 per week for 0- to 4-year-olds; £119 for 5- to 10-year-olds; £137 for 11- to 15-year-olds; and £159 per week for each over-16. Recommended London/south-east England rates are about 15% higher. However, the *Fostering Network*, a U.K. charity that represents foster carers, argues that to cover costs of fostering, basic allowances need to be about 30% higher. Their annual survey reveals that 1 in 11 local authorities nationally pay below the government recommended minimum fostering allowance. Two-fifths pay below the *Fostering Network* suggested rates (Fostering Network, 2009). They conclude that significant extra investment is still required from local authorities.

Foster carers are more likely now to have some involvement in key decisions. It is the preferred placement of choice, especially for younger children who have experienced abuse and inconsistent parenting. A recent overview of fostering in England concluded that it is an impressive service that caters for a wide variety of children with pressing problems (Sinclair & Wilson, 2009). Its success depends on the quality of foster carers, whose recruitment and retention are key. More attention in England is often given to organizational change, with little evidence that this is the key to greater success (Sinclair & Wilson, 2009).

Fostering with relatives is an area that has received increasing attention in England, although interestingly its scale has remained similar over the decade; the bulk of its expansion occurred in the early 1990s. Policy and local procedures have sometimes been unclear about the status of relatives as carers. Research has shown that outcomes of relative care are mainly positive, although frequently at some considerable costs to carers themselves, mainly grandparents (Farmer & Moyers, 2008). Practitioners also need to appreciate that relative care should not be seen as a panacea and that placement with unrelated carers is often preferable.

The use of children's residential care in England has levelled out at around 13% of the total group. It is perceived as an expensive although necessary service, with total individual costs averaging approximately £120,000 per annum (Berridge et al., 2008). Most residents are older adolescents, with more disrupted backgrounds and displaying a wider range of behavioral problems than those in foster care. Maltreatment affects teenagers, not just younger children, and the study cited above found that some two-thirds of residents were living away from home partly due to abuse or neglect.

Residential care especially, and to some extent the care system in England generally, has been criticized for its poor educational and other outcomes for children. The Berridge et al. (2008) research included a comparative, 9-month follow-up study across placements of outcomes for 150 adolescents posing a range of challenging behaviors. Using a variety of measures, in fact, most young people were judged to be making progress in their behavioral, emotional, social, and educational difficulties. This applied across placement categories, but the fostered group was doing better than those in residential children's homes. This was not due solely to background differences. Overall, young people were mainly positive about the care they received, and a good range of study supports was in place to help with their education. However, over the 9 months, instability was high: half of the young people had a change of social worker and four in 10 changed placements, although the impact of moves was felt to be mainly positive.

CONCLUSION

The Death of Baby Peter and its Consequences

What we have suggested in this chapter is that the period since 1994 has seen considerable change in policy and practice in England. More particularly, we have argued that, while far from straightforward, the general trend has been one which has attempted to broaden approaches to child protection and tried to prioritize prevention and early intervention. A clear attempt has been made to develop a much more explicit family service orientation, and there has been a growing emphasis on attempts to improve the well-being of *all* children. The changes have been driven by a strong performance management, centrally driven framework, one in which the role of information communication technology (ICT) has become key, and managers and practitioners have been spending an increasing amount of time inputting information into computers. The administrative and bureaucratic demands of the work have increased inexorably.

However, as we suggested in the introduction, the period since November 2008 has been one of considerable turmoil, if not crisis. It has the potential to undermine the aims of the *Every Child Matters: Change for Children* program and the other attempts to refocus child protection over the previous 15 years.

On November 11, 2008, two men were convicted of causing or allowing the death of 17-month-old Baby Peter, including his stepfather. The baby's mother had already pleaded guilty to the charge. During the trial, the court heard that Baby Peter was used as a "punch bag" and that his mother had deceived and manipulated professionals with lies and on one occasion had smeared him with chocolate to hide his bruises. There had been over 60 contacts with the family from a variety of health and social care professionals, and he was pronounced dead just 48 hours after a hospital doctor failed to identify that he had a broken spine. He was the subject of a child protection plan with Haringey local authority in London—the local authority that had been at the center of failures to protect Victoria Climbié back in 2000.

The media response was immediate and very critical of the services, particularly the local authority. The largest selling daily tabloid newspaper, *The Sun*, ran a campaign aimed at getting the professionals involved in the case sacked from their jobs under the banner of "Beautiful Baby P: Campaign for Justice" (*The Sun* November 15, 2008). Two weeks later, the newspaper delivered a petition to the Prime Minister containing 1.5 million signatures and claiming it was the largest and most successful campaign of its sort ever. In addition, a large number of Facebook groups, comprising over 1.6 million members, were set up in memory of Baby Peter and seeking justice for his killers. This weight of expressed opinion put major pressure on the government Minister, Ed Balls, to be seen to be acting authoritatively in order to take control of the situation. He responded by:

- Ordering the Office for Standards in Education, Children's Services and Skills (Ofsted), the Healthcare Commission, and the Police inspectorate to carry out an urgent Joint Area Review (JAR) of safeguarding in Haringey;
- Ordering the preparation of a new and independent Serious Case Review following the publication of the original one on 12 November, one which he deemed to be inadequate and insufficiently critical;

- Appointing Lord Laming to carry out an urgent review of child protection in England to report in 3 months;
- Establishing a Social Work Task Force to identify any barriers that social workers faced in doing their jobs effectively and to make recommendations for improvements and the long-term reform of social work, to report in the autumn of 2009.

On receipt of the JAR on December 1, 2008, which he described as "devastating," the Minister announced he was using his powers under the Education Act 1996 to direct Haringey to remove the Director of Children's Services. Later that month, she was sacked by the council without compensation and with immediate effect. In April 2009, Haringey Council also dismissed four other employees connected to the Baby Peter case—the Deputy Director of Children's Services, the Head of Children in Need and Safeguarding Services, the Team Manager, and the Social Worker. In addition, the pediatrician who examined Baby Peter 2 days before his death but missed the most serious injuries was suspended from the medical register, and the family doctor who saw Baby Peter at least 15 times and was the first to raise the alarm about the baby's abuse was also suspended from the medical register.

Very quickly, reports surfaced that it was becoming very difficult to recruit and retain staff nationally to work in children's social care, particularly social workers, and that morale was at an all time low (LGA, 2009). The case was clearly having wide-scale reverberations. A number of influential commentators, including the House of Commons Children, Schools and Families Parliamentary Committee (House of Commons, 2009) began to argue that the threshold for admitting children into state care was too high. Not only should Baby Peter have been admitted to care some months before his death, but his situation was not seen as unusual. Similarly, the Children and Family Court Advisory and Support Service (CAFCASS, 2009) produced figures that demonstrated that there were nearly 50% more care applications to court in the second half of 2008–09 compared with the first half of the year; demand for care cases was 39% higher in March 2009 compared to March 2008; and the demand for care continued to remain at an unprecedentedly high level for the first two quarters of 2009–10, with June 2009 having the highest demand for care ever recorded for a single month.

A survey produced by the Association of Directors of Children's Services (Brookes, 2010), based on responses from 105 local authorities in England (69% of the total) covering 73% of the under-18 population, compared the increases in child protection activity and workload between the two quarters, October–December 2007 and October–December 2009. There were increases of 25% in initial contacts, 17% in referrals, 21% in Section 47 enquiries, 23% in initial assessments, 20% in initial child protection conferences, of 33% for children subject to a child protection plan, 39% in police protection orders, 32% in emergency protection orders, and 38% in interim care orders. There was also a 17% increase in the number of children starting to be "looked-after," so that the number of children looked after at December 31, 2009 was 8.1% higher than at December 31, 2007.

Although it is early days to assess the likely long-term impact of the Baby Peter case on policy and practice, it has clearly engendered a sense of very high anxiety among government officials, children's services managers, and practitioners; all the indications are that concerns about child protection have moved center stage. It is also notable that the report produced by Lord Laming in March 2009 was entitled *The Protection of Children in England*, and that both this and the government's response (HM Government, 2009) were framed in terms of child protection, whereas before policy and practice had been framed more generally in terms of safeguarding and promoting the welfare of the child.

In addition to rediscovering child protection, England also seems to have rediscovered professional social work. It is a particular irony that the area in which social work has been so heavily criticized for over 30 years, child protection, is the area of practice in which it continues to be seen as having a key role to play, and the failures in the Baby Peter case seem to have reinforced this even further. The work of the Social Work Task Force, which reported in late 2009 (Social Work Task Force, 2009) is clearly central in this regard. The New Labour government made it clear that a major contribution to the improvement in child protection practice was crucially dependent on the rejuvenation of a well-trained, respected, and professionalized social work service. It seemed that it was recognized that child protection work was complex, skilled, and very demanding. Although improving systems and inter-agency communication were important, improving the service was now seen as being vitally dependent on supporting and investing in a professional social work workforce.

However, the situation is made more complex by the growing impact of the global economic crisis. Since late 2008, England has experienced a growth in unemployment and house repossessions, and the pervasive negative impact upon the well-being of children and families has become more evident. In the May 2010 general election, a change of government occurred. After 13 years of rule, New Labour lost power, to be replaced by a coalition government made up of the Conservative and Liberal-Democrat parties. This was the first time since World War II that a coalition government had been formed. The new government immediately made it clear that it was to embark on a series of public expenditure cuts, to try to reduce the government debt and balance the public finances. Although this will have a direct impact upon all areas of public services it is, as yet, very unclear what the detail of the cuts will be. This changing political, social, and economic context is of considerable significance, but how it will impact on the more specific reforms to child protection and social work outlined by the previous New Labour government is difficult to anticipate. However, clearly, we cannot assume that the *Every Child Matters* reforms will be developed and implemented in the way originally envisaged.

NOTES

1   We are grateful to Lorna Henry from the School for Policy Studies, University of Bristol, who helped with gathering some statistical data for this chapter.

2   Victoria Adjo Climbié was born on the Ivory Coast in West Africa on November 2, 1991. Her aunt, Marie Therese Kouau, brought her to London in April 1999. In the following 9 months, the family was known to four different local authority social service departments, two hospitals, two police child protection teams, and a family center run by the National Society for the Prevention of Cruelty to Children (NSPCC). However, when she died on February 25, 2000, the Home Office pathologist found 128 separate injuries on her body as a result of being beaten by a range of sharp and blunt instruments. It was the worst case of deliberate harm to a child that he had ever seen. Marie Therese Kouao and her boyfriend, Carl Manning, were convicted of her murder in January 2001. The government immediately set up an inquiry chaired by Lord Laming to investigate the involvement of the various public agencies in the case and to make recommendations for change to ensure that such a death could be avoided in the future. Lord Laming's report was published in January 2003 (Laming, 2003).

3   "Foster care" in the U.K. refers only to family-based, not residential care.

REFERENCES

Berridge, D. (1997). England: Child Abuse Reports, Responses, and Reforms. In N. Gilbert (Ed.), *Combatting child abuse: International perspectives and trends.* New York: Oxford University Press.

Berridge, D. (1997). *Foster care: A research review.* London: Stationery Office.

Berridge, D., Dance, C., Beecham, J., & Field, S. (2008). *Educating difficult adolescents: Effective education for children in public care or with emotional and behavioural difficulties.* London: Jessica Kingsley.

Brookes, C. (2010). *Safeguarding pressures project: Results of data collection.* Manchester: Association of Directors of Children's Services.

Bullock, R., Courtney, M., Parker, R., Sinclair, I., & Thoburn, J. (2006). Can the corporate state parent? *Children and Youth Services Review, 28,* 1344–1358.

Byrne, D. (2005). *Social exclusion,* 2nd ed. Buckingham: Open University Press.

Chief Secretary to the Treasury. (2003). *Every child matters.* London: Stationery Office.

Children and Family Court Advisory and Support Service. (2009). *CAFCASS care demand–Latest quarterly figures: October 20, 2009.* London: CAFCASS

Corby, B., Doig, A., & Roberts, V. (2001). *Public inquiries in abuse of children in residential care.* London: Jessica Kingsley.

Department for Children, Schools and Families. (1999). *Children looked after by local authorities. Year ending March 31, 1998, England.* London: DCSF.

Department for Children, Schools and Families.(2009a). *Children looked after by local authorities. Year ending March 31, 2009. England.* London: DCSF.

Department for Children, Schools and Families. (2009b). *Preventable child deaths in England: Year ending March 31, 2009.* London: DCSF.

Department for Children, Schools and Families. (2009c). *Provision for children under five years of age in England. January 2009.* London: DCSF.

Department for Education and Skills. (2004a). *Every Child Matters: Change for children.* London: Department for Education and Skills.

Department for Education and Skills. (2004b). *Every child matters: Next steps.* London: Department for Education and Skills.

Department for Education and Skills. (2006). *Children in need in England: Results of a survey of activity and expenditure as reported by local authority social services' children and families teams for a survey week in February 2005.* London: DES.

Department of Health. (1995). *Child protection: Messages from research.* London: Her Majesty's Stationery Office.

Department of Health. (2001). *The Children Act Now: Messages from research.* London: Stationery Office.

Department of Health, Department of Education and Employment, Home Office. (2000). *Framework for the assessment of children in need and their families.* London: Stationery Office.

Department of Health, Home Office, Department of Education and Employment. (1999). *Working together to safeguard children: A guide to inter-agency working to safeguard and promote the welfare of children.* London: Stationery Office.

Farmer, E., & Moyers, S. (2008). *Kinship care: Fostering effective family and friends placements.* London: Jessica Kingsley.

Featherstone, B. (2004). *Family life and family support: A feminist analysis.* Basingstoke: Palgrave Macmillan.

Fostering Network. (2009). *The fostering network annual survey of allowances 2008–09.* London: Fostering Network.

France, A., & Utting, D. (2005). The paradigm of "risk and protection-focussed prevention" and its impact on services for children and families. *Children & Society, 18*(2), 77–90.

Frost, N., & Parton, N. (2009). *Understanding children's social cares: Politics, policy and practice.* London: Sage.

HM Government. (2006). *Working together to safeguard children: A guide to inter-agency working to safeguard and promote the welfare of children.* London: Stationery Office.

HM Government. (2008). *Staying safe: Action plan.* London: Department for Children, Schools and Families.

HM Government. (2009). *The protection of children in England: Action plan.* The Government Response to Lord Laming. Cm758. London: Department for Children, Schools and Families.

HM Government. (2010). *Working together to safeguard children: A guide to inter-agency working to safeguard and promote the welfare of children.* London: Department for Children, Schools and Families.

HM Treasury. (2009). *Public expenditure statistical analyses 2009.* London: HM Treasury.

Home Office. (2007). *Homicides, firearms offences and intimate violence 2005–2006: Supplementary volume 1 to Crime in England and Wales.* London: Home Office.

Home Office, Department of Health, Department of Education and Science, the Welsh Office. (1991). *Working together under the Children Act 1989: A guide to arrangements for inter-agency cooperation for the protection of children from abuse.* London: Her Majesty's Stationery Office.

House of Commons. Children, Schools and Families Committee.(2009). *Looked-after children.* Retrieved August 6, 2009 from http://www.publications.parliament.uk pa cm200809 cmselect cmchilsch 111 11106.htm

Hudson, B. (2005). Partnership working and the children's services agenda: Is it feasible? *Journal of Integrated Care, 13*(2), 7–17.

Laming Report. (2003). *The Victoria Climbié inquiry: Report of an inquiry by Lord Laming.* Cm5730. London: Stationery Office.

Laming Report. (2009). *The protection of children in England: A progress report.* HC 330. London: Stationery Office.

Levitas, R. (2005). *The inclusive society? Social exclusion and New Labour,* 2nd ed. Basingstoke: Palgrave Macmillan.

Local Government Association. (2009). *Councils struggling to recruit social workers in wake of Baby P.* London: LGA.

Melhuish E., et al. (2008). *The impact of Sure Start local programmes on three year olds and their families.* The National Evaluation of Sure Start (NESS). London: HMSO.

OECD. (2009). OECD Social Expenditure Statistics. Retrieved August 6, 2009 from http: stats.oecd.org brandedviewpilot default.aspx?datasetcode=socx_agg

Parton, N. (1997). *Child protection and family support: Tensions, contradictions and possibilities*. London: Routledge.

Parton, N. (2006). *Safeguarding childhood: Early intervention and surveillance in a late modern society*. Basingstoke: Palgrave Macmillan.

Parton, N. (2008). The "Change for Children" programme in england: towards the preventive surveillance state. *Journal of Law and Society, 35*(1), 166–187.

Parton, N. (2010). "From dangerousness to risk": The growing importance of screening and surveillance systems for safeguarding and promoting the well-being of children in England. *Health, Risk and Society, 12*(1), 51–64.

Peckover, S., White, S., & Hall, C. (2008). From policy to practice: Implementation and negotiation of technologies in everyday child welfare. *Children & Society, 23*(2), 136–148.

Powell, M. (Eds.). (2008). *Modernising the welfare state: The Blair legacy*. Bristol: The Policy Press.

Secretary of State for Social Services. (1974). *Report of the inquiry into the care and supervision provided in relation to Maria Colwell*. London: Her Majesty's Stationery Office.

Selwyn, J., Harris, P., Quinton, D., Nawaz, S., Wijedasa, D., & Wood, M. (2010). *Pathways to permanence for Black, Asian and mixed ethnicity children*. London: BAAF.

Sinclair, I., & Wilson, K. (2009). Foster Care in England. In G. Schofield & J. Simmonds (Eds.). *The child placement handbook: Research, policy and practice*. London: BAAF.

Simmonds, J. (2009). Adoption: Ethical Stalemate–Does Evidence Help?. Presentation to the British Agencies for Adoption and Fostering (BAAF) conference on The Future of Child Placement Practice: Messages from Research. London, March 26, 2009.

Social Work Task Force. (2009). *Building a safe, confident future: The final report of the Social work Task force: November 2009*. London: Department of Children, Schools and Families.

Stein, M., & Munro, E. (Eds.). (2008). *Young people's transitions from care to adulthood: International research and practice*. London: Jessica Kingsley.

Thoburn, J.(2007). *Globalisation and child welfare: Some lessons from a cross-national study of children in out of home care*. Social Work Monographs. Norwich: University of East Anglia.

Thoburn, J., Chand, A., & Procter, J. (2005). *Child welfare services for minority ethnic families: The research reviewed*. London: Jessica Kingsley.

Stafford, A., Vincent, S., & Parton, N. (2010). *Child protection reform across the U.K.* Edinburgh: Dunedin.

PART II

NORDIC SYSTEMS

5

THE DARK SIDE OF THE UNIVERSAL WELFARE STATE?: CHILD ABUSE AND PROTECTION IN SWEDEN

MADELEINE COCOZZA AND SVEN E.O. HORT

Children are entitled to care, security, and a good upbringing. Children are to be treated with respect for their person and individuality and may not be subjected to corporal punishment or any other humiliating treatment.

Swedish legislation: Children and Parental Code, Chapter 6 (1983: 47)

CHILD ABUSE AND NEGLECT IN THE WELFARE STATE

On more than one occasion, Sweden has been singled out as the most successful contemporary example of a harsh industrial class society transformed into an advanced human welfare society. Grounds for the claim are not lacking. Beginning the 20th century as the poorhouse of Europe, Sweden became one of the richest societies in the world while remaining one of the most egalitarian in culture. Family forms, as well as family law, went through remarkable transformations. So has childhood and adolescence. Following in the footsteps of neighbouring Denmark, through the welfare state—and not least through an active labour market policy and comprehensive social provisions in kind and cash—young persons as well as old, women and men, workers and farmers, all were recognized as worthy members of society and citizens with voices and social rights to lives of decency and dignity. Finland and Norway followed suit, and out of this process was born the renowned Nordic, or Scandinavian, welfare model (Alestalo, Hort, & Kuhn, 2010; see also Therborn, 2004; Hobsbawm, 2005). However, as was apparent already in the precursor to this book and which is still visible through reading all four Nordic contributions in this volume, child welfare policy and practice, in particular when protection of the poorest sections of society is in focus and the most controversial issues come to the fore, is a bone of contention throughout the far north of Europe. Sweden, being the largest nation in this part of the world with a population of almost 10 million people, out of which about 2 million are children aged 0–18, is no exception to this pattern. Although a pioneer in underwriting and implementing the United Nations (UN) Convention of the Rights of the Child, there is much to add about the limits of child-friendly policies and practices in Sweden (Rasmusson, 2009). For the great majority of children, no doubt Sweden is almost a paradise on earth, and their voices have been heard much more frequently in recent decades in social research, particular the voices of middle- and upper-middle-class girls and boys. But, for those on the margins of society, as for instance, the so-called *apathetic children*[1], it is closer to hell.

In the Shadows of the Past

For the last decades, two ghosts have haunted Swedish child protection and welfare services. First and foremost, the historical accusation that the state intervenes too frequently in the private lives of a changing social nucleus called the family. In 1982, from the German weekly *Der Spiegel* to the BBC, Sweden was portrayed as a "Kinder Gulag" with a world record for "the numbers, more precisely the percentage of children taken into custody" (Gould, 1988, p. 88). For many years, Swedish officialdom had a hard time shaking off this label, and although no longer seen in this light, it has continued to be regarded as a threat even into the end of the first decade of the new millennium. Second, local social workers, employed by municipal welfare services and responsible for child protection in Sweden, have been depicted as overly cautious, unenterprising, and even incompetent in taking care of the best interests of children. For instance, in early 2009, a 15-year-old girl committed suicide the day before the court was supposed to start hearing her sexual abuse case. This media story created an outcry against local social authorities for being too lenient and unwilling to immediately intervene. Such criticisms have, on and off, come to the fore, although cases such as this have been extremely rare. Nevertheless, intervention—including the prevention of child abuse and other kinds of maltreatment and neglect of children—into the private lives of families became a sensitive issue for social authorities, including politicians responsible for municipal welfare services, and social workers. Not to mention law- and policy makers at the national level of government who, as a rule, have preferred to hide behind local authorities.

Lately, a third, rather new phenomenon has received critical attention from foreign human rights observers: the isolation of children either in separate cells in central state youth reformatories or refugee camps, and perhaps even more egregious, the spectacle of youngsters under threat of deportation

(Andersson et al., 2009; Westerberg et al., 2009). In the former case, state institutions and their employees are accused of using more force than necessary (and than the law permits); in the latter case, due to ever more restrictive immigration policies, the state is held responsible for severely impairing the health of adults and children (as in the case of "apathetic" refugee children). Immigration authorities have kept families and their children under strict surveillance after an application for residency has been turned down but is under appeal or while these families await deportation. National authorities, including social welfare agencies, are held responsible for manipulating data, information, and knowledge following media coverage (Tamas, 2009). In the wake of these occurrences, the question of ethnicity in child welfare policy has reached the public agenda. In the spotlight is the relationship between the harsh national state and the least powerful members of a global class society.

Framed in the universality of the highly decentralized post-war welfare state model, child protection has been deliberately integrated into a system of general municipal family welfare services. In Sweden, universal services start before the delivery of the child, in the form of prenatal health check-ups, abortion, and paternal education, and continue until the child's entrance into adult life and further into old age. All citizens and most residents are included under a tax-financed social safety net. Local authorities—municipalities as well as county councils—are in charge of free or highly subsidized educational and health services for the younger generation, which includes pre-school as well as free education. Moreover, the central state provides, for instance, a general child allowance, and income-related paternal insurance ensures the standard of living for most families. Public spending on social protection, including child welfare, is thus substantial and looked upon as an investment in human beings and the future of society (Hort, 2003; Platzer 2009). In a comparative perspective, social spending is substantial and in this sense, Sweden is no exception to the current pattern of fairly generous public child welfare in Scandinavia.

Thus, throughout the post-war decades there has been a consistent trend toward a deresidualization of welfare policy and practice in Sweden, an attempt to move its poverty-relief focus away from targeting services to only the poor and toward scrutinizing worthy as well as undeserving claimants and clients. Nevertheless, with a history of rather harsh intrusion in family life, residual practices were part and parcel of the old, predominantly pre-war system of poor relief. Despite the fact that the 1982 Social Service Act—which integrated child welfare legislation and other branches of special social legislation, and which boasted a voluntary, child- and parent-friendly approach—was looked upon by many experts in this field as a landmark achievement, child protection and welfare services have not been fully integrated and developed all over the country (see several articles in Andersson, 2006; Eliasson-Lappalainen et al., 2009).[2] In this chapter, we first outline the characteristics of the current formal Swedish child protection system. Next, we turn to systemic changes and trends in social practice during the last 15 years. And we end by examining the prospects inherent in the present overview of the system initiated by the national government in December 2007 and presented to the public as a proposal for a new child protection law in June 2009. In the concluding section, this political intervention, as well as other challenges to the present Swedish child protection system, will be discussed 2009).[2] In this from a macro-sociological perspective.

FAMILY WELFARE SERVICES VERSUS CHILD PROTECTION

An analysis of welfare systems dealing with child abuse, maltreatment, and neglect in nine countries grouped them around two central dimensions: child protection versus family service orientation (Gilbert, 1997). In countries that emphasized child protection, the prevention of child abuse demands the protection of children from harm by potentially harmful relatives, "the child saving approach." In countries with a family service orientation, the psychological, marital, and socio-economic problems of the parents are considered more central, with child maltreatment conceived as an aspect of family conflicts and dysfunctions that are responsive to welfare service and public aid. A second difference concerns the reporting system. Primary intervention in the child protection system emphasizes an investigatory process, in contrast to the therapeutic family-need assessment of the service-oriented system. A third distinguishing characteristic is that, in a service-oriented system, representatives of public authority function more in partnership with parents compared to those in the child protective system. Using this classification, the system in Sweden was family service-oriented with a mandatory reporting system (see also Wiklund, 2006; Lagerberg, 2009).

In 1980, the enactment of new social service legislation in Sweden was an important step in a general trend toward developing a broader and integrative approach to child welfare policy and practices. Such policies and practice were supposed to become part and parcel of an all-encompassing, universal welfare state. That was the political intention both at the national and local levels of government at a time when the welfare state was still expanding and was looked upon as the model for the future. Political parties as well as strong lobby groups had advocated a sincere policy shift in an ambitious attempt to implement a truly democratic, egalitarian, and solidaristic universal welfare state. Thus, policy makers looked upon residual social policies as a thing of the past, a descendant of the old "poor relief" system, with its high degree of social control and human surveillance. Policy makers agreed that child welfare services belonged to local government, an important intrastate distinction in Sweden.

However, as mentioned, the enactment of new national legislation occurred at a time during which certain types of child services were heavily criticized. In the early 1980s, the international press, orchestrated by domestic lobby groups, had campaigned against a (welfare) state that"snatched children" from their parents.

Child welfare and social services were to meet family needs while ensuring that few children were taken into compulsory care or into foster homes. This law has been amended several times, but the general aims and fundamental principles set forth in the 1982 legislation are the same as in the legislation in force today. The current Social Service Act regulates different areas of social support and intervention, such as financial assistance, preschool child care, care of the elderly and handicapped, and care of substance abusers. The Act states that the local social service authority shall work in partnership with families to support children's personal, psychosocial, and social development. In addition, social services shall monitor families and children who show signs of unfavourable development and work in partnership with families to make sure that children at risk get protection and support. When it is determined to be in the best interest of the child, social services shall place the children in care outside their families (out-of-home care).

The legislation has two objectives: one is voluntary (family service), the other coercive (child protection). The two objectives result in two different kinds of inflow to the social services. The first type is a result of someone asking for social support; the second occurs when an official files a mandated report. Both can result in the same kind of support; thus, no intervention is specifically linked to child protection or to family support.

Child abuse and neglect is not defined in the legislation. What constitutes maltreatment is to be assessed within the three levels of child protection. In order not to restrict the conditions that could constitute detriment to a young person's health or development, the legislation does not specify such conditions. The child protection process in Sweden is composed of three gate-keeping posts, identified in the Social Service Act: reporting (chapter 14), investigation (chapter 11), and voluntary (chapter 4) or compulsory care (in the latter case, according to the supplemental Care of Young Person Act). Chapter 14 of the Act notes:

> Any person receiving information of a matter, which can imply a need for the social welfare committee to intervene for the protection of a child should notify the committee accordingly. Authorities whose activities affect children and young persons are duty bound, as are other authorities in health care, medical care, other forensic psychiatry investigation services, social services, and prison and probation services to notify the social welfare committee immediately of any matter which comes to their knowledge and may imply a need for the social welfare committee to intervene for the protection of a child. . . . (Ministry of Health and Social Affairs, 2005)

Comparatively speaking, it is a rather unusual approach to call for all citizens to act simply on the basis of suspicion and direct them to inform Social Services about children or youths who may need help or protection. In the Swedish case, the whole community is involved in the process of protecting children, although many abstain, of course, and the citizen reporter has the right to remain anonymous. Mandated reporters are those who have contacts with children on the job: school personnel, child care, child health care, child and adolescent psychiatry departments, paediatric departments, and the like. The first gate-keeping point involves an initial assessment by the municipal social services. Here, the validity of the report regarding child maltreatment is evaluated. If a social worker decides that the report does not present evidence that meets the legal standards for child maltreatment, then the case will be closed without further consideration. Reports that do not fit legal standards for a judgment of child maltreatment are supposed to be sorted out. There is no formal requirement to register cases when the reports do not lead to investigation (e.g., those screened at this first gate-keeping point). Such reports do not figure in Swedish national statistics or in the archives of the local social welfare departments. Reports determined to indicate the likelihood of child maltreatment are to be passed on to the next gate-keeping point: the investigation specified in chapter 11 of the Social Service Act:

> The social welfare committee shall without delay open an investigation of matters which have been brought to its knowledge by application or otherwise and which may occasion action by the committee. Information emanating from an investigation and material to the determination of a matter shall be securely stored. (Ministry of Health and Social Affairs, 2005)

This section of Swedish law applies both to investigations initiated by a parent and to those initiated by a mandated reporter. Children who are abused or neglected are first subjects of processes outlined in the Social Service Act. The ambition is to provide help to the child by offering additional public support or care. The legislation allows the authorities to look into a family's life and to decide if the child has been maltreated. If the investigation substantiates that the child has been maltreated, she or he must be supported. The case will then pass to the third gate-keeping point: the intervention level, where the authorities decide what kind of support the child needs. If parents agree to the intervention and supportive services that a social worker finds necessary, then this is given voluntarily. If a parent or youth refuses the help that the social worker calls for, then the coercive legislation—Care of Young Persons Act (1990:52)—is applicable, and care can be given without consent:

> A care order is to be issued, if due to physical or mental abuse, exploitation, neglect, or other circumstance in the home, there is a palpable risk of detriment to the young person's health or development. (Ministry of Health and Social Affairs, 2005)

It should be added that the inflow to social services then will also encompass those cases that, for example, in many other countries would be handled by a juvenile court. Swedish children who possibly have committed a crime are taken into custody by the police and then are handed over to social services. The same public authority then handles families' applications for support, juvenile criminality, and child protection. With this construction, the child protection process as a whole is difficult to distinguish from a system simply providing supportive measures.

The child welfare protection system is administered by municipal social service agencies. Social service is the legal and financial responsibility of local government; this occurs without much control or supervision when welfare services are privately delivered. Otherwise, the 290 Swedish municipalities are free to organize their services as they like, and consequently services may differ from one local authority to another. As long as the basic standards of the legislation are met, local authorities have the right to arrange their child welfare as it suits them. For instance, no cost levels are regulated for child welfare by law. Most of those working with these issues are trained as social workers, although their degree of professionalism in recent years has been under review. The average allocation of personnel resources in Swedish child welfare is one full-time worker per 30.9 referrals and investigations. When considering that one-third of the referrals are screened out and that 60% of these concern adolescents, the density of personnel must be considered high. Furthermore, each municipality has an elected council (politicians) that makes decisions on a wide range of matters, and in every specific case where, for example, a child is to be separated from his parents. Thus, in Sweden, the latter is not a professional decision but one made by elected officials followed up by a judicial review (if the separation does not have parental consent; i.e., coercive). Coercive decisions within social child care must first be presented to and accepted by the elected council in the municipality; then, the elected council applies for coercive care at the county court.

Until 2009, the work of the municipalities was supervised by one of the 21 central state county administrative boards that Sweden is divided into. The overall responsibility for supervising the child protection process lies with the National Board of Health and Welfare, and as of 2010, their regional offices will be in charge of inspecting municipal child protection services, reflecting the increased attention being given to this issue at the national level.

THE SOCIAL PRACTICE

The legislative policy that frames the child protection process provides general guidelines within which the municipalities and their employees are left to design the specific features of protection and support. In the following section, the everyday practice of child welfare protection services at the local level will be scrutinized based on available estimates and research.

The Filtering Process

Several comparative studies have described the handling of reports as a filtering process, following a fairly similar pattern despite different legislation (Parton et al., 1997). The reports were organized into a top level, representing the inflow, and a bottom level, representing children receiving services. The majority of referrals for child maltreatment received few services. In the only Swedish study of a total population of referrals made to a municipality in 1 year, the filtering process began with a total of 1,570 reports filed regarding 1,051 children. Sixty percent of the children were between 13 and 18 years old. The results show that after 41% of the reports were filtered out at gate-keeping point one, 802 reports were processed into gate-keeping point two. Out of these, 32% were filtered out after an investigation was completed. These children were not assessed to have been maltreated at the level specified in the Care of Young Persons Act, and the parents did not want assistance from social services. Few children remained in the child care system when the process was completed at gate-keeping point three. Overall intervention was provided for 16% of the cases; 14% on a voluntary basis and 2% on a compulsory basis. There are different interpretations of the small percentage of children receiving an intervention—16% remained at the end—as a result of the child protection process. One possibility is that families were helped in other ways during the child protection process (e.g., talks, referred to other institutions), and this is one of the purposes of a family service orientation. Another interpretation is that the number who received services is linked to the resources that are designated for that purpose, and that the number receiving services reflects this constraint within the system. When discussing the relation between the high inflows to the agencies relative to the outflow, several authors have argued that the vague criteria in legislation dealing with "suspicion of maltreatment" and the extension of child protection into the domain of child welfare has resulted in an overwhelming demand for services. Resources that are intended for maltreated children are "used up" in the filtering process, and therefore these at-risk children receive less attention and support than they deserve. Researchers question whether this is due to children in Sweden being more in need than in other countries, or if this could be an effect of "diagnostic inflation," as Parton (2006) maintains.

Mandatory reporting creates an inflow that brings more children to the notice of the social services in an attempt to support those children in need, but only a relatively small percent of these children receive services. The findings from one municipality (Cocozza, 2007) suggest that, when compared internationally, the Swedish system did not provide more services. The child protection process in a family service organization whose character strongly favors help and assistance and working in partnership with parents does not provide more services than do countries with different systems. One explanation for this finding lies in the organizational child protection system. The Social Service Act covers both family service and child protection processes. Since relatively few children get assistance, a question arises as to whether the organization of child protection may counteract the intended aim of the family service provisions. Families might turn down the assistance offered to avoid contact with a controlling authority. These issues suggest the need for a closer examination of the costs and benefits of having the child protection processes organized as family services.

How Many Children are Reported?

Studies of referrals in municipalities have resulted in a more accurate estimate of the number of children referred to the social services, although the variation is still considerable: from 11 to 24/1,000. Studies of who files reports in Sweden (Sundell & Egelund, 2001; Kanuitz et al., 2004) found a congruous pattern. When looking into who files mandated reports in Sweden, as a consequence of the lack of a juvenile delinquency system, the police have the highest rates of filing referrals to the Social Services. The police account for about one-third of referrals. Although most of the police reports are not filed due to a suspicion of maltreatment, they are automatically passed to the social services as a mandated report, and this procedure may distort the figures. In the total Swedish population study, 715 cases, including those reported by the police, remained after the filtering process. But when police reports are excluded, only 348 cases remained. Another finding from this study is that only 13% of the police reports were investigated. School personnel and the social services were the second most frequent mandated reporters. In the study of all reports in one municipality, it was notable that institutions meeting minors (child health centers and child care centers) reported only 11 children (2%) and institutions meeting parents with mental disorders reported only one case (Cocozza, 2007).

It appears that Swedish child welfare workers often refrain from their duty to report. One study found that child care personnel reported only 37% of the cases in which maltreatment of children was suspected (Sundell, 1997). The low reporting rate was explained by a lack of awareness on the part of directors of their obligation to report; that few of the reports led to an investigation; negative experience of previously reporting; and the absence of proof that a report actually helped the child. Investigating the identification of abuse and neglect by child health nurses another study came to the conclusion that out of 6,044 children that the nurses categorized as possibly being maltreated, only 11% were reported to social services. Determinants of nurse reporting to social services correlated with small district populations, regular contact with social services, and personal interest (Lagerberg, 2004). In a study of the experience of reporting child abuse and neglect among primary care and hospital-based physicians, 80% stated that they had filed a report regarding child abuse or neglect to Social Services, two-thirds had suspected and decided not to report, and 20% had never reported a case of child abuse or neglect during their working career (Borres & Hägg, 2007). Most noteworthy, as the major reason for not reporting, these professionals claimed a lack of confidence in social services.

The current legislation indicates the following situations in which a child could be in need of protection due to maltreatment: physical violence, psychological violence, sexual abuse, and emotional and/or practical neglect. The categories sexual and physical abuses have, in some studies, been found to constitute about 3%–6% of all cases. When report conditions were presented in one study, for children aged 0–12, the referrals concerned neglect 62%, abuse 34%, and child's own conduct 8% (multiple conditions can be register for the same child, so the total is more than 100%). When the referral regarded adolescents aged 13–18, the figures were child's own conduct 67%, neglect 26%, and abuse 7% (Kaunitz et al., 2004).

Gate-Keeping Points

There is sparse knowledge of the characteristics and proportion of cases screened out. Research has shown that practice varies widely, and systematic evaluations are lacking also in Sweden. Dissatisfaction with this vagueness has led researchers to argue that screening should be more formalized and that child protection agencies should develop policies to specify the criteria that should determine which reports should be accepted for investigation (Besharov, 1990; Zellman & Fair 2001).

The initial point of contact—the municipal social welfare office—having received a report, has to determine the seriousness of a case reported as suspected maltreatment and 2009).[2] In this decide whether to investigate the case or screen it out. The exclusion at the first gate-keeping point has in several studies been found to be approximately 30% (Kaunitz et al., 2004; Wiklund, 2006). The number of screened-out referrals is difficult to evaluate, and to increase knowledge of the screening process a study of 220 reports not investigated was carried out in 2000 (Cocozza, 2007). The written files of the 220 reports indicating possible child maltreatment were analyzed and re-evaluated. As a measure of the justification for the decisions, a 5-year follow-up study was done. The finding was that 76% of the reports still indicated child maltreatment after the initial assessment was done. In the follow-up study, 45% of the children had been investigated. The social worker used the family as the only source of information in 74% of the cases, in 6% someone outside the family was contacted, and in 11% no further information in addition to the report was collected. In 9%, data on information sources were missing. The findings are rather discouraging, as they challenge the belief that a report is a mean of ensuring that maltreatment does not continue. The study shows, that depending upon the way in which the initial assessments are made, maltreated children may run a risk of not being identified, even though the maltreatment has been reported. When the supervising county boards later conducted an inquiry, they came to the same conclusions (Länsstyrelserna, 2008).

The second decision made about a report is whether an investigation should lead to an intervention or not, or gate-keeping point number two. In Sweden, the substantiation rates vary considerably from one municipality to another. On the basis of existing evidence, a group of researchers has estimated the proportion of children subject for an investigation in social child care to be 3%–5% (Sundell & Egelund, 2007). In the study by Kaunitz et al. (2004), 65% of the reported children were investigated. The percentage investigated varied within geographic district, and could not be explained by socioeconomic factors such as the proportion of low-income earners, single mothers, recently arrived immigrants, etc. Another study found a major discrepancy between social workers over when an investigation should be initiated (Östberg et al., 2004). One result common to all the studies is that police reports were least likely to lead to an investigation being initiated.

A research group estimates that 20% of the children who had been investigated some time during childhood had a social child care measure (intervention). Among this group, 75% had been placed out of home on some occasion. The average age at which they had a measure was 5 years, and 20% of the children had had the measure for at least 10 years. The occurrence of social child care was stable for teenagers at 3%, increased to 4% for 17-year-olds, then dropped to 1% for 20-year-olds. Cohort studies of out-of-home placed children born 1970–1980 shows that 3%–3.5% had been placed voluntary or with compulsions some time during their childhood (Sundell et al., 2007). To summarize, it is estimated that of the approximately 100,000 children are investigated each year, half get support, which would correspond to 3% of all children and youth.

FROM INVESTIGATIONS AND INTERVENTIONS TO OUT-OF-HOME PLACEMENT

Investigations and interventions take place under the auspices of the municipal social welfare committee and its employees, although the judicial system is involved if, as a last resort, compulsory measures are deemed necessary. The notion of preventive measures or early intervention (i.e., that relevant measures should be taken by authorities as early as possible in each case) is the guiding principle, together with the principle of least possible intervention. In the latter case, the meaning is that out-of-home placements—separating child and parents—should not take place before other and less radical supportive alternatives have been considered and tested in cooperation with the custodians and with the consent of the child if she or he has reached the age of 12. Apart from coordinated preventive support from various parts of the social welfare apparatus—from preschools and schools to the health system, and in a wide sense including special child psychiatric clinics—supporting contact families and contact persons contracted by the social welfare agencies may facilitate the everyday life of children at risk and select families who have voluntarily agreed to receive public assistance after an investigation has begun. Since its inception with the new law in 1982, the latter measure has increased and received much acclaim. The official Swedish national collection of statistics changed in 1998, and earlier figures are not comparable to later; figures are shown from 2000.

In Table 5.1, noninstitutional care is presented. These measures could be a contact person, a contact family, or in-home service, which could be delivered to children living with their parents but also to children being placed in institutional care.

Despite the emphasis on the least-intrusive intervention, out-of-home placement, both residential and foster care, is clearly part of the child protection process. In this type of intervention, parental responsibility is, in principle, temporarily, but in practice, more or less permanently transferred to the social welfare authorities ("the state snatches children"). Placements outside the home environment, including foster care, normally take place with parental consent, whereas the alternative of adopting a child rarely is considered a viable option (Sallnäs, 2006; Vinnerljung, 2006; Andersson 2009a). Foster care is still the dominant form of out-of-home placement for young children, but kinship care has gradually become more accepted as an alternative by both politicians and social workers. Thus, voluntary out-of-home placement combined with the intention that, under normal circumstances, the child shall return to his or her biological parents is the guiding parental bonding and family reunification philosophy, which is far from the "state child snatching" approach. However, the distance between normality and deviance may be larger in practice than in theory, and the alternative to out-of-home placement by consent is often compulsory placements (Levin, 1998). Abandoned and abused "swinging door" children may be moving back and forth between the homes of their parents and a multitude of out-of-home placements, despite the fact that the right of a child to grow up under stable and secure conditions with affectionate adults has been thoroughly stressed (Höjer & Sjöholm, 2009). Purely voluntary care is of shorter duration than compulsory

Table 5.1: Children Receiving Noninstitutional Measures November 1, 1998–2007

Year	2000	2002	2005	2007
Total	28,000	28,600	28,000	28,300
Per thousand	13/1,000	13/1,000	12/1,000	12/1,000
Age				
0–12	9/1,000	11/1,000	10/1,000	10/1,000
13–17	13/1,000	18/1,000	18/1,000	18/1,000

Source: Barn och unga – insatser år 2000, 2002, 2005, 2007
Official sources, reports, and statistics for the relevant period are more or less fully documented in SOU 2009:68. Official statistics are also published on an annual basis by the National Board of Health and Welfare, sometimes in cooperation with Statistics Sweden (Barn och unga–insatser, Annual reports, various years).

intervention but the step from preventive measures in the home of the child to out-of-home placement in both types of intervention signify much to maintain long-lasting relationships between children and parents.

Moreover, in recent years, Sweden has experienced a shift from charitable, philanthropic, nonprofit and public residential care to a new private market of companies offering out-of-home placements. Foster parents have been portrayed as entrepreneurs and profit-minded businessmen, and together with consultants contracted by local authorities to facilitate placements, have driven the increase in the growth of out-of-home placements, in particular for adolescents. In addition, an increasing number of larger corporations that offer residential care have taken their share of the growing out-of-home placement market for children at risk.

So far, this chapter has examined the Swedish response to child abuse based mainly on estimates and figures from more or less critical social research. In examining reporting and out-of-home placement trends, we have to rely on administrative official statistics. Thus, it is pertinent to stress that it is difficult to obtain indications of reporting trends concerning child abuse or neglect per se. As mentioned, reports that are not considered cases for investigation and intervention by municipal social welfare committees and local social workers are not systematically filed, archived, and passed on to national statistical authorities. Moreover, as long as social child care is classified as voluntary, no specific reason is given in the national official statistics based on local agency practice. However, when care is of a compulsory nature, it is possible to make a distinction between cases related to the behaviour of the child—or, more correctly, of teenagers and adolescents—and those that involve inadequate parental attention, which often reflects some form of abuse or neglect of younger children (see Table 5.2).

Certain child abuse offenses are registered under the penal code, and furthermore some placement figures are related to such legislation. As discussed

Table 5.2: Out-of-Home Placements 1998–2007

Year	2000	2002	2005	2007
Total	14,000	15,000	15,200	15,100
Per thousand	6/1,000	6.6/1,000	6.6/1,000	6.6/1,000
Without consent	4,000	4,300	4,600	4,600
With consent	9,500	10,400	10,400	10,300
Immediate custody	150	160	200	200
New children	4,000	4,400	4,900	5,900
Per thousand	1.8/1,000	2/1,000	2.3/1,000	2.6/1,000

Source: Barn och unga – insatser år 2000, 2002, 2005, 2007
Official sources, reports, and statistics for the relevant period are more or less fully documented in SOU 2009:68. Official statistics are also published on an annual basis by the National Board of Health and Welfare, sometimes in cooperation with Statistics Sweden (Barn och unga–insatser, Annual reports, various years).

in earlier research, the number of allegations of child abuse and family violence continues to increase, reflecting the growth in the awareness of these types of offenses rather than an actual increase in the number of crimes committed (Olsson Hort, 1997). What has not been discussed (and is much harder to detect through official statistics) is the changing focus toward children raised by parents born outside of Sweden (Lundström & Sallnäs, 2003). The demographic shift toward a more ethnic heterogeneous population has been given considerable attention in recent years, not least in relation to youth and even "gangs." As for trends over the past decade, the total number of children and young persons for whom care outside the home was in effect on November 1 during the last year for which statistics are available—regardless of when placement began was 15,100 or roughly 6/1,000 of the population aged 0–17 (2007). This figure includes those in both voluntary and compulsory care, placements were due to a variety of reasons including child abuse and neglect, and for 5,900 of these children, care was initiated in 2007 (see Table 5.2). About 75% of the out-of-home placements are constituted of foster family care and 25% institutional care; this breakdown between foster family care and institutional care has been rather stable over the years. In a comparative Nordic perspective, Sweden has a low rate of out-of-home placements (Bengtsen & Jacobsen, 2009). The proportion of children under the age of 13 has been rather stable over the period, at 1.3/1,000. The majority of placements are found among persons between 13 and 17 years of age, thus reflecting a focus on the behavior of the (teenage) person, and thus not child abuse. The data on out-of-home placed children show an increase in children aged 13–17 who were new to the municipal social services.

COMPELLING ISSUES AND CHALLENGES

When child protection was reframed as a family welfare service, the change was definitely ideological and political, although consensual at the national level. Social liberal and democratic welfarism defined the agenda, reflecting a major transformation of Swedish society: the absence of widespread material poverty considerably reduced the placement of children in out-of-home residential care and, thus, the taking of children from their loved ones. Multiculturalism and its challenges were still in its infancy. Children or parents were no longer to blame; instead, the extended family was looked on as a resource for change. Those initiating the law assumed that child maltreatment, irrespective of social origins (class, gender, race, sexuality, etc.), was to be prevented by and children protected within the family welfare service system. National data on the process were, however, never collected and evaluated, and no other measure was implemented to know whether the new orientation was successful. When the child protection process was organized into a family service organization in 1982, the old child protection system seemed to disappear. Questions were seldom asked as to what extent children were protected under the new organization.

Since the late 1980s, however, with the death of several children due to the lack of social services intervention, there has been an increasing awareness that child maltreatment did not disappear, once the process of protection changed to a family service frame. The system has gone from being invisible to becoming a more visible one, and one that, in operation, cannot be regarded as safe from the point of view of maltreated children. Over the years, several attempts have been made to upgrade the child welfare protection system. The ratification of the UN child convention in 1990, articles 3 and 12 in particular, has, as in other countries, led to changes in the Social Service Act; the best interest of the child must be considered, whatever that is and whoever defines it (Rasmusson, 2009). When a measure regards a child, the will of the child must be taken into consideration, depending on the age and maturity of the child. What impact this change in legislation has had on social practice is still difficult say, despite recent efforts to evaluate it.

Throughout the post-war decades, the relationship between laymen and professionals has been a bone of contention in the social sector in Sweden. The reasons for the vague specifications in the Social Service Act may be because, in Sweden, the role of professionalism in the social welfare sector is not yet firmly grounded. The very nature of the Swedish welfare sector is a mix of areas of interests that frame a rather weak semi-professional estate. Child welfare decisions are not only made on the basis of knowledge but also on political and economic grounds. As explained previously, although social workers conduct the investigations in the child protection process, the final decisions are made by elected laypeople in local government positions, the child welfare committees, and, if the decision concerns compulsion, then the judicial system as well. Not all legislation in Sweden defines the professional role and level in this way. For example, in the Health and Medical Services Act (1982:763), legislation that defines health and medical services, professional levels are specified, and a nurse or a doctor is required to have specific specializations within health and medical care (Health and Medical Services Act, 1998:1513).

Even though the professional level is not defined in legislation, municipalities seem mostly to employ social workers (Bergmark & Lundström, 2000). In 2004, the National Board of Health and Welfare (NBHW) surveyed 100 municipalities and found that four out of five workers within the social child care system had completed a degree in social work. During the last decade, a discussion has emerged about the shortcomings of the professional level in the social child care system, and the views of teachers at the departments of social work have been studied (Egelund et al., 2000; Hindberg 2006). The National Board of Health and Welfare (2004) stated that there is a consensus about the fact that social work education in Sweden does not provide the specific knowledge needed to work within the social child care system, and that the social work degree is to be regarded as generalist education. Without some form of subspecialization, the education of social workers in Sweden is inadequate training for those engaged in such difficult work as child protection. Thus, there is an ongoing discussion about how to improve existing university programs for child protection work.

In 1995/96, the national government gave an assignment to the NBHW to develop methods and treatment in work with maltreated children, specifically sexually abused children. The results of this process and the focusing on methods laid a foundation for the development of Swedish child protection during the following years. Abuse, and sexual abuse in particular, has been a major concern. This has resulted in written documents about how to work with abuse. In the Swedish system, these categories of child maltreatment target other authorities than the social services, and there has been an effort to create units in which child psychiatry, police, prosecutors, pediatricians, and social services work together. Two such national projects; a national center for sexual and psychical abuse and joint centers of action and investigation ("child houses") have come out of this process.

Another challenge has been to develop specific methods to work with maltreated children (Eriksson et al., 2008). One is represented by the implementation of an assessment instrument in many municipalities called the BBIC. This is a tool adjusted for Swedish conditions imported from England; the acronym is from the Swedish for Framework for the Assessment of Children in Need and Their Families). Studies of the implementation of this instrument show that the quality of investigations has increased when the tool is used (Börjesson, 2009). Another effort in increasing the evaluation and implementation of social practice was to create a national Institute of Social Methods (IMS), which evaluates methods used by local social services. When national audits and inspections of the different levels of child protection have been made, the municipal social services have often been criticized for their approach to specific issues of child protection (Swedish National Audit Office, 2001/02; National Board of Health and Welfare, 2003).

In 2006, the government gave the county administrative boards the mandate to investigate the work by the social services with children in need of protection. The investigation resulted in a booklet that found major differences among the municipal social services, regarding what services were delivered, their quality, and the basic legal rights of the individual. In most municipalities, a range of noninstitutional services was provided, and the quality of investigations had improved. Almost all municipalities are or are considering using BBIC. There were still some municipalities failing to consider the child's perspective. Collaboration with other operators had increased. Referrals were found to be recorded adequately, but several municipalities waited for an unacceptably long time to decide whether an investigations should be initiated or not. The social services in some municipalities did not investigate serious cases of suspected child maltreatment. The county administrative boards found that, rather than the content of referral, it was the municipality in which the child lived that determined whether the referral was investigated or not. The social services foster home assignments were revealed as flawed in several areas. Foster homes were not thoroughly investigated, and some children were placed in foster home without the benefit of legal due process. Children placed in foster homes were seldom visited and when they were visited, social workers rarely spoke to the child privately. In contrast, there were several municipalities in which social workers visited children more than prescribed and involved children in deciding meeting arrangements (Länsstyrelserna, 2008).

Looking back over the past decade to describe perspectives and trends in child protection in Sweden, the question remains as to why children were not protected within the family service organization. As the system of supporting maltreated children by offering family service measures becomes more visible, through government commissions and research, about five to seven children are still dying per year due to abuse and neglect—this conclusion is by no means satisfying (Nordlund & Temrin, 2007). To address this situation, in December 2007, the government appointed a commission to review the legislation of social child care. The objectives pointed out for revision were the overall aims and responsibilities, the obligation of mandated reports, the investigations, and the follow-ups of measures in general and foster homes in particular given to children within social chid care. Another objective was to review the present specification of the professional level in the legislation. The commission has presented a proposal for a new legislation (SOU, 2009:68) that, if approved will be made effective during 2010.

In the meantime, the government reorganized the national structure for supervising local child welfare protection systems by moving the inspectors from the 21 central state county administrations to the six regional offices of the National Board of Health and Welfare. Nevertheless, the missing link in this governmental process is the lack of robust analysis of the issues and practices that underlie the system's failures to prevent child maltreatment.

CONCLUSION

Child Protection During the Neo-liberal Era

Although in no sense uncontested, the universal welfare state is still alive in Sweden. Many municipal services are rights-based, although tested against need, and only in a few cases means-tested. The beneficiary is both a citizen and a customer, both a taxpayer cum wage earner and a voter. Child welfare services are in general universal, although a fee is most often part of the system, in particular for services aimed at young children. From the 1980s, the role of local government in financing and providing such welfare services has been strengthened, although there is a tendency toward privatization of the delivery of services and a very marked movement in this direction in the residential care of young persons. Child protection is part of the system of municipal welfare services but is of a somewhat different kind. As a service, it is aimed at a select group of families and children nonetheless defined as universal. Although still voluntary in principle, the possibility of compulsory intervention is an alternative lurking behind the relationship between clients and authority, between family members and state powers. The providers of social services—the municipalities and their employees, the social workers—have the upper hand in dealing with families characterized by social problems, whether it is the child, parent(s), or the social order that is to be protected. Since the shake-ups of the 1980s, child abuse and neglect have occasionally topped the public agenda in Sweden, and practices have been scrutinized. Good intentions is one thing, actual practices another. During the first 15 years of new universal welfare legislation, at the different levels of policy and practices, the pattern was rather contradictory. On the one hand, a deliberate attempt was made to break with history and make welfare a social citizenship right, free from intrusive social control; on the other hand, attempts were made to intervene when things went wrong for children in atypical or deviant families. In theory, preventive, voluntary services had priority over coercive practices against families and children, which were considered a marginal phenomenon in social work practice.

What has happened in this field during the last 15 years? The universal welfare state is still around, although operating under different (and from a global perspective, neo-liberal), market conditions, which were to some extent already visible during the 1980s and early '90s. Although not very much has changed at the policy level, as of late 2007, the central government gave a state commission the task to investigate child protection policy and formulate new legislation and other types of central state support. Thus, change is in the air, so to speak. But on the ground, there are too few studies investigating variations in approaches to child protection at the local level to illuminate the pattern and full details of 290 independent practices. Without comprehensive and robust empirical evidence, the State Commission in June 2009 proposed a new Child Protection law, and most likely Parliament will make a decision later this year or early next year (SOU, 2009:68). More or less indefinite postponement is another, less plausible, alternative. Training of professionals will most likely get priority in the years to come, which may have repercussions on the quality of work at the grassroots level (Andersson, 2009b). However, the conclusion here is that there has come forward no unanimous response to the systemic flaws, and most likely uncertainties in this area of social action will prevail. The appearance of a rather unregulated private out-of-home placement market is further evidence in this direction. Decision-makers in the municipalities and their child protection workers are left alone in yet-uncharted territory.

Finally, although not very effectively shown in official statistics or academic research, there are definitely groups of children in Sweden who have not been sufficiently included in the general pattern of increased welfare and material progress, despite considerable public and private efforts in this direction during the most recent decade. Poverty has become more visible, not least among children (Salonen, 2007). The records of central state immigration authorities are a critical case. Moreover, most indicators point toward an overrepresentation in residential care of children with roots in countries other than Sweden; residential care is still thoroughly class-biased—now with an added ethnic twist. In domestic affairs, policies have indicated that the state should not strip parents of their responsibility, but through the municipalities, offer individual families a spectrum of supportive measures and also encourage enabling networks of friends and relatives. After the implementation of the 1982 welfare legislation, many municipal social services have been criticized for paying too little attention to the needs of socially marginalized children. Of course, some municipalities have made child protection and welfare a top priority; and some deserve criticism.

Throughout the most recent decades, media coverage has focused on bureaucratic failures, and several municipal officials have been scorned and scrapped. Already in the mid-1990s, the national government made maltreated children an official priority group under an initiative to improve the situation of vulnerable and disadvantaged children, and to strengthen the rights of children significantly following the UN Convention on the Rights of the Child. This has included the creation of the office of a national Ombudsman for Children. The efforts of lobby organizations, such as Save the Children and BRIS—The Rights of Children in Society—receive considerable public attention and enjoy widespread popular support. The welfare of children, including the most vulnerable, remains a highly emotional affair in Swedish civil society.

How much multiculturalism Sweden can absorb will most likely provide some of the key parameters for the answer to the future of welfare for children in the far north of Europe. Child protection has, as in other countries, not grown out of its poverty-relief shell, a conclusion that poses a continuing challenge for the numerous rhetorical adherents of the practices of the universal welfare state, as well as of uncompromised rights of children, including the maltreated. The paragraph from the Children and Parental Code quoted at the start of this article is still in force, if not always enforced, but carries a high legitimacy in both Swedish society and state.

NOTES

1   Refugee children suffering lying in bed in coma-like conditions, no longer eating or talking, whose parents are waiting for residence permit.

2 Some of these issues were dealt with in detail in the precursor (Gilbert, 1997) to this book. Thus, for a detailed historical perspective, the curious and devoted reader is recommended to consult that work

REFERENCES

Alestalo, M., Hort, S. E. O., & Kuhnle, S. (2010). The Nordic Model: Communalities, continuities, constraints, challenges. In S. Kuhnle, C. Yingzhang, K. Petersen, & P. Kettunen (Eds.), *The Nordic welfare state*. Shanghai: Fudan University Press. (In Chinese). [This chapter is available as a Working Paper from Hertie School of Government (Berlin).]

Andersson, G. (2009a). *Adoption som barnavårdsinsats [Adoption as a social child care measure]*. In Appendix volume to SOU 2009:68, pp.189–225. (In Swedish.)

Andersson, G. (2009b). *Snäll som kvalitetsindikator i social barnavård [Good as an indicator of quality in social child care]*. In Eliasson-Lappalainen, R., Meeuwise, A., & Parcan, A. (Eds.). (In Swedish.)

Andersson, G. (2006). Child and welfare in Sweden. In N. Freymond & G. Cameron (Eds.). *Towards positive systems of child and family welfare: International comparisons of child protection, family service and community caring systems*. Toronto: Toronto University Press.

Andersson G., Andersson, K., Hollander, A., Lundström T., Mattsson, T. Sallnäs, M., & Överlien, C. (2009). *Isolering hjälper inte utsatta barn [Imprisonment does not help vulnerable children]*. Svenska Dagbladet. Date - 2009-07-18. (In Swedish.)

Bengtsen, T.T., & Jacobsen, T.B. (2009). *Institutionsanbringelse af unge i Norden [Institutional upbringing of children in Nordic countries]*. Köpenhamn: SFI (Report 09:12). (In Norwegian.)

Bergmark, Å., & Lundström T. (2000). *Kunskaper och kunskapssyn [Knowledge and epistemological approach]*. Stockholm: Socionomernas forskningssupplement no. 12. (In Swedish.)

Besharov, D.J. (1990). *Recognising child abuse: A guide for the concerned*. New York: The Free Press.

Borres M.P., & Hägg A. (2007). Child abuse study among Swedish pediatricians and medical students. *Paediatrics International, 49*, 177–182.

Börjesson, B. (2009). "Det är ju ett svårt och oerhört kvalificerat jobb"–om förutsättningarna för att utveckla det sociala arbetet med barn och ungdomar [It is a difficult and enormously qualified job - about the conditions to develop social work with children and youth]. In Appendix to SOU 2009:68 pp. 227–307. (In Swedish.)

Cocozza, M. (2007). *The parenting of society: A study of child protection in Sweden–from report to support*. (Medical Dissertations no. 1027). *Linköping: Faculty of Health Sciences*.

Egelund, T. et al. (2000). *Social barnavårdskunskap och professionalisering* [*Social childcare knowledge becoming professionalized*]. Stockholm: Centrum för utvärdering av socialt arbete. (In Swedish.)

Eliasson-Lappalainen, R., Meeuwise, A., & Parcan, A. (Eds.). (2009). Den berusade båten–vänbok till Sune Sunesson [*The drunken boat- book to my friend Sune Sunesson*]. Lund: Arkiv. (In Swedish.)

Eriksson, M., Källström Cater, Å., Dahlkild-Öhman, G., & Näsman E.(Eds.). (2008). *Barns röster om våld* [*Children's voices about violence*]. Malmö: Gleerups. (In Swedish.)

Gilbert, N. (Ed.). (1997). *Combatting child abuse: International perspectives and trends.* Oxford: Oxford University Press.

Gould, A. (1988). *Control and conflict in welfare policy–the Swedish experience.* London: Longman.

Hindberg B. (2006). *Sårbara barn–att vara liten, misshandlad och försummad* [Vulnerable children- to be a child abused and neglected].Stockholm: Gothia. (In Swedish.)

Hobsbawm, E. (August 4, 2005). The retreat of the male. *London Review of Books.*

Hort, S.E.O. (2003). Back on track–to the future? The making and remaking of the Swedish welfare state during the 1990s. In N. Gilbert & R. Van Voorhis (Eds.), *Changing patterns of social protection.* New Brunswick: Transaction.

Höjer, I., & Sjöholm, Y. (2009). *Ungdomar i utsatta livssituationer och deras väg till självständighet* [Youth in exposed life situations and their ability to become independent]. In Appendix SOU 2009: 63 pp. 41–77. (In Swedish.)

Kaunitz C., Andrée Lövholm, C., & Sundell, K. (2004). *Social barnavård i Stockholms stadsdelar* [Social childcare in the districts of Stockholm]. Stockholm: Socialtjänstens FoU-enhet. (In Swedish.)

Lagerberg, D. (2009). *Skydd och stöd i social barnavård* [*Protection and support in social childcare*]. In Appendix to SOU 2009:68 pp. 79–188. (In Swedish.)

Lagerberg, D. (2004). A descriptive survey of Swedish child health nurses' awareness of abuse and neglect. *Acta Paediatrica, 93,* 692–701.

Lagerberg, D., & Sundelin, C. (2000). *Risk och prognos i socialt arbete med barn* [Risk and prediction in social work with children]. Stockholm: Centrum för utvärdering av socialt arbete. (In Swedish.)

Levin, C. (1998). *Uppfostringsanstalten–om tvång i föräldrars ställe* [Institutions of upbringing- about compulsion care instead of parent]. Lund: Arkiv Förlag. (In Swedish.)

Lundström T., & Sallnäs M. (2003). *Kön, klass och etnicitet i den sociala barnavården* [Gender, class and ethnicity in social childcare]. *Socialvetenskaplig tidskrift, 10,* 193–213. (In Swedish.)

Lundström T., & Winnerljung, B. (2001). Omhändertagande av barn under 1990-talet [Compulsion care of children in 1990]. In M. Szebehely (Ed.), *Välfärdstjänst i omvandling* [Welfare service in change]. Stockholm: Fritzes (SOU 2001:51). (In Swedish.)

Länsstyrelserna. (2008). *Socialtjänsten och barnen–länsstyrelsernas granskning av den sociala barn- och ungdomsvården 2006–2007* [Social services and the children- county administrative board check of the social childcare 2006–2007]. Stockholm: Länsstyrelserna i respektive län. (In Swedish.)

Nordlund, J., & Temrin, H. (2007). Do characteristics of parental child homicide in Sweden fit evaluation criteria? *Ethology, 113*(11), 1029–1035.

Olsson Hort, S.E. (1997). Sweden: Towards a de-residualization of Swedish child welfare policy and practice. In N. Gilbert (Ed.), *Combatting child abuse: International perspectives and trends.* New York: Oxford University Press.

Östberg, F., Wåhlander, E., & Milton, P. (2000). *Barnavårdsutredningar i sex kommuner. En vinjettstudie* [Social childcare investigations in six municipalities. A study]. Stockholm: Socialstyrelsen, Centrum för utvärdering i socialt arbete [Official statistics and government publications]. (In Swedish.)

Parton N., Thorpe, D., & Wattam, C. (1997). *Child protection risk and the moral order.* London: Maxmillan Press Ltd.

Parton N. (2006). Every child matters: The shift to prevention whilst strengthening protection in children's services in England. *Children and Youth Service Review, 28*, 976–992.

Platzer, E. (2009). De ekonomiskt värdelösa och emotionellt oersättliga barnen [The financially worthless and emotionally irreplaceable children]. In E. Fasth, et al. (Eds.), *Mellan hantverk och profession–samhällsvetenskap på klassisk grund: en vänbok till Gunnar Olofsson* [Between craft and profession - social science on classic foundation: a festschrift to Gunnar Olofsson]. Växjö: Växjö University Press. (In Swedish.)

Rasmusson, B. (2009). *20 år med barnkonventionen* [20-year child convention]. In Appendix to SOU 2009:68 pp. 7–39. (In Swedish.)

Sallnäs, M. (2006). Fosterhemsvård [Foster family care]. In V. Denvall, & B Vinnerljung (Eds.), *Nytta & fördärv–socialt arbete i kritisk belysning* [Benefit & ruin- social work in a critical elucidation]. Stockholm: Natur och kultur. (In Swedish.)

Sallnäs, M. (2000). *Barnavårdens institutioner–framväxt, ideologi och struktur* [The institutions of the social childcare–growth, ideology and structure]. Stockholm: Institutionen för socialt arbete. (In Swedish.)

Salonen, T. (2007). *Barns ekonomiska utsatthet–årsrapport 2006* [The financial exposure of children- annual report 2006]. Stockholm: Rädda Barnen. (In Swedish.)

SOU. (2009:68). *Lag om stöd och skydd för barn och unga* (LBU) [Legislation of support and protection for children and youth]. Stockholm: Ministry of Social Affairs (with an appendix volume consisting of five separate expert reports). (In Swedish.)

SFS. (1980:620). *Socialtjänstlag* [The Social Service Act]. (In Swedish.)

SFS. (1983:47). *Föräldrabalken* [Children and Parental Code]. (In Swedish.)

Sundell, K. (1997). Child care personnel's failure to report child maltreatment: Some Swedish evidence. *Child Abuse & Neglect, 21,* 91–105.

Sundell, K., & Egelund T. (2001). *Barnavårdsutredningar–en kunskapsöversikt* [Social childcare investigations- a survey of the body of knowledge]. Stockholm: Centrum för utvärdering av socialt arbete. (In Swedish.)

Sundell, K., & Egelund T. (2007). *Barnavårdsutredningar–en kunskapsöversikt* [Social childcare investigations- a survey of the body of knowledge]. Stockholm: IMS & Gothia. (In Swedish.)

Tamas, G. (2009). *De apatiska–om makt, myter och manipulation* [The apathetic- about power, myths and manipulation]. Stockholm: Natur och Kultur. (In Swedish.)

Therborn, G. (2004). *Between sex and power: Family in the world 1900-2000.* London: Routledge.

Westerberg, B., Ascher, H., Blennow, M., Florin, T., & Wiborn, K. (October 4, 2009). *Regeringen måste ändra sig om papperslösas sjukvård* [The government must change opinion about medical treatment to people without documents]. *Dagens Nyheter.* (In Swedish.)

Wiklund, S. (2006). *Den kommunala barnavården–om anmälningar, organisation och utfall* [The social childcare of the municipalities- about report, organisation and outcome]. Stockholm: Socialtjänstens FoU-enhet. (In Swedish.)

Vinnerljung, B. (2006). Institutionsvård av barn och unga [Institutional care of children and youth]. In V. Denvall & B Vinnerljung (Eds.), *Nytta & fördärv- socialt arbete i kritisk belysning* [Benefit & ruin- social work in a critical elucidation]. Stockholm: Natur och kultur. (In Swedish.)

Zellman, G., & Fair, C. (2001). Preventing and reporting abuse. In J. Briere, L. Berliner, J.A. Bulkley, C. Jenny Eliasson-Lappalainen, R., Meeuwise, A., & Parcan, A. (Eds.). (2009), & T Reid (Eds.), *The APSAC handbook on child maltreatment,* 2nd ed. Thousand Oaks, CA: Sage Publications.

6

COMBATTING CHILD ABUSE IN FINLAND: FROM FAMILY TO CHILD-CENTERED ORIENTATION

TARJA PÖSÖ

In the early and mid-1990s, child abuse was far from being a prominent issue in Finnish social policy. Within the existing system of services provided by local authorities or nongovernmental organizations (NGOs), interest was more or less focused on the welfare of families, with services and interventions functioning accordingly. The philosophy was metaphorically described as an hourglass model: when services are targeted to the family, the outcome profits the children as benefits, like the trickle of sand in an hourglass, filters down to them (Hurtig, 2003). Family-service orientation was strong, and Finland could easily be classified as belonging to such an orientation model, as suggested in *Combatting Child Abuse* (Gilbert, 1997).

There have, however, been considerable changes since the mid-1990s. Finland, with its 5.3 million inhabitants, 1 million of them being children under the age of 18, tries to balance providing universal benefits and services to all families with children in the tradition of the Nordic welfare states with recognizing the specific needs and problems some children and families have. The expenditure on cash benefits and services to families and children totaled 3% of the gross domestic product (GDP) in 2005 (Social protection…, 2007, p. 70). Changes suggest that Finland has moved away from the family service orientation, especially when treating child abuse.

This chapter examines the Finnish system, policy, and practice in relation to child abuse, first by giving an overview of the present system and subsequently by locating some tendencies that affect the present situation and have characterized the period since the early 1990s. The chapter is, however, fraught with definitional controversies that not only concern linguistic but also cultural translation. Special attention is therefore given to concepts and their local/national meanings at the beginning of the chapter.

CHILD MALTREATMENT, CHILD ABUSE, AND CHILD WELFARE: CONCEPTUAL CONFUSION

Finnish child welfare was fundamentally changed in 1983 when the Child Welfare Act (Act 683) was introduced. It identified child protection more sharply than ever as a form of social service provided by the public authority to families with children. The practises were framed accordingly, with a wide-angled approach to service needs given priority over an approach strictly focused on child abuse. Subsequent reforms reflected in the Child Welfare Act (417) of 2007 did not fundamentally alter that approach.

Consequently, as the vocabulary of legislation and practice side-steps fixed problem formulations, the terms "child abuse" and "child neglect," recognized by the Child Welfare Act before 1983, have almost disappeared from the child welfare vocabulary. Instead, system-based definitions are more common than phenomenon-based ones when describing Finnish child welfare as institutional practice: We speak about "the need for child welfare," "child welfare clienthood," or "decisions about taking the child in care" rather than about the particular children's or families' problems, such as abuse and neglect. This is reflected, among many other issues, in knowledge production. The national and most of the local and regional child welfare statistics are framed by such system-based definitions.

Translating the concepts used in Finnish social and child policy into English as "child abuse" or "child maltreatment" is therefore not without problems. Child abuse, for example, refers literally to violence or abuse of some kind, which was a standard concept in practice in the early part of the 20th century, but has given way to other concepts when talking about violence or related issues met with in child welfare. In the 1990s, the concept of *child maltreatment* was reintroduced, mainly from the point of view of health practitioners and nursing science (Paavilainen et al., 2001), and the concept, including abuse and neglect issues, has since become rooted in some health and social welfare practices. It is not, however, commonly used in child protection. At the other extreme, there is a tendency to address childhood social problems as "children's ill-fare" or "social exclusion," both in the media and among social welfare practitioners and policy makers. These are nonspecific concepts, used in a variety of ways to address the state of children and young people in general (Forsberg & Ritala-Koskinen, 2010).

Concepts are rarely innocuous; rather, they often contribute to the construction of social reality. The concepts used in Finnish social and child welfare policy, practice, and research should be understood in their own sociohistorical and cultural context. The English translation used for cross-cultural communication might not pay enough attention to these particulars (Hearn et al., 2004). Furthermore, in Finland, these concepts are mutable, varying depending on time, context, and actors. I have, therefore, some uneasiness about using these concepts in writing this chapter.

Keeping in mind these problems, I use the concepts "child abuse" and "child maltreatment" as they are relevant to the context of this book, even they do not fit the Finnish situation well. I present them in this chapter as social problem categories that are addressed by the child protection system. Therefore, issues of youth social problems, including criminality, will be taken into consideration since they are included in the Finnish child welfare system by legislation, ideology, and practice. Child welfare refers here, above all, to all the ways that society, including social policy and child protection, considers children's and families' welfare. I will use the concept "child protection" to describe the particular statutory activities of public authorities to support/protect children/families by providing them with special services, such as taking them into care. This differentiation is made bearing in mind that the formal translation of the Act uses the term "child welfare" instead of "child protection" in order to emphasize the welfare and service character of child-specific child protection.

CRITERIA FOR CHILD MALTREATMENT: NATIONAL LEGISLATION, DECENTRALIZED PRACTICE

Legislation

The key regulations about child maltreatment are presented in the Child Welfare Act (417/2007), which, according to Finnish legal principles, should be read in relation to the Finnish Constitution, the United Nations (UN) Convention on the Rights of the Child, and other legislation. In this chapter, the Act will be considered in terms of the child maltreatment criteria it presents. The criteria, as we shall see, are not detailed or explicit, as the entire Act takes the form of a *skeleton law*: It only defines the general frames for child welfare.

The task of child welfare in a general sense belongs to all public authorities. The Finnish Child Welfare Act (417/2007) begins with statements about what it provides to parents—namely, support, assistance, and services—and what it requires from public authorities: that is to say, providing families with necessary assistance at a sufficiently early stage. It also sets certain requirements for parents and outlines legal reasons to change the care and custody of children when necessary. It highlights municipal child protection authorities, whose task is to provide "child-specific" services for children and families in need of them.

The child-specific activities consist of an investigation of the need for child welfare measures, the provision of support in open care (in-home services), emergency placement of the child, and taking the child into care, as well as substitute care and after-care related to these. The general intent is that open-care and supportive measures should be prioritized over substitute care. Child welfare should be available to those who need it. All those measures should meet the child's best interest.

The principle of the child's best interest is presented in the Act in language that has some psychological undertones when describing the child's needs for human interaction and closeness. In a similar manner, the discourse on children's rights is also influential in the formulations of children's participation and involvement in determining "best interest." Most importantly, the child's best interest is formulated as a general principle, giving a lot of room for interpretation in individual situations—as so often seems to be the case when introducing the notion of "the child's best interest" as a guiding principle (Sandin & Halldén, 2003).

A similar lack of specificity is used when identifying the point at which child- or family-specific interventions are needed. Child maltreatment or child abuse are not mentioned in the legal text at all. The Act avoids any specific problem formulations and only mentions illegal acts (other than a minor offence), substance abuse, or other comparable behavior as specific grounds for child welfare measures. Child maltreatment and child abuse are, self-evidently, included in the wider formulations, which, for open-care measures, are:

- The circumstances in which the child is being brought up are endangering or failing to safeguard his or her health or development; *or*
- The child's behavior is endangering his or her health or development.

To take a child into care, the set criteria are

- The child's health or development is seriously endangered by lack of care or other circumstances in which he or she is being brought up; *or*
- The child seriously endangers her or his health or development by abuse of intoxicants, by committing an illegal act other than a minor offence, or by any other comparable behavior.

Additional criteria are that the open-care measures have turned out to be unsuitable or insufficient and that substitute care would be in the best interest of the child.

Due to the general and unspecific approach employed by the Child Welfare Act, the municipal authorities, and professional social workers in particular, are entitled to specify for themselves how they view those factors, situations, and processes that may endanger the children, as well as the signs of endangerment itself. In consequence, the criteria for child maltreatment are defined in local practices. Although this might be the case in any country with a more specific and child-abuse focused legislation, what is noteworthy here is that there is a legal agreement that it should be so.

Practice

In child protection practice, the criteria of child maltreatment are negotiated in different formal contexts, such as when receiving reports, taking a child into care, or terminating custody, as well as in every institutional encounter between the social worker and the child. The criteria are far from being uncontested, despite attempts to make them more straightforward. In the 2000s, several guides were published to instruct professionals on how to recognize different forms of abuse, physical and sexual in particular. Additionally, open websites were established for professionals, as well as for children and families, either by NGOs or the Ministry of Social Affairs and Health. These increases in activity over those conducted in the early or mid-1990s could be seen as a sign of a growing interest in formulating a practise in which the criteria for interventions would be somewhat shared if not similar.

There is, however, very little documentation about the criteria used for assessing child maltreatment. Research in Finnish child welfare does not tend to focus on such issues, and the statistical documentation is limited. The national statistics do not list any reasons for child protection interventions (Heino, 2007). Some local reports look at the criteria presented for registering a child as an open-case client or for taking the child in care (e.g., Heino, 2007; Hiitola, 2008).

The criteria for child maltreatment in those local reports show a pattern indicating that problems associated with parents—substance abuse, mental health problems, and "problems in parenting" in particular—are common reasons for interventions with small children, whereas the child's own behavioral problems, such as substance abuse and "uncontrolled behavior," are mentioned as reasons for interventions in the case of teenagers. Young people's criminal offences do not form a distinctive category but are somewhat hidden (Kuula & Marttunen, 2009). A variety of other reasons for intervention are possible as well. However, Finnish social workers often stress that interventions are not based on reactions to single problems but are more or less based on a holistic analysis of the child's social situation, which a social worker has assessed in relation to social and cultural norms and expectations about a "good-enough childhood" or "good-enough family life" (Pösö, Heino, & Ritala-Koskinen, forthcoming).

The criteria for child maltreatment are put into practice in the 348 municipalities, each with its own local culture. There is reason to believe that the criteria vary between the municipalities just as they vary within the municipalities among teams and offices due to different organizational cultures, communities, and related social and cultural norms and expectations about appropriate childhood and parenthood. From the practice point of view, it is therefore difficult to demonstrate what the criteria for child maltreatment are: The main message is that *they vary*.

MANDATORY REPORTING FOR AUTHORITIES AND THE RESPONSIBILITY TO NOTIFY

A mandatory reporting system exists in Finland. The Child Welfare Act demands a wide range of authorities working with children and families with children to fulfil their duty to notify if there is reason to believe that *the child is in need of child welfare assessment.*

The duty to notify is strong; regulations are stricter and more expansive now than they were under the previous Child Welfare Act, when there was confusion among authorities and professionals about how they should balance their duty to maintain client confidentiality and their duty to notify. Indeed, the Parliamentary Ombudsman had previously remarked how poorly notifications were done in cases of serious violence within the family toward children; a remark that supported the expansion of the duty of notification (Hallituksen esitys…, 2006, p. 31). Such confusion is eliminated according to the present Act since the duty to notify must always be given first priority. Consequently, the number of reports has grown since the new Act. Also under the new Act, municipalities are expected to keep a register of child welfare notifications and their content. Before the 2007 Act, such registers were only occasionally kept and published.

The Act also requires child welfare workers to notify the police about situations in which the child has been the object of a crime for which the maximum penalty prescribed is at least 2 years of imprisonment; such reporting was previously often avoided by social workers (Pösö, 1995). This regulation has been interpreted by some scholars as leading to the intensification of criminal control over parents and as a sign of a new punitive culture (Satka & Harrikari, 2008). On the other hand, it sends a message that authorities must take seriously children's experiences of violence.

In addition to the mandatory reporting system, everyone has the right and responsibility to notify child protection services. A recent report about reporting practice in the towns of central Finland demonstrates that during a 10-month period in 2006, 76% of all reports were made by other authorities, most of them working within the social care, health, or education sectors. Seventeen percent of reports were made by private persons outside the family, and 7% by family or kin. Again, if one looks at all the new clients entering the system at that time in those municipalities, 38% of them began when the child, his or her parent, or other family members contacted child welfare to ask for help (Heino, 2007, pp. 40–41). Child welfare clienthood, in other words, is not established only on the basis of reports about various kinds of child maltreatment, but on the basis of seeking for help and support as well.

RESPONDING TO CHILD MALTREATMENT

Due to its legal position, the key body for responding to child maltreatment is municipal child protection. Unlike the previous Act, the present Act (417/2007) sets a time restriction for such activity: The preliminary assessment must be done within 7 days of the notification or application having been received. The preliminary assessment may lead to a proper assessment of "need for child welfare," or to a decision not to include the child in the child protection system. The Act specifies this part of the process in detail by stating, for example, that the beginning of being formally identified as a client should be documented in the case files and that the child and his or her guardian(s) must be informed about the decision. This might sound a self-evident part of any ordinary bureaucratic process; nevertheless, studies from the late 1990s demonstrated that, at that time, a discrepancy existed between the bureaucratic practice and the information received by the children and families: the latter were not always informed that they had been treated as child protection clients or that their information was included in the child protection files. This was due largely to the practice custom that did not specify the beginning of clientship (Heino, 1997; Oranen, 1997).

Another element of the new, more formally structured child protection process is to be found in the "investigation"—as it is called in the translation of the Act—of the need for child welfare intervention. Again, a time limit is placed, with the Act specifying that the investigation should be carried out within 3 months of the preliminary assessment. In the investigation, social workers are asked to make a judgement about whether the child is in need of child welfare interventions. What is noteworthy here is that the task is not specified in terms of assessing the particular needs, risks, or problems the children might have but in terms of *entitlement to service*.

The frame or the instruments for the investigation process are not specifically defined by the Act or similar nationwide guidelines. No particular model for assessment is employed in all assessments, and practices differ among social workers and municipalities. There have, however, been several development projects attempting to create the principal outlines and actual tools for assessing the need for child welfare. In those proposals, special attention has been given to the everyday life of children in particular, and to supporting a strengths-based approach instead of focusing on problems or risks, such as examining the characteristics of child abuse (Ervast & Tulensalo, 2005; Oranen, 2006).

Finnish child protection prioritizes *open-care measures*, which should always be tried as the first step if the child is included in the child protection system. These measures include a wide range of psychosocial, financial, and practical supportive services, taking place most often within the child's community with the exception of placing the child outside of his or her home for a short period of time. Open-care measures are always of a voluntary nature for clients. The child may be taken into care only if open-care measures turn out to be insufficient or inappropriate.

Taking a child into care and placing him or her into substitute care is a measure introduced as a last resort. In 2007, there were 10,207 children in care (1.2% of all the under-aged population). In addition, a child may also be taken into care for 30 days temporarily as an emergency measure, if an "immediate danger" exists. A child may be in care for as long as the need for such a measure exists, but the care order terminates at latest when the child becomes an adult (18 years of age). Care orders are supposed to be temporary, and the task of social work is to support family reunification. As a care order is based on "joint guardianship," this means that parents—or other guardians—remain as guardians, even though the municipal authority also has guardianship and looks after the child's everyday life. The majority of care orders (about 80%) are agreed to by both parents (guardians) and the child, whose point of view is considered when she or he is 12 years of age or older. Decisions about involuntary care orders are made by the county courts; the so-called *voluntary care order* decisions are made by the local authorities. The Child Welfare Act does not include adoption as a measure.

Taking a child into care means that the child is placed into substitute care; that is, a foster home or institutional care. The placement must be in the child's best interest, and it is up to social workers to judge the form of placement. Residential institutions host children of all ages, but the custom is to place younger children into foster homes.

In 2007, the majority of children who had been placed out-of-home were in institutional care: 8,095 in residential care and 5,526 in foster homes (Lastensuojelu, 2007).[1] In 2006, there were 108 public residential units and 568 privately owned ones (Heino, 2009). The number of private enterprises has been increasing recently, replacing public or charity-run institutions even to the extent that some critics have questioned possible links between the simultaneous growth of out-of-home placements and the private residential industry (Marttunen, 2008).

At the moment, several policy initiatives are aimed at prioritizing foster care over residential care. Kinship care is seen as a form of foster care, and is being increasingly encouraged, with the number of placement in kinship care being estimated as 15%–20% of all foster home placements (Koisti-Auer, 2008, p. 28). One key argument for foster care is financial: the six largest Finnish towns have estimated that the annual costs of a foster home placement per child is around 19,000 Euro, whereas a residential placement may cost up to 52,000 Euro. Their estimate is that a child entering the child protection system costs the system 11,000 Euro a year; 85% of the costs are attributed to residential care (Kumpulainen, 2009).

Children and young people who have been in substitute care are entitled to *after-care*, which terminates 5 years after the placement or at latest when the person reaches 21 years of age.

The data in Table 6.1 demonstrates that most of the children in the child protection system are in open care and that these figures have been growing since 1994. The figures show the total number of children in open care or out-of-home

Table 6.1: The Number of Children in the Finnish Child Protection System by Year

Year	Children Per 1,000 in Open Care (in-Home Services)	Children Per 1,000 in Out-of-Home Placements	Children Per 1,000 in Residential Units	Children Per 1,000 in Foster Care
1994	24	8	4	4
1995	26	8	5	4
1996	26	8	5	5
1997	28	9	5	5
1998	31	9	5	5
1999	35	9	6	5
2000	40	9	6	5
2001	40	10	7	5
2002	44	10	7	5
2003	47	10	8	5
2004	50	11	8	5
2005	49	11	9	5
2006	50	12	7	5
2007	53	12	7	5

Source: *Lastensuojelu 2007.* [Child Welfare in 2007]. (2008). Statistical report 23. Helsinki: Stakes & Suomen virallinen tilasto; and *Suomalainen lapsi* [The Finnish Child]. (2007). Helsinki: Tilastokeskus & Stakes.

placement throughout the year since the national register does not include figures about out-of-home placements on a set day. The figures concerning open care are, however, problematic, and changes have been made to the registration system over the years (Heino & Pösö, 2003). Regarding the out-of-home placements, the figures cover placements of every duration (and also so-called open-care placements). A child may have been both in residential and foster care, which explains the inaccuracy of some figures.

Annually, more children enter the child protection system than exit it (Heino, 2009). Of all the children placed in out-of-home placements, there are more boys (53%) than girls (47%). The number of children belonging to ethnic minorities in child protection is not known (Anis, 2008). Teenagers are overrepresented in child protection. In 2007, 55% of children taken into care were between the ages 12 and 17, compared with 48% in 1995 (Heino, 2009).

The key tasks of child protection are carried out by social workers who are responsible for each child's affairs in child protection. To become a qualified social worker requires a master's degree in social work (5 years university training). The present Child Welfare Act, however, sets requirements that multiprofessional expertise and multiagency work should be utilized in child protection. Health and school professionals, as well as police, play an important role.

The role of the police—as part of the force's traditional work in criminal investigation and reflecting the recent ethos of crime prevention—has become more evident in working with children and young people (Niemi, 2010). On the other hand, child protection and child and youth psychiatric clinics tend to cooperate greatly, due to joint clients: Many children tend to be in need of psychiatric treatment as well as protection services, and the professional expertise of both sectors is coordinated in their care (Enroos, 2006).

In addition to the interventional responses just described, general services for children and families also shape the response to child maltreatment. Such services are mainly given in the forms of cash (e.g., child allowance, home care allowance) and in-kind services (e.g., day care, family guidance). These are typically universal services to which everyone is entitled; the share of all costs for families and children is about 11% of all expenditures on social and health care (Sosiaali- ja terveydenhuollon taskutieto, 2006, p. 31). As the most recent analysis suggests (Eydal & Kröger, 2010), these services tend to be rather similar across Nordic countries, and they have a long history that must viewed within the context of the genesis of the Finnish/Nordic welfare state (Eydal & Satka, 2006). As a maltreated child may use the services of child protection as well as universal services, universal and specific responses can easily overlap.

CHANGES IN THE PHILOSOPHY AND PATTERNS IN COMBATTING CHILD ABUSE

Changes in the philosophy and practices regarding child maltreatment since 1994 are reflected in the Child Welfare Act of 2007. Although generally in tune with the philosophy of the previous Act, the 2007 Act has formalized the process of intake, documentation, and decision-making and strengthened the role of children and their participation. Besides the Act, other changes have occurred as well, in society in general and in social, family, and child policy more specifically, with the result that more children than ever before are ending up in the child protection system.

The period of the last 10 years or so has been recognized in Finland as an era during which the ethos of the welfare state has been replaced to some extent by the ethos of market orientation, competitiveness, efficiency, and private responsibility (Julkunen, 2008). The period has also been marked by a restructuring of public welfare services: for example, smaller municipalities have merged with bigger ones or formed coalitions to provide joint services; health and social services are united organizationally more than previously; and the purchaser–provider model has been employed in several municipalities. Concerns about improving management, leadership, and finances have to some extent replaced concerns about reinforcing equality and solidarity. Both the issues of the aging population—with its needs and the corresponding adequacy of services—and of children and young people (education, day-care, enrollment in the labor market, early health promotion, and tackling "social exclusion") have been given major attention.

The period since 1994 has been marked by contradictory trends that are linked to ways of approaching child abuse and child maltreatment. The following discussion analyzes four of the major developments during this period.

The Well-Being of Children and Tackling Social Exclusion as an Ethos

In 2007, the center-right coalition government launched a policy program for "the well-being of children, youth, and families" with three special targets: a child-oriented society, the well-being of families with children, and the prevention of social exclusion (The Policy programme..., 2007). The key instruments include early intervention and a variety of multiprofessional and multiorganizational services. The program encompasses a wide interest in childhood and youth because

> [T]he best security for the ageing population in Finland is provided by healthy and happy children and young people. It is advisable to invest in the well-being of children, young people, and families. The Government's goal is to achieve a more child-friendly Finland. (The Policy programme..., 2007)

The policy program seeks to promote a new approach that underlines the importance of investing in childhood. The ethos of social investments is known in many countries, and the program demonstrates that it has arrived in Finland as well. The focus is on children and young people in general, as a population group whose health and welfare must flourish for the sake of society.

Since the mid-1990s, a number of concerns regarding the risks of childhood and youth have been voiced with moral undertones (Harrikari, 2008). Childhood and youth are obviously associated with an abundance of worries and problems, from more traditional ones like child obesity and school bullying, to some new ones as well (e.g., the risks caused by information technology). According to Mirja Satka and Timo Harrikari (2008), the "moral turn" in the Finnish context refers to the ideological and concrete changes that have taken place since the early 1990s and that represent a control-based interest on childhood and families.

The moral influence of approaching childhood and family issues has been demonstrated empirically in media presentations (Jallinoja, 2006; Forsberg & Strandell, 2007; Harrikari, 2008) and in political debate (Harrikari, 2008). This influence has also been expressed in welfare practices by the growing numbers and types of "early intervention programmes" (Satka, 2009) and the new discourse of describing childhood problems using unspecific terms, such as "ill-fare"

(Forsberg & Ritala-Koskinen, 2010). Moral concerns lend support to more regulation of childhood. Hannele Forsberg and Harriet Strandell (2007) argue that the target is childhood in general and not just a certain type of behavior or certain groups of children and young people; childhood is going through cultural reshaping. Increasingly, professional interventions and services are called to monitor, support, and help children and families in order to avoid risks.

The Expansion of Child Protection and Holistic Approaches

The number of children in the child protection system has been increasing greatly since 1994, as demonstrated earlier in this chapter. This growth may be seen on one hand as a reflection of increased social and moral control on children and families; on the other hand, the numbers may inform us that there is a growing number of children whose development and welfare is threatened, so that they need the services child protection can offer and their needs are not met by other form of services (Heino, 2009). Furthermore, changes in the system of services for children and families may have resulted in more service needs being directed to child protection instead of being channeled to other service providers. It should be noted that family values in general are strong in Finnish society (Jallinoja, 2006) and that there is a basic agreement among people that the services provided by the state may be used to assist families in trouble (Hearn et al., 2004).

Heikki Hiilamo (2009) analyzed the number of out-of-home placements in relation to general socioeconomic indicators and other so-called risk factors known to child welfare. Analyzing the period between 1991 and 2007 on the national level, the study shows clearly that out-of-home placements are associated with long-term economic hardships. The results also indicate that the rate of change in the share of children placed outside the home is associated with alcohol and substance abuse. Indeed, the early 1990s was marked by strong economic recession, and the period since 1994 by increased alcohol consumption in Finnish society, which is reflected in the number of out-of-home placements.

It is, however, difficult to estimate how general economic hardship or increased consumption of alcohol are transformed into out-of-home placement on the individual level. The message from social workers underlines that no one individual factor, such as poverty or parents' substance abuse, triggers child protection interventions. Instead, the interventions are based on multiple factors and on the social work assessment about their implication on the child's life. As social workers consider these factors *holistically*, they are not willing to explain the growth of out-of-home placements by any single category of social problem. This is seen as unfair from the point of view of the grassroots practice of child welfare (Pösö, Heino, & Ritala-Koskinen, forthcoming).

The holistic approach places specific social problems out of focus, and even violence may be excluded. In the municipal institution of child welfare, violence is approached as an issue interwoven with other problems and not easily separated from them. For example, when social workers analyzed the situation of children who had been registered in child protection in 2006, violence was very rarely described as a key factor; it did, however, play a role among many other issues (Heino, 2007). This tendency was noted already in the mid-1990s (Pösö, 1995). In a violence-rich society, marked by an internationally high number of homicide, among other factors (Lehti & Kivivuori, 2008), it seems to be possible to ignore violence experienced by children as a "special" issue in municipal child protection; as a matter of fact, pioneering models on work with children exposed to violence have been launched by NGOs. Corporal punishment was forbidden by law in 1983. Still, the 2007 national victim survey addressed to children aged 12 and 15 ($N = 13,515$) notes that a comparison of victimization surveys reveals that children are exposed to considerably higher levels of violence than are adults (Ellonen et al., 2008, p. 158.) The key forms of violence tend to be violence in their homes among family members and violence experienced in peer groups. Furthermore, in 2007, six children under the age of 14 died due to homicide or other violent criminal acts. The number of violent child deaths has been between four and eight during the period of 2003–2007, with more than half the deaths having been caused by mothers (Lehti & Kivivuori, 2008).

Currently, there are no comprehensive follow-up studies of children who have been taken into the child protection system. Very little is known about the implications of this system, which influences the lives of so many, and this reflects the lack of interest in child protection and its functioning.

Client Work Under Pressure in Child Protection

Despite the strong present interest in childhood and the emphasis on "investing" in childhood, the child protection system is continuously lacking financial and human resources to cope with its task properly. The number of social workers in municipalities has increased: in 1995, there were 8.6 social workers per 10,000 inhabitants, whereas in 2005, the corresponding figure was 9.8 (Sosiaali- ja terveydenhuollon…, 2006, p. 28). However, this increase does not tend to meet the requirements set by child protection.

Just before the Child Welfare Act was introduced in 2008, the trade union for professionals in social welfare expressed its concern that the expansion of tasks given to social workers could not be realized without a considerable increase in their numbers. Since the new Act, the lack of human resources has created a new phenomenon in child protection: children and their parents have to queue for services. Child protection agencies have also experienced difficulties as a result of the high turnover of social workers and heavy work loads (Huuskonen & Korpinen, 2009). There were 59 children per social worker served by child protection in 2008 in the six largest towns, and 60% of their social workers were unqualified (Kumpulainen, 2009, p. 10). The municipalities tend to profile child protection as necessary but still as a last-resort activity and invest resources accordingly (Heino & Pösö, 2003); moreover, the long-lasting shortage of qualified social workers has not led to any considerable increase in education.

Not surprisingly, citizen complaints to legal bodies about child protection are not rare. The amount of involuntary care orders has been increasing since the early 1990s (Heino, 2009). The Ombudsman for Children, a national post since 2005, is contacted in personal matters mostly in relation with child protection (Lapsilla on oikeus…, 2008, p. 47). Media scandals about the failures of child protection are, however, rare.

The heavy work loads, high turnover of social workers, and new organizational structures for child protection both within and between municipalities have not created an environment conductive to new working methods or research-informed practice. The period since the mid-1990s has, however, been marked by new centers of expertise excellence, among others, which have been established to develop social work practice. A special development project on child protection was carried out by the Ministry of Social Affairs and Health in 2004–2007. The Ministry has also launched a new model for sharing the tasks of child protection client work between social workers and social educators, in order to tackle the shortage of qualified social workers and to enrich services to clients.

The economic crisis beginning in 2009 is threatening to further reduce resources for municipal services, despite strong civic and political campaigns claiming that children should not suffer from the economic crisis and that services for children and families with children should not be cut. Preventative and universal services are in the front lines of these campaigns and policy programs. Overall child protection services might, however, be threatened because it is argued that resources from corrective child protection should be redirected to preventative work. This policy reaction demonstrates that the emphasis on universalism in services has a reverse side, as suggested by Keith Pringle (1998) and Hannele Forsberg and Teppo Kröger (2010): the nonuniversal needs and situations of children and families may be excluded from or given low priority on the public agenda.

Focusing on Children

The family-centered approach to child welfare, influential especially since the 1980s, was challenged in the early years of the 21st century by a child-centered approach which, according to some authors (Forsberg, Ritala-Koskinen, & Törrönen, 2006, p. 5), has been the theme of the liveliest discussion in the field of Finnish social work. The child-centered approach is both about methods of working with children, as well as about an overall way to looking at social work from the point of view of children. It addresses children both as individuals and as members of their generational group. The norm of children's participation is strongly written into the Child Welfare Act (2007) and the Youth Act (2006), together with other pieces of legislation, including the Constitution and policy program measures. The message here is that children should be entitled to practise their right to express their views on issues that concern them in society in general and especially to participate in any decision-making about their own affairs.

The focus on children has become rooted in child protection work in several ways. In the mid-1990s, clients in open care, for example, were documented in the child protection case files according to the custodian's name, whereas now the child's name is the key code. Working methods, such as interviewing children and running children's groups, have been developed and implemented in practice to some extent. Even physical arrangements have changed in some social welfare agencies: chairs, tables, toys, and books for children are more common than in the early 1990s, when agencies looked like very standard bureaucratic offices for adults. The shift is not, however, all that clear or straightforward. Hannele Forsberg with her colleagues (2006) notes that the rise of child-centeredness has supported general concerns about the state of childhood—increased attention is paid to children, and more and more regulations and interventions are called for when problems occur. The risk is to ignore the social, cultural, and historical context of childhood when the focus is on individual children and their childhood. At the same time, the focus on children has not been applied equally to all areas of children's lives. Child-centered methods appear to flourish more in NGOs than in municipalities' social work (Forsberg et al., 2006). The differences among children and young people and their different needs might not have been adequately recognized either. Rosi Enroos (2008), for example, has demonstrated vividly how small children are residing in prison with their parents, without any monitoring or support from authorities, even though the situation could be threatening to children.

AWAY FROM THE FAMILY SERVICES MODEL

The period since 1994 has been marked by considerable changes. The very phenomenon of "child abuse" or "child maltreatment" has been given more attention in practice, policy, and research than before; equally, the importance of seeing children as the key focus of services has been emphasized and put into practice to a certain degree. Several legal and policy reforms also have had an impact on how services respond to child and social problems, and welfare services for children and families have undergone widespread restructuring. Even more, the cultural landscape regarding children, families, and the role of public authorities currently looks different from that of the early and mid-1990s: the present landscape is rich in concerns and regulations about childhood and youth. Furthermore, the child protection system serves considerably more children now than it did in the early 1990s.

Since the mid-1990s, Finland has shifted away from the family service emphasis toward a new focus, with a strong interest in the well-being of children. The emphasis on children's well-being covers children's and young people's lives in general and aims to manage risks and stop social exclusion. This emphasis generates a variety of health, educational, social services, and monitoring measures targeted at childhood and provided by a wide set of professionals from different sectors. It includes families as well, but the aim is more or less in "investing in children" for the sake of society.

Despite the strong interest in the well-being of children and young people in displayed by the media, policy, and practice, the actual policy and practice of combatting child abuse and child maltreatment on the individual level has remained more or less marginal. Established programs and guidelines suggest how to tackle abuse, and new agencies and teams are working on the psychiatric, forensic, or legal elements of abuse. The social work response to abuse, especially that taking place in municipal child protection, is, however, more diffuse and suppressed. Most ironically, the public institution of municipal child protection tends to lack resources of any kind to invest in abused and maltreated children, even though it is dealing with a larger group of children than ever before. In the era of investments, abused and maltreated children are, it seems, a poor investment, as is municipal child protection.

NOTE

1   In addition to child welfare institutions, a good number of children and young people are treated in psychiatric facilities: in 2007, the number of minors in psychiatric hospital care was 3,502 (5.1 children/1,000 minors) whereas only two or three under-aged children are serving a prison sentence (Marttunen, 2008).

REFERENCES

Anis, M. (2008). *Sosiaalityö ja maahanmuuttajat.* [Social Work and Migrants]. Helsinki: Väestöliitto.

Ellonen, N., Kääriäinen, J., Salmi, V., & Sariola, H. (2008). *Lasten ja nuorten väkivaltakokemukset* [Children and young people's experiences of violence]. Report 71. Tampere: Poliisiammattikorkeakoulu.

Enroos, R. (2006). *Lastensuojelun sosiaalityöntekijän asiantuntijuus lastenpsykiatrian kanssa tehtävän yhteistyön rajapinnoilla* [The expertise of child protection social work in cooperation with child psychiatry]. Unpublished thesis for a master's degree in social sciences. Tampere: University of Tampere.

Enroos, R. (2008). *Vankila lapsuudessa – lapset vankilassa. Tutkimus lapsista, joiden elämää vankeus värittää* [Prison in childhood – Children in prison. Study on children affected by imprisonment]. Publication 1. Helsinki: Rikosseuraamusvirasto.

Ervast, S. -A., & Tulensalo, H. (2005). *Sosiaalityötä lapsen kanssa*. [Social work with a child]. Reports 8. Helsinki: SOCCA and Heikki Waris–instituutti.

Eydal, G.B., & Kröger, T. (2010). Nordic family policies: Constructing contexts for social work with families. In H. Forsberg & T. Kröger (Eds.), *Social work and child welfare politics through the Nordic lenses*, pp. 29–46. Bristol: Policy Press.

Eydal, G.B., & Satka, M. (2006). Social work and Nordic welfare policies for children – present challenges in the light of the past. *European Journal of Social Work, 9*(3), 305–322.

Forsberg, H., & Strandell, H. (2007). After-school hours and the meanings of home: Re-defining Finnish childhood space. *Children's Geographies, 5*(4), 393–408.

Forsberg, H., Ritala-Koskinen, A., & Törrönen, M. (2006). *Lapset ja sosiaalityö*. [Children and social work]. Jyväskylä: PS-kustannus.

Forsberg, H, & Ritala-Koskinen, A. (2010). From welfare to illfare: Public concern for Finnish childhood. In H. Forsberg & T. Kröger (Eds.), *Social work and child welfare politics through the Nordic Lenses*, pp. 47–64. Bristol: Policy Press.

Forsberg, H., & Kröger, T. (Eds.). (2010). *Social work and child welfare politics through the Nordic lenses*. Bristol: Policy Press.

Hallituksen esitys Eduskunnalle lastensuojelulaiksi ja eräiksi siihen liittyviksi laeiksi [The Government proposal to the Parliament for the child welfare act and other acts related with it]. HE 252 2006 vp.

Harrikari, T. (2008). *Riskillä merkityt* [Marked with risk]. Helsinki: Nuorisotutkimusverkosto.

Hearn, J., Pösö, T., Korpinen, J., Smith, C., & Whyte, S. (2004). What is child protection lastensuojelu? Historical and methodological issues in comparative research on lastensuojelu child protection. *International Journal of Social Welfare, 13*(1), 28–41.

Heino, T. (1997). *Asiakkuuden hämäryys lastensuojelussa : sosiaalityöntekijän tuottama määritys lastensuojelun asiakkaaksi* [The obsure nature of clienthood in child protection: The social workers producing the definition of a client]. Report 77. Helsinki: Stakes.

Heino, T., & Pösö, T. (2003). *Tilastot ja tarinat lastensuojelun tiedonlähteinä* [Statistics and stories as forms of child welfare knowledge]. *Yhteiskuntapolitiikka, 68*(6), 584–596.

Heino, T. (2007). *Keitä ovat lastensuojelun uudet asiakkaat?* [Who are the new clients in child welfare]. Working Papers 30. Helsinki: Stakes.

Heino, T. (2009). Lastensuojelu–kehityskulkuja ja paikannuksia [Child protection–Tendencies and locations]. In J. Lammi-Taskula, S. Karvonen, & S. Ahlström (Eds.), *Lapsiperheiden hyvinvointi 2009* [The well-being of families with children], pp. 198–213. Helsinki: Terveyden ja hyvinvoinnin laitos.

Hiilamo, H. (2009). What could explain the dramatic rise in out-of-home placement in Finland in the 1990s and early 2000s? *Children and Youth Services Review*, 31(2), 177–184.

Hiitola, J. (2008). *Selvitys vuonna 2006 huostaanotetuista ja sijaishuoltoon sijoitetuista lapsista* [A report about children who had been taken in care and been in care in 2006]. Working Papers 21. Helsinki: Stakes.

Hurtig, J. (2003). *Lasta suojelemassa: Etnografia lasten paikan rakentumisesta lastensuojelun perhetyön käytännöissä* [Protecting the child: Ethnography on children's position in family work within the context of child welfare]. Rovaniemi: Lapin yliopisto.

Huuskonen, S., & Korpinen, J. (2009). *Runsas vuosi lastensuojelun avohuollon asiakkuuden alkamisesta: Mitä lapsille kuuluu nyt?* [About one year since being registered in open care in child welfare: How are the children now?]. Report 1. Tampere: Pikassos Oy.

Jallinoja, R. (2006). *Perheen vastaisku* [Counterattack of the family]. Helsinki: Gaudeamus.

Julkunen, R. (2008). *Yhteisvastuusta julkisen vastuun prioriteetteihin* [From joint responsibility to prioritising public responsibilities]. In P. Niemi & T. Kotiranta (Eds.), *Sosiaalialan normatiivinen perusta* [The normative ground of social welfare], pp. 146–182. Helsinki: Palmenia.

Koisti-Auer, A. -L. (2008). *Sukulaissijaisvanhemmuuden profiili* [Profile of kinship care]. Research Reports 1. Jyväskylä: Pesäpuu.

Kumpulainen, A. (2009). *Kuuden suurimman kaupungin lastensuojelu 2008* [Child protection in the six largest towns in 2008]. Helsinki: Kuusikko-ryhmän julkaisusarja.

Kuula, T., & Marttunen, M. (2009). *Laitoksessa rikosten vuoksi* [In residential care for the sake of crime]. Researh reports 89. Helsinki: Oikeuspoliittinen tutkimuslaitos.

Lapsella on oikeus osallistua [Children have the right to participate]. Lapsiasianvaltuutetun vuosikirja (2008). Helsinki: Sosiaali-ja terveysministeriö.

Lastensuojelu 2007 [Child Welfare in 2007]. (2008). Statistical report 23. Helsinki: Stakes & Suomen virallinen tilasto.

Lehti, M., & Kivivuori, J. (2008). *Kuolemaan johtanut väkivalta* [Violence leading to death]. In Rikollisuustilanne 2007 [Crime trends in Finland 2007], pp. 15–50. Research report 238. Helsinki: Oikeuspoliittinen tutkimuslaitos.

Marttunen, M. (2008). *Nuorisorikosoikeus. Alaikäisten rikosten seuraamukset kriminaalipoliittisesta ja vertailevasta näkökulmasta* [Juvenile criminal justice: Comparative and criminal policy perspective on sanctioning juveniles]. Publication no. 236. Helsinki: Oikeuspoliittinen tutkimuslaitos.

Niemi, M. (2010). *Moraalijärjestystä tuottamassa. Tutkimus poliisityöstä lasten parissa* [Producing Moral Order. A study on police work with children].

Jyväskylä Studies in Education, Psychology and Social Research 391. Jyväskylä: University of Jyväskylä.

Oranen, M. (1997). *Semmonen pikkunen huoli. Diskurssianalyyttinen tutkimus lastensuojelun arviointikeskustelusta* [A tiny issue of concern. A discourse analytic study on the assessment discussion in child protection]. *Janus, 1*(5), 3–25.

Oranen, M. (2006). *Tutkimista ja tunnustelua. Lastensuojelun alkuarvioinnin käytäntöjä, malleja ja kehittämissuuntia* [Examining and exploring. The models, practices and directions for child protection assessment]. Alkuarviointi ja avohuolto-työryhmän loppuraportti 22.3.2006, Lastensuojelun kehittämisohjelma. Retrieved May 13, 2009 from http://www.sosiaaliportti.fi.

The Policy Programme for the Well-being of Children, Youth, and Families. Programme as set out in the Government Programme of Vanhanen's second Cabinet 19.4.2007. Retrieved May 13, 2009 from http://www.valtioneuvosto.fi toiminta politiikkaohjelmat lapset lapsiohjelma-hallitusohjelmassa en.jsp.

Paavilainen, E., Åstedt-Kurki, P., Paunonen-Ilmonen, M., & Laippala, P. (2001). Caring for maltreated children: A challenge for health care education. *Issues and Innovations in Nursing Education, 37*(6), 551–557.

Pringle, K. (1998). *Children and social welfare in Europe.* Buckingham: Open University Press.

Pösö, T. (1995). *Lasten pahoinpitely lastensuojelussa - ollako vai eikö olla?* [Child abuse - To be or not to be?]. In A. Jokinen, K. Juhila, & T. Pösö (Eds.), *Sosiaalityö, asiakas ja sosiaaliset ongelmat - konstruktionistinen näkökulma* [Social work, clienthood and social problems - A constructionist view], pp. 32–53. Helsinki: Sosiaaliturvan Keskusliitto.

Pösö, T, Heino, T., & Ritala-Koskinen, A. (Forthcoming). Making statistics of child protection: A case study about "important" and "available" information. Manuscript to be published.

Sandin, B., & Hallden, G. (2003). *Barnets bästa-en antologi om barndomens innebörder och välfärdens organisering* [The best of child-an anthology of childhood's dimensions and organising welfare]. Stockholm Stehag: Brutus Östlings Bokförlag Symposium.

Satka, M., & Harrikari, T. (2008). The present Finnish formation of child welfare and history. *British Journal of Social Work, 38,* 645–661. doi:10.1093 bjsw bcn037. Advance access publication April 15, 2008.

Satka, M. (2009). *Varhainen puuttuminen, moraalinen käänne ja sosiaalisen asiantuntijat* [Early intervention, moral turn and the expertise of social]. *Yhteiskuntapolitiikka 74*(1), 17–32.

Suomalainen lapsi [The Finnish Child]. (2007). Helsinki: Tilastokeskus & Stakes

Social protection in the Nordic countries. (2005). Scope, expenditure and financing. (2007). Kobenhavn: Nordisk Social-Statistical Committee.

Sosiaali- ja terveydenhuollon taskutilasto [The short statistics of social and health care]. (2006). Tasku2006suomi.pdf. Helsinki: Stakes.

7

DENMARK: A CHILD WELFARE SYSTEM UNDER REFRAMING

ANNE-DORTHE HESTBÆK[1]

With approximately 5.5 million inhabitants, lots of possibilities open to every citizen, and a tight social security net, Denmark considers itself a small, efficient welfare state. Yet, a relatively large number of Denmark's 1.2 million children and young persons (corresponding to 21.8% of the total child and youth population 0–17 years old) are placed in out-of-home care. Next to Finland, Denmark has the highest proportion of children and young people in out-of-home care in the Nordic countries (Bengtsson & Böcker Jacobsen, 2009).

The Danish welfare system is based on the principle that all citizens are guaranteed certain fundamental rights in case they experience social problems. The social sector is highly decentralized, and the 98 local municipalities have the main responsibility for implementing and administrating the child welfare legislation and provisions issued at the state level. The local bodies have a high degree of autonomy when implementing social protection schemes, leaving room for considerable differences between municipalities. Denmark does not have a Children's Act, but rather a broad-spectrum Consolidation Act on Social Services, covering, for example, children with special needs, disabled people, preventive measures, out-of-home care with and without consent, activation, sheltered employment, and the like. The overall aim of the legislation concerning children and young persons in need of special support is "providing them with the same opportunities for self-expression, personal development, maturity, and health as their contemporaries, despite their individual problems" (Consolidation Act on Social Services, Art. 46). Also, the social worker must conduct an individual assessment of the needs of each child (characterized in the legislation as case-by-case assessment adapted to the specific situation of the individual child).

In the first half of the 1990s, Denmark was the only Nordic country that had not yet fully abolished the parental right to inflict corporal punishment on children. Another issue debated in child protection and child welfare at the end of the 1990s concerned the limited involvement of parents and children in the processes of the local welfare agencies. Also, placement in out-of-home care without consent was discussed, which led to a (slightly) more precise definition, where respite care was separated from more long term care in the legislation.

Like several other countries in this book, Denmark has faced media scandals in the child welfare field, as for example, in the "Tønder" case, in which a father sexually abused his two daughters from the time they were 6 and 2 years old. When the eldest daughter was 11 years old, the father made her available for paid and unpaid prostitution in their own home, and the mother knew about it. Several years later, 12 men were sentenced to long prison terms for sexual interaction with the girl. Two different local authorities apparently had had their attention drawn to the family, but did not react adequately. The case revealed that moving from one local authority to another easily left room for unintended gaps in the social security net. However, it is important to note that irrespective of the character of these scandals, they have never reached the importance of setting sociopolitical agenda as, seems to be true, say, in England in similar cases.

This chapter examines the development in legislation and policy from 1994 on, focusing on three main periods, characterized by different trends in legislation and policy. Next, Danish procedures for reporting child maltreatment will be described, followed by an analysis of the out-of-home care field in Denmark, with figures regarding the number and proportion of children in out-of-home care, and the distribution of children in alternative-care settings.

DEVELOPMENTS IN LEGISLATION AND POLICY

According to an analysis from the mid-1990s, Denmark was characterized as a welfare state with a child welfare system emphasizing voluntary, family-oriented interventions (Pruzan, 1997). However, developments since then indicate that this regime might slowly be turning into a system more characterized by child protection, with a stronger focus on legal interventions.

This movement has taken place over three main periods since 1995: the continuation period, 1995–2000; the reform period, 2001–2005; and the "reframing" period, from 2006 onward.

The Continuation Period, 1995–2000

The end of the 1990s, may be broadly characterized as continuing the social policy paradigm of the first part of the decade without major changes. This is partly due to the extensive amendments of the Social Welfare Act in 1993 (Act No. 501 of June 24, 1992), based on a thorough expert committee report, "On the Legal Framework for Efforts to Support Children and Adolescents," (Betænkning/Report No. 1212, 1990).

However, the concept of continuation refers not only to continuing an ongoing legislative process, but to the concept of continuity in the relationship between parent and child. The Betænkning report made clear that the principle of continuity in childhood and adolescence is the key principle of Danish child welfare legislation (Betænkning/Report No. 1212, 1990; Ebsen, 2007). A core theme of continuity is the relation between the child and his or her biological parent. The 1993 law drew on the psychologically oriented theory of object relations, in which biological parents are integrated into the self of the very young child and thus are irreplaceable. Thus, local authorities must actively support contact between children in out-of-home care and their parents (Egelund & Hestbæk, 2003; Ebsen 2007).

Other important 1993 amendments, of which there were several, involved a considerable increase in the number of preemptive measures mentioned in the law; new procedural requirements for the caseworkers, such as better investigations; and individual written plans for each child subject to interventions. There was an increased demand for involvement of the child and the parents, who were also given more rights, as new principles for deciding on interventions without consent were introduced.

Although other Nordic countries had abolished corporal punishment relatively early, Denmark had, in 1985, introduced a statement more open to interpretation in the Act on Parental Responsibility, which gave the parents an obligation to protect children from corporal and emotional abuse. As this statement gave rise to ambiguous interpretations, in 1997, the Parliament decided to abolish corporal punishment fully and include its use in the penal code.

In 1998, the Social Welfare Act was replaced by the Consolidation Act on Social Services and the Consolidation Act on Legal Service and Administration in Social Matters. To a large extent, these new acts continued the overall principles of the Social Welfare Act. The aim of creating equal opportunities for development for children with special needs was introduced, and the need for early intervention was once again underlined. The concept of "interdisciplinary cooperation" was introduced into child welfare legislation for the first time, as well as a mandatory obligation for citizens to report on children in need of special support.

The Reform Period, 2001–2005

The "reform period" label refers to the large number of legislative amendments and action plans concerning child welfare and child protection occurring during the period 2001–2005. In 2001, Denmark also experienced a change in the political regime, as the Social Democratic government was replaced by a liberal government after 8 years in office. The new government launched ideas reflecting the beginning of an ideological shift in the child and family welfare climate. More weight was given to the responsibility of each individual family, preferably sanctioned by stronger interventions toward parents who might not live up to these expectations (e.g., through parental orders). The main amendments and action plans launched in 2001–2005, the most important of which is the Consolidation Act on Social Services in 2001, are described below.

The 2001 Amendment of the Consolidation Act on Social Services

The first important change during this period involved amendments to the section on children and young people in need of specialized support in the Consolidation Act on Social Services (Act No. 466 of May 31, 2000). These amendments were motivated by, among other things, the fact that expenditures on child welfare and child protection interventions were rapidly expanding, mirrored by the absence of evidence-based knowledge about the effects of the most frequently used measures and services.

As mentioned previously, the overall aim of the amendments was to provide disadvantaged children "with the same opportunities for self-expression, personal development, maturity and health as their contemporaries…" (Art. 46.1.). A central change was the strengthening of the child's rights, through the inclusion of the provision from the United Nations (UN) Convention of the Child stating that any intervention must be "in the best interest of the child."

More specifically, the 2001 amendment included a range of measures aimed at increasing stability in the lives of children living in out-of-home care. Thus, it was made possible to refuse parents permission to take home a child who had been placed in out-of-home care (with the parent's consent) for a given period, if the child had developed a close relationship with adults in the caregiving environment. This amendment was one of the first examples of the possibility of using forcible measures without fulfilling the usual criteria for interventions without consent (to be described later in this chapter).

Another notable amendment was the formal introduction of after-care measures targeted at young people coming of age, giving them the possibility of gradually leaving the care system with different types of support from the age of 18 through the age of 22. This amendment reflected what social workers (and international research as well) had known for years; namely, that the need for special support does not disappear when a young person in care reaches 18 (Stein 1994; Egelund & Hestbæk, 2003; Espersen, 2004). On the contrary, young people who have spent a number of years in out-of-home care typically have performed poorly in school; lack certain social and practical competences; are relatively poor; often have weak support networks, with limited access to apprenticeships, education, and training; and have few possibilities to obtain low-cost accommodations. The new measures include the possibility of remaining in out-of-home care, a gradual reentry into society, and the appointment of a welfare officer or a more permanent contact person for the young person. Since 2001, the implementation of these after-care measures has been mirrored in a steadily increasing number of 18- to 22-year-olds previously placed in care using these options.

Another new procedural measure was the organizational requirement that all local authorities set up interdisciplinary committees, with the aim of obtaining early, coherent interventions and of securing the involvement of experts—medical, social, pedagogical, and psychological. The interdisciplinary committees are examples of measures aimed at increasing casework quality through new working procedures and reorganization of the local administration.

Last, the 2001 amendment also included measures designed to increase the involvement of parents, such as a right of the biological parent with custody of the child to be assigned a specific "support person" whose task is to help the parent in coping with the placement in the best possible way. This service is based on the assumption that the better the parent copes with the placement, the more the child will be able to benefit from it.

All in all, the 2001 amendments included a mix of substantial changes in measures, such as after-care and support persons on the one hand, and of procedural changes aiming at increasing casework quality on the other.

Action Plans in the Reform Period on Combatting Sexual Abuse of Children and Violence Against Children

The reform period introduced (at least) two governmental action plans in the child abuse field. In 2003, the government published an action plan to combat sexual abuse of children. One of the initiatives was the establishment of SISO, the Danish National Centre for Social Efforts Against Child Sexual Abuse. SISO prepared teaching aids and materials concerning sexual abuse for professional groups working with children, young people, and families. Also, another center was established, offering assessment, outpatient psychological treatment of young offenders, and educational activities, as well as advisory services for professionals.

In 2004, the government also launched an action plan to combat violence against children, giving priority to children aged 0–7 years. This action plan focused on raising awareness and encouraging the population to notify public authorities if they suspected that a child was being abused. The measures included training, campaigns, and other informative activities to ensure that cases of child abuse would be discovered early and addressed. The plan also sought to prevent abuse in high-risk population groups (e.g., families with drug abusing parents) and to increase cooperation between various sections of the public sector. In 2006, a follow-up to the action plan was adopted, to upgrade the skills of professionals to identify signals of distressed children and to ensure that the local authorities received correct notifications of violence against children.

The Reframing Period, 2006–Onward

Since 2006, child welfare and child protection policy have entered a new period, one in which legislative amendments gradually reflect changes in the political climate that started at the beginning of the decade. One of the main trends involves a slow movement away from voluntary family and child welfare measures (as characterized by Pruzan's [1997] earlier analysis of the Danish system) toward a more interventionist child protection regime, marked by an increased focus on the responsibility of the individual citizen, on the ability to employ punitive sanctions, and on compulsory measures.

In 2006, Parliament adopted a new Act on Parental Responsibility. According to this, local authorities can instruct parents to perform certain actions in relation to their children, which aim at increasing the child's possibilities for developing positively (going to a kindergarten, receiving homework coaching, etc.). An order to parents for active support of the child can, for example, be issued when it has been impossible to establish efficient cooperation between parents and the authorities. If the parents fail to follow instructions, their family allowance may be withheld.[2]

The 2006 Foster Care Reform was another amendment of the section concerning children and young people in need of specialized support in the Consolidation Act on Social Services. The aim of the Foster Care Reform is to strengthen early preventive activities for disadvantaged children, young people, and their families, while also improving casework services handled by local authorities. A central feature of this measure is to ensure that the consideration for the child outweighs everything else, taking the principle of the best interest of the child seriously. The reform promotes early intervention and an increased involvement of and partnership with families and children.

The Foster Care Reform also places an increased emphasis on the responsibility of the individual citizen, and of the family as a whole, for solving their own problems, possibly by involving their personal networks. Looking more closely at the concrete measures of the Foster Care Reform, this ideological shift toward private responsibility and involvement is reflected in, for instance, the new provisions promoting kinship care. From now on, kinship care (placement with biological family) or network care (in which the child is placed with, say, a teacher or friends of the parents to whom the child is not biologically related) always has to be considered as an option in any case involving placement in out-of-home care. This development has been strongly inspired by the considerable international evidence that quite a few children may benefit from kinship care (Winokur, Holtan, & Valentine, 2009; Knudsen, Egelund, & Hestbæk, 2010). Although "traditional" foster care in Denmark is salaried according to fixed rates, kinship and network care provides a smaller compensation for reduced salary due to constraints on employment and the extra expenses incurred by having the child in residence (Knudsen, Egelund, & Hestbæk, 2010). Thus, the Foster Care Reform was also followed by a political expectation that the total expenditure on out-of-home care would be reduced. For decades, Denmark has had a relatively low level of children cared for in kinship and network care (all in all, about 4%–5% of all children in care; Knudsen, Egelund, & Hestbæk, 2010; Lindemann & Hestbæk,

2004; www.ankestyrelsen.dk). In continuation of the Foster Care Reform, the former Minister of Welfare expressed an expectation of increasing the number of children in kinship care to a level of about 15% of all children in care; this, however, still remains to be implemented by the local authorities.

Besides a new priority for kinship and network care, the Foster Care Reform placed increased emphasis on school performance. Research has almost unanimously pointed to the poor school performance of children in care and the subsequent difficulty in achieving social integration (Jackson, 2001; Christoffersen, 2003; Egelund, Hestbæk, & Andersen, 2004; Berridge, 2007; Andersen, 2008; Ottosen & Christensen, 2008; Egelund et al., 2009). With a heightened focus on school performance of young people in care and better social reintegration when exiting care, the government wants to contribute to breaking "the vicious circle of deprivation,. . . as it is called in the government's strategy 'Equal opportunities for all children and young people.'" Thus, when undertaking a so-called Article 50 investigation of the child's conditions, and when later outlining the mandatory action plan for the child, the child's school performance, behavior and development, family relations, health issues, leisure time activities, friendships, and other relevant factors must be examined. This list of items reflects the reform's objective of encouraging cooperation and coordination across sectors. For example, cross-sectorial cooperation between the social system and the school system seems to present an almost never-ending challenge.

Another important change is that the period is extended during which local authorities may decide that a child placed in care with parental consent may be denied going back to his or her parents, if these same local authorities find that it is in the best interest of the child not to do so. This is true even if the criteria for placing a child without parental consent are not fulfilled (these criteria are described below). Thus, the breach in the principle of continuity in biological relations mentioned above has widened a bit.

A final amendment to the 2006 Foster Care Reform worth noting is that the government gave priority to the implementation of the new law by allocating a considerable amount of resources for training and education targeted at local case workers, in order to facilitate the performance of good casework.[3]

Along with the Foster Care Reform in 2006, the government launched a cross-ministerial comprehensive strategy called Breaking the Vicious Circle of Deprivation—Equal Opportunities for All Children and Young People. The "vicious circle" refers to the processes of intergenerational transmission, in which different forms of inequality, barriers, and lack of resources are passed on from one generation to the next. The expression suggests how people to some extent come to resemble their parents not only physically, but also in terms of education, social status, income, culture, habits, values, mentality, resources, networks, interests, and qualifications—even in a welfare state like Denmark. The government's vision is to offer the right child the right support at the right time, thus providing all children the same opportunities.

Status: A New Children's Reform in the Pipeline

The Ministry of Social Affairs (until spring 2009, the Ministry of Welfare, and until January 2010, the Ministry of Interior and Social Affairs) is involved in an ongoing process with the Children's Reform legislation, the objective of which is to improve initiatives targeted at disadvantaged children and young people. As part of the reform process, the Ministry initiated a dialogue with a large number of stakeholders including researchers, nongovernmental organizations, professionals, representatives from the local authorities, and unions.

A few amendments to the Consolidation Act of Social Services have been passed in 2009, as the first part of the Children's Reform legislation. The power of local authorities to keep a child in care against the parents' will has been strengthened further. For instance, local authorities must now decide on the duration of a "waiting period" before a child placed with parental consent may exit out-of-home care. The child must remain in care up until 6 (additional) months, in order to give the local authorities an increased possibility of planning the child's return to the birth home, prepare new measures to be taken, or investigate whether there is reason to substantiate a placement without parental consent. Also, in particular cases, a 0- to 1-year-old infant may be placed in out-of-home care for up to 3 years without the usual requirements for trial.

An even more radical measure is the possibility to decide that a child placed in out-of-home care must remain permanently with the foster parents, if he or she has been living with them for a number of years and is more closely attached to them than to the biological parents. This is true even if the biological parents want their child back home, and/or they withdraw their consent to the placement. The legislation in this area clearly reflects a fundamental dilemma: that there are no easy answers as to what is in the best interests of the child. On one hand, remaining in care may be in the best interest of the child if the child really is closely attached to the foster parents (and not to the biological parents). On the other hand, this amendment is another breach in the continuity principle that ruled throughout the 1990s, which strived for a continuous and stable relationship between the child and her or his parents. Legally, it seems now practically possible to place a young child in out-of-home care for his or her entire childhood and adolescence without meeting the criteria concerning care without parental consent.

As a part of the Children's Reform legislation, the amended Act on Parental Responsibility has been tightened, too. Where the former Act opened the possibility of issuing an order for active parental support, the amended Act now states that the local authority *must* decide on a parental order if the criteria are met. Further, the principle of parental order has been extended to cover children and young persons from 12 to 17 years of age. The local authority must decide on a "youth order" when there is a risk that the child's health or development will suffer significant harm, and when the authorities simultaneously find that the possibilities for consensual cooperation with the parents are not sufficient to relieve the problems of the child.

Finally, in 2009, the Act on Adoption has been changed as a part of the Children's Reform legislation (Act no. 105 of May 28, 2009). It has become easier to put up a child for adoption without the consent of the parents, especially *if* the child is younger than 1 year; or *if* the child, typically less than 3 years old, has developed a close attachment to the foster parents; *and if* it has been substantiated that the biological parents will never be able to take proper care of the child *and* that they will not be able to play a positive role when having access to the child. Until now, adoption without consent has been used only rarely in Denmark (approximately 2–3 children during a 5-year period), and never as open adoption.

Debureaucratization is a central goal for the government. Therefore, the political agreement on the amendments of the Consolidation Act to come also includes removal of selected regulations that were part of former amendments made at the beginning of the century. For example, the procedural regulations of the Article 50 investigation and the action plan for the child following such an investigation are to be reduced, as are those regulations connected with placement in out-of-home care without consent. The newly introduced interdisciplinary committees will be abolished as well.

As may be apparent from the descriptions of the three developmental periods, in almost every reform and every legislative amendment of the last two decades, the "buzz words" have included early intervention and the use of preemptive measures; more involvement of children and parents; more responsibility on the part of families and their networks; and improved measures for disadvantaged children and young people. Despite common rhetoric in these areas, the current trend seems to be moving away from a broader family welfare ideology and toward a child protection ideology with a stronger element of compulsive measures and punitive devices, and with increased demands on individual families, and especially, their 12- to 17-year-old young people.

What is very interesting is that these developments might leave room for increased consideration of the best interest of the individual child. However, they might also result in (further) exclusion of biological parents, depending on how local municipalities interpret and implement the amendments.

CHILD ABUSE AND NEGLECT IN DANISH LAW

This section examines the Danish definitions of child abuse and neglect, as illustrated through the criteria for intervening with and without parental consent in the Consolidation Act on Social Services. I will also review the procedural requirements concerning notifications.

Key Criteria Defining Child Abuse and Neglect

Several Danish studies have examined child abuse and neglect using a typology in which child abuse is divided into two dimensions: active or passive abuse/neglect, and physical or emotional abuse/neglect, thereby constructing four main types of abuse/neglect (Christensen, 1992; Pruzan, 1997). According to the legislation and government guidelines, social workers in the local authorities and other groups of professionals are supplied with somewhat different criteria for interventions with and without parental consent.

As noted below, the criterion for interventions with parental consent is rather vague, leaving considerable room for interpretation:

> The municipal council shall decide on measures. . . where this must be deemed to be *of material importance*, having regard to a child's or young person's special needs for support. (Consolidation Act on Social Service, Art. 52)

Any such decision shall be subject to the consent of the parents and also of the young person over the age of 15. Thus, applying the law requires an assessment of whether the intervention seems to be of material importance. Procedurally, the government guidelines for "material importance" convey that the support must be of essential importance to the child; an investigation of the child may have revealed the need for intervention, and the parents and the child over the age of 15 must have given their consent. The municipal council may implement preventive measures of the following types:

- Consulting assistance relating to the conditions of the child or young person; among other things, that the child or young person must seek admission to a daytime facility, youth club, training or education establishment, etc.
- Practical, pedagogical, or other support in the home
- Family therapy or specific treatment of the child's or young person's problems
- Residential accommodation for both the custodial parent, the child or young person, and other members of the family
- A relief care arrangement
- Appointment of a welfare officer for the child or young person, or a permanent contact person for the child or young person and possibly for the whole family
- In-service training of the young person with a public or private employer
- Placing the child or young person in a care facility outside the home (out-of-home care with consent) (Consolidation Act on Social Service, Art. 52)

The municipal council is always supposed to choose the least restrictive suitable measure(s) for the resolution of the problems uncovered in the course of such an investigation. If out-of-home care is the most suitable measure, placement in care may be the very first intervention.

Regarding the criteria for placement *without* parental consent, here we find the most precise specification for intervention:

> Where there is an obvious risk that the health or development of the child or young person will suffer *significant harm* due to:
>
> 1. inadequate care for or treatment of the child or young person;
> 2. violence or other serious ill-treatment;
> 3. substance abuse, criminal conduct, or other serious social difficulties on the part of the child or young person; or
> 4. other behavioural or adjustment problems in the child or young person, the children and young persons' committee may decide, without the consent of the custodial parent or other person having custody and the young person over the age of 15, that the child or young person is to be placed in care... where there is a reasonable presumption that the problem cannot be resolved during the child's or young person's continued stay in the home. (Consolidation Act on Social Services, Art. 58)

Here, the threshold for compulsory intervention is tightened considerably, compared with interventions with consent, and the focus is placed on significant harm, much like similar statements in the United Kingdom's Children Act of 1989. The government guidelines emphasize (Section 332) that it is the risk of harm that is decisive. By using the terms "obvious risk" and "health or development," it is indicated that due consideration must be given to both the present conditions of the child or adolescent and to the future conditions while growing up. Decisions on care without consent are made by the children's and young people's committees of the local authorities, consisting of a judge, an educational/psychological consultant, and three lay members of the local council.

The government guidelines mention examples of situations that may cause placement without consent: maltreatment or other severe forms of assault, for example sexual abuse; severe neglect or inadequate fulfilment of the child's needs; adult-centered parental behavior that neglects the needs of the child (e.g., caused by substance abuse); and notable child behavioral problems, such as substance abuse, delinquency, learning disabilities, emotional problems, etc. The definition of abuse creates the social frame within which reporting, investigation, and substantiation take places.

Responsibility for Reporting Suspected Cases of Maltreatment

Denmark has a mandatory reporting system placing all citizens under obligation to report on neglect/abuse:

> Any person who learns or becomes aware that a child or young person under the age of 18 is being neglected or abused by his/her parents or other

persons involved in his/her upbringing, or is living under conditions endangering his/her health or development, shall notify the municipal authorities. (Consolidation Act on Social Services, Art. 154)

If a person suspects that a child or young person is being sexually abused, that person must also notify the police.

The Act also specifies that the municipality must acknowledge the receipt of the notification within 6 business days. In the past, local municipalities had been criticized because the reporting citizen rarely received any kind of response from the authorities. Still, the person reporting to the municipality is not a party to the case, meaning that the authorities must acknowledge the receipt but cannot divulge how they will react to the notification.

One of the 2001 amendments to the Consolidation Act on Social Services was that, if a family moves from one municipality to another, and the local authorities find that one or more children are in need of special support at this point, then the local authorities have an obligation to notify the new municipality in which the family takes residence (Section 152). As mentioned in the beginning of the chapter, a frequently noted problem, however, has been that families with children in need could move from one municipality to another, where their case then had to start all over again. This often led to months or years passing before the new municipality had a sufficient base for intervention.

Persons holding public office or providing public services have a heightened responsibility for reporting child maltreatment/child abuse to the local authorities, overriding the rules of professional confidentiality. This heightened obligation to notify is conditional on the premise that the professional is not able to relieve the child's problems. The professional also has a duty to prevent social problems if possible.

A pilot study undertaken by the National Social Appeals Board found that professionals, particularly those in day care centers and child-minders in private homes, rarely made notifications. The study, based on approximately 1,900 notifications, showed that 7% of the reports came from day care centers, whereas 18% originated from teachers and 14% from health care personnel (Table 7.1). Further, 13% of the notifications were a result of the general mandatory reporting system. The last 13% of the notifications came from the holders of parental custody (12%) or from the children or young persons themselves (1%) (www. ankestyrelsen.dk). This study only listed formal notifications. An earlier study on children in care in Denmark showed that 11% of the children or young persons in care in Denmark had been in contact with the child protection system on their own initiative before they were taken into care (Hestbæk, 1997).

In continuation of this study, the government asked the National Social Appeals Board to conduct a media campaign in 2009, including advertising in the newspapers and television, and the establishment of websites targeted at professionals. The aim of the campaign was to underline the importance of

Table 7.1: Reporters of Notifications in Denmark 2007 (%)

Notifications from Professionals with Heightened Obligation to Report	%
School teachers	18
Day care centers, day care homes, etc.	7
Health care nurses	3
Other health care professionals	11
Police	8
Courts	1
Other municipalities	4
Others with heightened obligation to report	21
Persons with general obligation to report	
Anonymous	5
Family, network, friends	5
Others	3
Holders of parental custody or the child/young person	
The child/the young person	1
Holders of parental custody	12
All	**99**

Source: Based on a pilot study on 1,900 notifications made by The National Social Appeals Board (www.Ankestyrelsen.dk).

reporting suspected cases of child abuse. A preliminary impact analysis shows that, in the first 6 months of 2009, the National Social Appeals Board received 175 notifications, which is almost three times as many as throughout 2006.

Inquiry into Reports and Substantiation of Allegations

The local authorities are responsible for the situation of children and adolescents in their community. As mentioned, local authorities must acknowledge all reports of child abuse no later than 6 business days after the notification is received.

When local authorities receive a notification regarding child maltreatment/child abuse, they assess whether it will be necessary to undertake an investigation under the rules of Article 50 of the Consolidation Act on Social Services. If the local authorities decide on an Article 50 investigation, they then ensure that the conditions of the child or the young person are investigated thoroughly. Any decision to do so usually (but not always) needs to be made with the consent of the custodial parent or other person having custody and the young person if over the age of 15. The Care Reform implied that, during the course of investigation, the case worker prepares an overall evaluation of several factors relating to the child's or young person's life; these factors include development and behavior, family, school, health, leisure time activities, and friendships. As previously indicated, however, as part of a debureaucratization process, the Article 50 investigation will in future be subject to fewer procedural claims, the effect of which is unknown.

In general, an Article 50 investigation "shall not be any more comprehensive than required by their purpose and shall be conducted as gently as possible in the given situation." If it is necessary, the examination of the child or young person can be undertaken without the parents' approval:

> Where it is deemed necessary in order to determine whether there is an obvious risk of serious damage to the health or development of a child or young person, the children and young persons' committee may decide, without the consent of the custodial parent or other person having custody and the young person over the age of 15, to conduct an examination of the child or young person during his/her stay at an institution or admission to a hospital, including a psychiatric ward. Any such examination must be completed within two (2) months of the decision by the children and young persons' committee. (Consolidation Act on Social Services, Art. 51)

OUT-OF-HOME CARE IN DENMARK

Placement in out-of-home care with the consent of the custodial parent and the young person over the age of 15 is counted as one measure along a continuum of preventive measures. The social worker or an administrative board has been delegated the authority to decide on placements with consent when this is deemed to be of material importance to the child or young person's special needs for support.

According to results from Western countries, out-of-home care has produced poor long-term outcomes for socially disadvantaged children (Fanshel & Shinn, 1978; Bohman & Sigvardsson 1979, 1980, 1985; Osborn & Clair 1987; Christoffersen, 1996, 1999).[4] Although lacking longitudinal studies with control groups, British and Scandinavian research shows unambiguously that, as young adults, formerly cared-for children are disproportionately poorly educated; they are often unemployed and poor; and they often suffer from mental and physical illnesses or are substance abusers.[5] Despite these results, the public costs of out-of-home care have risen dramatically during the last decades. Therefore, efforts are being made to develop and test better forms of out-of-home care treatment that can meet the extraordinary needs of children and young people placed in care (these efforts include, for example, Multidimensional Treatment Foster Care/MTFC).

In 2001, a remarkable change in after-care made it possible for young people coming of age to remain in care or to maintain the relationship with their former foster home or residential institution while gradually developing an independent life.

During the last 25 years, foster care has continually been the preferred out-of-home care environment in Denmark, covering more than 40% of all children aged 0–22 years in out-of-home care (including after-care) in 2008. However, changes have occurred in the conceptualization of foster care. As part of the Foster Care Reform in 2006, kinship care and network care were introduced as legal concepts (prior to that, any kind of 24-hour foster care with a private family was labelled "foster care"). The Consolidation Act on Social Services now stresses the responsibility of parents, wider kin, and the family's own networks for assistance in solving the problems of children. As a part of the Foster Care Reform, municipal child protection authorities are obliged to consider if kinship care might be a suitable option in all new decisions on placement in out-of-home care.

The Rate of Out-of-Home Care Placements

Since Denmark has extensive national administrative data on child protection and child welfare interventions based on annual reports from local authorities on any child who enters and exits the system, it is possible to give relatively precise descriptions of developments in the field over the last several decades.[6]

During the past 40 years, around 10/1,000 of the child and youth population aged 0–17 years have been placed in out-of-home care, measured as of 31 December of any given year; amounting to just under 13,000 children in out-of-home care in 2007 (Figure 7.1). The 10/1,000 (i.e., 1%) seems to be a number hard to escape regardless of legislation, regardless of government, and regardless of social policy reforms and numerous efforts to put more weight into prevention. In addition to this, new rules on after-care entail the continuous placement of slightly less than an additional 2,700 young persons aged 18–22 years in 2007 (not displayed in Figure 7.1). Thus, together with Finland, Denmark has the highest proportion of children up to 22 years of age placed in care in the Scandinavian countries, and, simultaneously, the smallest proportion of children placed without consent (Bengtsson & Böcker Jacobsen, 2009).

A tight social security net and a high proportion of children and young people subject to either preventive measures or to being placed in out-of-home care (or both!) leave their marks on child welfare and child protection spending. In 2008, out-of-home care amounted to approximately DKK 9.4 billion (or $2 billion), and costs for the child protection sector as a whole amounted to approximately DKK 13 billion (or $2.9 billion; Table 7.2).

There is an ongoing discussion between the 98 local authorities and the national government concerning the extent to which local authorities should be compensated for their child protection spending. Some find that, too often, an inappropriate balance is struck between professional and economic considerations (in favor of economy) when considering the potential measures to be implemented for a child (and the costs following).

Figure 7.1: The amount and proportion per 1,000 of children 0–17 years of age in out-of-home care in Denmark 1983–2007 (number/per thousand)

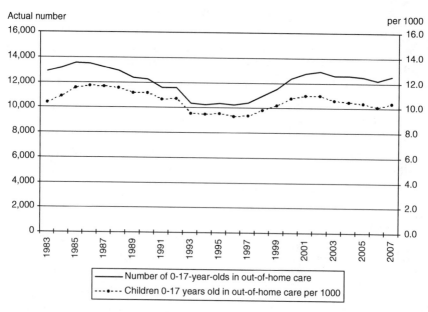

Source: Statistics Denmark www.statistikbanken.dk.

Types of Caring Environment

The Danish out-of-home care landscape is highly diversified. As shown in Figure. 7.2, a little less than 45% of 0- to 17-year-olds in out-of-home care are placed in some type of foster care. Of this 45%, only 2%–3% are placed in kinship care or network care, respectively; and the remaining 40% in foster care are placed in "traditional" professionalized foster care. It is remarkable that the incidence of children in kinship care has been rare in the Denmark (and the other Scandinavian countries). Among other factors, researchers explain the low incidence of kinship care by pointing to skepticism about the suitability of kin as an alternative source of care (Holtan, 2002; Mehlbye 2005; Knudsen et al., forthcoming).

Table 7.2: The Expenditure on Out-of-Home Care and Preventive Measures 2001–2008 (DKK billion)

	2001	2002	2003	2004	2005	2006	2007	2008
Out-of-home care[1]	8,375	8,756	9,027	9,221	8,698	8,888	8,824	9,443
Preventive measures	2,951	3,167	3,231	3,402	3,266	3,352	3,558	3,761
Secure care	–	145	163	178	211	223	258	279
Total DKK billion	**11,326**	**12,068**	**12,421**	**12,834**	**12,175**	**12,463**	**12,640**	**13,483**

Source: The Ministry of Interior and Social Welfare 2010.
[1] The 2001 expenditures to out-of-home care includes secure care.

Figure 7.2: Children 0–17 years of age in care, distributed on type of care 1983–2007 (%)

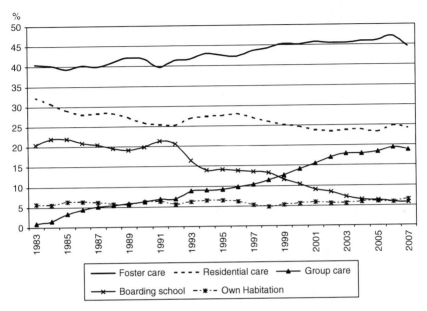

Source: Statistics Denmark www.statistikbanken.dk.

Residential institutions are the second most frequently used type of care regime, but their use has decreased during the last 25 years. A little less than 25% of all children 0–17 years old in care were placed in different types of residential institutions during 2007. These are either public institutions or private institutions with public funding. Residential institutions are often targeted for specific groups, be it infants and toddlers, children with school problems, or antisocial adolescents (for instance, in secure or open accommodation). Some offer therapeutic environments for children with severe emotional or behavioral problems of different kinds.

About 18% of out-of-home placements involve group care or so-called "sociopedagogical homes," which are privately organized, often highly professionalized and specialized, nonprofit units, usually caring for 5–10 children or young people. The use of this type of caring environment has seen considerable growth since its emergence in the 1970s, amid a severe critique of the old-fashioned "children's home." Finally, around 12% are placed in either boarding schools or in some kind of independent dwelling. Boarding schools have internal classrooms and accommodations; the child in care is placed at the boarding school by the local authorities and lives there with other children, including other young people who have just one or two years of school left away from home (e.g., due to the posting of parents abroad). Being placed in an independent dwelling means that young people—typically 16–18 years old and without severe problems—will be offered a room or a small apartment, and will be in close contact with the authorities, eventually being appointed a welfare officer or a permanent contact person.

Figure 7.3: Children 0–17 years of age in care, distributed by age group 1983–2007 (%)

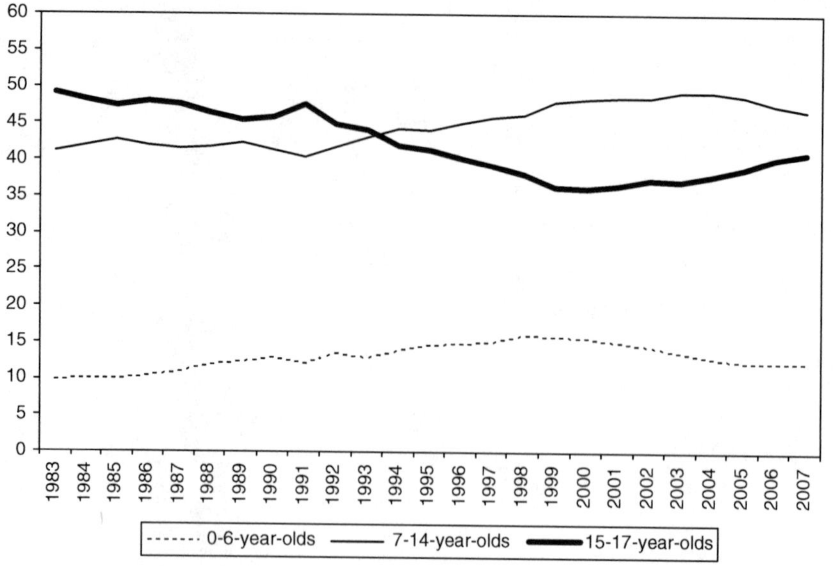

Source: Statistics Denmark www.statistikbanken.dk.

Age Distribution of Children and Young Persons in Out-of-Home Care

If we look at children and young persons in care by age, it is evident from Figure 7.3 that the youngest group of children, those 0–6 years old, only constitutes a minor part of all children in care (10%–12%). The remaining school-aged children and the eldest teenagers (15–17 years old) constitute the largest share (around 90% in 2007). Thus, being in out-of-home care is mainly a teenage phenomenon in Denmark, and during the last 10 years, 13- to 17-year-old teenagers form an increasing part of this population, growing from approximately 53% in 1999 to 63% of all 0- to 17-year-olds in care in 2006. So, although the average proportion of the whole child population 0–17 years old (1.2 million) in care is 10/1,000, only 4/1,000 of 3-year-olds are placed in care, but as many as 30/1,000 of 17-year-olds are in care. There are no unambiguous explanations for this statistic. Presumably, it reflects the fact that we cannot document positive effects for being placed in out-of-home care. And, although it is often possible to treat a preschool-aged child at home, throughout adolescence, an increasing number of young people with social problems have severe conflicts with parents and peers, delinquency problems, and like for which 24-hour care is often seen as part of the solution.

CONCLUSION

Denmark, together with Finland, holds a Nordic record for the proportion of youngsters up to age 22 in out-of-home care. It is subject to discussion whether this figure reflects a tight and efficient social security net, or a poor ability to implement prevention effectively. The fact is that we still cannot estimate the effects of the billions spent on interventions either at home or in out-of-home care; neither in the perceived quality of life of these children, nor in the performance of (previously) disadvantaged children and young people as concerns, say, school achievement, education, employment, physical and emotional health and well-being, and crime. However, as is the case in many other countries, Denmark is gradually putting more and more efforts into testing and evaluating intervention programs, seeking to cultivate an evidence-based social practice. These programs are most often imported from other countries, such as Multi Systemic Therapy (MST), Multidimensional Treatment Foster Care (MTFC), Incredible Years, MultifunC institutions, and Parent Management Training (PMT).

An obvious change since the mid-1990s is the considerable increase in the number of sections in the law and the interventions possible that have to do with children in need of special support. Also, casework routines in the local authorities are, to an increasing extent, the object of legislation and very specific government guidance. The processes of regulation and control have gone so far that the government has now started a debureaucratization process, repealing those regulations that are too costly.

For the last decade, the Danish child welfare regime has attached great importance to working cooperatively with the child and the family; and indeed, most interventions have been implemented with the consent of the parents. Only around 9%–10% of all children in care have been placed without the consent of the custodial parent and/or the child over 15 years. However, as mentioned in the historical overview of legal and political developments, the government has during the last few years launched new approaches that emphasize increased family responsibility. Parents with disadvantaged children are facing more demands on their individual ability to support their children, and to live up to the expectations of the law as implemented by the local municipalities. Further, the amended Consolidation Act on Social Services makes it easier to intervene in families without the consent of the parents, and it has become less bureaucratically burdensome to put up a child for adoption.

From the perspective of these changes, we observe the emergence of a movement away from a broader child welfare orientation based on voluntary partnerships toward a child protection regime characterized more by legalism and with an increased use of measures without the consent of the children and families involved. Seemingly, Denmark is slowly abandoning the child and family policy regime that, in the form of a "nonintervention" ideology, has been dominant for years. A study of the Nordic countries in the mid-1990s showed that Denmark at that time seemed to be much less intervening in families with children with special needs (reflecting an ideology in which family privacy was carefully protected), as was also the case for Norway and Sweden (Hestbæk, 1997). This new development may be conceived as a step away from the classical social democratic welfare state and toward a more liberal state, as far as individual responsibility is concerned. Interestingly, and conversely, this trend also is linked to a simultaneous movement toward a more interventionist child protection policy. However, because these amendments have taken effect only recently, the extent to which they will change social work, and their effects on children and families remains to be seen.

In the summer of 2010, the Minister of Social Affairs unveiled the government's visions for the next steps in the ongoing Children's Reform legislation, which will be subject to reading in the parliament. The proposed bills include inducements for young children to be placed in foster care instead of residential care, better financial compensation to kinship caregivers and network caregivers, assignment of a right for children to keep up contact with their parents and their network if it is in the best interest of the child, lowering the age limit for being a party to the case from 15 years to 12 years, measures to make it easier to decide on and implement interventions for children when the parents do not give their consent, and additional resources for the training and education of social workers and case workers. Also, the government has now lowered the age of criminal responsibility from 15 years to 14 years., a move for which there is no evidence for a positive result for the teenagers involved, rather the contrary. As all these amendments (apart from a lowered age of criminal responsibility) have not come into force yet, the effects for the children and young persons involved remain to be seen.

NOTES

1   Tine Egelund, Programme Director at SFI–The National Centre for Social Research, has contributed with invaluable comments to the manuscript. Senior Researcher Mette Lausten, SFI, has kindly produced Figures 7.1, 7.2, and 7.3. Also, Professor of Child and Family Welfare, David Berridge, University of Bristol, has contributed with insightful questions and comments.

2   Any family in Denmark is entitled to a family allowance per child, independent of the family's level of income.

3   It is worth noting that Denmark faced considerable structural reform in 2007, reducing the former 271 local municipalities to 98 entities. With this reform, the local authority is now fully responsible for child welfare and child protection, for the supply of services, and for the finances entailed.

4   It is important to know that these longitudinal studies are not based on a randomized design.

5   To be mentioned among longitudinal studies: Bohman & Sigvardsson 1979, 1980, 1985; Christoffersen, 1996, 1999; Clausen & Kristofersen, 2008 (includes children in out-of-home care as well as in-home care); Hjern, Vinnerljung, & Lindblad, 2004; Hodges & Tizard, 1989a, 1989b; Osborn &

Clair, 1987; Quinton & Rutter, 1984, 1985, 1988; Vinnerljung, 1996; Vinnerljung & Ribe, 2001.

6 Both The Social Appeals Board (www.ast.dk) and Statistics Denmark (www. statistikbanken.dk) provide a huge amount of free data on disadvantaged children, of which some may be downloaded in English.

REFERENCES

Andersen, D. (2008). *Anbragte børn i tal. Kvantitative analyser af data om børn, der er anbragt uden for hjemmet med fokus på skolegang. Delrapport 1* [Children in out-of-home care in figures. Quantitative analyses of data on children with focus on schooling. Sub report No. 1], p. 14. Copenhagen: The Danish National Institute for Social Research.

Bengtsson, T.T., & Böcker Jacobsen, T. (2009). *Institutionslandskabet for unge i Norden* [The landscape of residential care of young children in the Nordic countries]. Copenhagen: The Danish National Institute for Social Research.

Berridge, D. (2007). Theory and explanation in child welfare: Education and looked-after children. *Child & Family Social Work, 12*(1), 1–10.

Betænkning/Report No. 1212. (1990). *Betænkning om de retlige rammer for indsatsen over for børn og unge (Graversen-betænkningen)* [On the legal framework for efforts to support children and adolescents]. Ministry of Social Affairs.

Bohman, M., & Sigvardsson, S. (1979). Long-term effects of early institutional care: A prospective longitudinal study. *Journal of Child Psychology & Psychiatry*, Vol. 20: 111–117.

Bohman, M., & Sigvardsson, S. (1985).A prospective longitudinal study of adoption. In A.R. Nicol (Ed.), *Longitudinal studies in child psychology and psychiatry. Practical lessons from research experience*, pp. 137–155. Norwich: Wiley & Sons Ltd.

Christensen, E. (1992). *Omsorgssvigt. En rapport om 0–3-årige baseret på sundhedsplejerskernes viden* [Neglect. A report based on visiting nurses' experience of neglect among 0–3 year-old children]. Copenhagen: The Danish National Institute for Social Research.

Christoffersen, M. (1993). *Anbragte børns livsforløb. En undersøgelse af tidligere anbragte børn og unge født i 1967* [The life course of children placed in out-of-home care. A survey of children born in 1967 who have been placed in out-of-home care], p. 11. Copenhagen: The Danish National Institute for Social Research.

Christoffersen, M. (1996). A follow-up study of out-of-home care in Denmark: Long-term effects on self-esteem among abused and neglected children. *International Journal of Child & Family Welfare, 1*, 25–39.

Christoffersen, M. (1999). *Risikofaktorer i barndommen - en forløbsundersøgelse særligt med henblik på forældrenes psykiske sygdomme* [Childhood risk factors–a longitudinal survey with focus on parents' mental diseases]. Copenhagen: The Danish National Institute for Social Research.

Clausen, S.-E., & Kristofersen, L.B. (March 2008). *Barnevernsklienter i Norge 1990–2005. En longitudinell studie* [Children in out-of-home care in Norway from 1990–2005. A longitudinal study]. Oslo: Nova, Rapport.

Consolidation Act on Social Services (Serviceloven), (2010). (www.sm.dk).

Ebsen, F. (2007). *Børn og unge med behov for særlig støtte fra 1990–2005* [Children and young people with special need for support from 1990–2005]. HPA-SERIE NO.1 Working Paper 5A. Copenhagen: Danish University School, University of Århus.

Egelund, T., Andersen, D., Hestbæk, A.-D., Lausten, M., Knudsen, L., Olsen, R.F., & Gerstoft, F. (2009). *Anbragte børns udvikling og vilkår. Resultater fra SFI's forløbsundersøgelser af årgang 1995* [The development and conditions for children in out-of-home care. Results from SFI's longitudinal survey on birth cohort 1995], p. 23. Copenhagen: The Danish National Institute for Social Research.

Egelund, T., & Hestbæk, A.-D. (2003). *Anbringelse af børn og unge uden for hjemmet. En forskningsoversigt* [Children in out-of-home care. A research review], p. 4. Copenhagen: The Danish National Institute for Social Research.

Egelund, T., Hestbæk, A.-D., & og Andersen, D. (2004). *Små børn anbragt uden for hjemmet.* [Young children placed outside home], p. 17. Copenhagen: The Danish National Institute for Social Research.

Espersen, L.D. (2004). *Fra anbringelse til efterværn* [From residential care to after care], p. 25. Copenhagen: The Danish National Institute for Social Research.

Fanshel, D., & Shinn, E. B. (1978) *Children in foster care. A longitudinal investigation.* New York: Columbia University Press.

Hestbæk, A.-D. (1997). *Når børn og unge anbringes. En undersøgelse af kommunernes praksis i anbringelsessager* [When children and young peopled are placed in out-of-home care. A survey of the local authorities' placement practices], p. 6. Copenhagen: The Danish National Institute for Social Research.

Hjern, A., Vinnerljung, B., & Lindblad, F. (2004). Avoidable mortality among child welfare recipients and intercountry adoptees–a national cohort study. *Journal of Epidemiology and Community Health, 58,* 412–417.

Hodges, J., & Tizard, B. (1989a). IQ and behavioural adjustment of ex-institutional adolescents. *Journal of Child Psychology & Psychiatry, 30,* 1, 53–75.

Hodges, J., & Tizard, B. (1989b). Social and family relationships of ex-institutional adolescents. *Journal of Child Psychology and Psychiatry, 30,* 1, 77–97.

Holtan, A. (2002). *Barndom i fosterhjem i egen slekt* [Childhood in kinship care]. Doktorgradsafhandling (Doctoral thesis). The University of Tromsø.

Knudsen, L., Egelund, T., & Hestbæk, A.-D. (2010). *Kinship care in Denmark: Comparing kinship and non-kinship forms of care.* In E. Fernandez & R. P. Barth (eds.) *How does foster care work? International evidence on outcomes*, pp. 224–240. London: Jessica Kingsley Publishers.

Lindemann, A., & Hestbæk, A.-D. (2004). *Slægtsanbringelser I Danmark–en pilotundersøgelse* [Kinship care in Denmark–a pilot study], p. 21. Copenhagen: The Danish National Institute for Social Research.

Mehlbye, J. (2005). *Slægtsanbringelse–det bedste for barnet?* [Kinship care–in the best interest of the child?]. Copenhagen: AKF Forlaget.

Osborn, A., & Clair, L. (1987). The ability and behavior of children who have been in care or separated from their parents. *Early Child Development and Care, 28*(3), 187–354.

Ottosen, M.H., & Christensen, P.S. (2008). *Anbragte børns sundhed og skolegang. Udviklingen efter anbringelsesreformen* [The health and schooling of children in out-of-home care. The development following the Care Reform], p. 21. Copenhagen: The Danish National Institute for Social Research.

Pruzan, V. (1997). Denmark: Voluntary placements as a family support. In N. Gilbert (Ed.), *Combating child abuse: International perspective and trends*, pp. 125–142. New York: Oxford University Press.

Quinton, D., & Rutter, M. (1984). Parents with children in care I: Current circumstances and parenting. *Journal of Child Psychology and Psychiatry, 25* (2), 211–229.

Quinton, D. & Rutter, M. (1985). Parenting behaviour of mothers raised "in care." In A.R. Nicol (Ed.), *Longitudinal studies in child psychology and psychiatry: Practical lessons from research experience*, 157–201. Norwich: John Wiley & Sons Ltd.

Quinton, D., & Rutter, M. (1988). *Parenting breakdown: The making and breaking of inter-generational links*. Aldershot: Avebury.

Stein, M. (1994). Leaving care, education and career trajectories. *Oxford Review of Education, 20*(3), 349–360.

Vinnerljung, B. (1996). *Fosterbarn som vuxna* [Foster children as+ adults]. Lund: Arkiv.

Vinnerljung, B., & Ribe, M. (2001). Mortality after care among young adult foster children in Sweden. *International Journal of Social Welfare, 10*(3), 164–173.

Winokur, M., Holtan, A., & Valentine, D. (2009). *Kinship care for the safety, permanency, and well-being of children removed from the home for maltreatment*, p. 1. Oslo: The Campbell Collaboration, Campbell Systematic Reviews.

8

NORWAY: TOWARD A CHILD-CENTRIC PERSPECTIVE[1]

MARIT SKIVENES

[T]he child (shall) be put first in all assessments the Child Welfare Agency undertakes. . . the aim is to give children in need equal opportunities compared with other children in Norway. (Minister of Children and Equality, April 24, 2009)[2]

This quote illustrates an important goal for the present Norwegian government: to provide equal opportunities for all children in Norway. Norway, with a population of 4.8 million people, first established a Child Protection Act in 1896. Today, more than 100 years later, the Child Welfare Act of 1992 (effective January 1, 1993),[3] is the legal foundation for the Norwegian child welfare system.[4] It defines child welfare workers' responsibilities and guides their decision making.

Historically, the Norwegian child welfare system has undergone developments similar to those of the Swedish system, as described by Hort (1997). Looking at the taxonomy of child welfare systems that already have been discussed (cf. Gilbert, 1997), the Norwegian child welfare system can safely be classified as a family service–mandatory reporting system similar to those of Denmark, Finland, and Sweden. The Norwegian child welfare system takes a *family-sensitive* and *therapeutic* approach to families and children, and this has increasingly been the case during the past 15 years. In addition, the approach is based on a mandatory reporting system in which all public (and many private) employees are required by law to report any suspicions of maltreatment toward children. The system is also a legalistic system, in the sense that it emphasizes the rule of law for children and parents. In the Norwegian system, all actions toward a family must be anchored in the law, and all serious interventions, such as care orders and involuntarily intervention, are ordered by the court.[5] This means that the child welfare system aims to protect children, to provide services, and to promote equal opportunities within the framework of due process and the rule of law.

The overview of the Norwegian child welfare system that I provide in this chapter focuses on the period from 1994 to 2009. I will use a political science perspective to explore what the system does and how it works, but I will also discuss how policies and practice in general developed during this period. However, I will not try to cover all the possible interpretations of policies, and I will not outline the many ways in which frontline practice is implemented.

The chapter is organized in the following way. I will provide background information on the Norwegian welfare state and introduce the basic premises of the child welfare system. I will then present overall policy trends in child welfare during the last 25 years. Thereafter, I will outline how maltreatment is defined, who is responsible for making referrals of possible maltreatment, the process of enquiring into referrals, how allegations of maltreatment are substantiated, and the patterns of out-of-home placements. The final part of the chapter is devoted to policies and three major trends in the Norwegian child welfare system. The first trend concerns knowledge and competencies, the second covers political orientations on how to divide the responsibility for children between family and state. Finally, I discuss how the Norwegian child welfare system is increasingly aiming toward a child perspective by putting the child in the center of its policies and practice.

BACKGROUND AND BASIC FACTS

In Norway, the child welfare system is an integral part of the overall welfare state. The Norwegian welfare state tries to distribute services according to universal principles of human dignity and justice, wherein all citizens are guaranteed "minimum standards of income, livelihood, housing accommodation, and education" (Eriksen & Loftager, 1996, p. 2). Children are included in these welfare arrangements as part of a family but also as individuals in their own right. They have rights to education, health services, and a decent childhood protected from neglect and abuse. For the last 10–15 years, the Norwegian child welfare system has conceptualized child protection as the integration of child welfare in the narrow sense of the term (by protecting children from risk of maltreatment) *and* the promotion of social equality in the wider sense, by providing equal opportunities to all children in society. Hence, the Norwegian child welfare system is both protective and supportive in its approach to children at risk, and it can provide a wide range of welfare services, as well as undertake compulsory actions when necessary. This reflects the fact that Norway is a social democratic welfare regime

(Esping-Andersen, 1999, 1990): the state provides services to all children, through universal access to health care, education, and other public services. The state provides these services more extensively than the so-called liberal welfare regimes do (Esping-Andersen, 1999). In the United States and the United Kingdom, for example, the family (or the market, through private services) is expected to provide many of these services (see the Introduction to this book).

The Norwegian government invests hugely in the child welfare system, and it has made major improvements during the last 20 years. However, there has been much criticism of the system by academics and the public, and many issues have remained unsolved (e.g., Backe-Hansen et al., 2002; Skivenes, 2002; Grinde, 2005; Kristofersen & Clausen, 2006; Križ & Skivenes, 2009). The most serious complaint, which is also evident in other countries, is based on longitudinal research showing that children who receive child welfare services do not have the same opportunities to lead healthy and successful lives that other children do (Clausen, 2004; Kristofersen, 2005; cf.; Felitti et al., 1998; Felitti, 2002 for the U.S.). These studies show that children who use the child welfare system have lower education levels and are statistically more likely to use social and disability benefits, engage in substance abuse and criminal activities, and suffer violent deaths. Thus, even with a broad set of welfare services available, we must admit that Norway could do better in guaranteeing that all children will be safe, will be treated in accordance with their best interests, and will have equal opportunities to fulfill their potential.

Demographics and Expenditures

In 2008, 1,099,279 Norwegians were below the age of 18, and 10% of these were immigrants.[6] In that same year, 60,500 children were born, and about 3.6% (N = 44,200) of all children in Norway received child welfare services. Eighty percent of all child welfare services were in-home services, especially economic support and day care, and most out-of-home placements were in foster homes (87%). Norway has historically been comparatively homogeneous society that is experiencing changes due to immigration levels in recent years. About 10% of the Norwegian population are first- or second-generation immigrants (SSB, 2009). Children of first-generation immigrants are overrepresented in out-of-home placements (6.7/1000 children) in the child welfare system, whereas children of third-generation (and more) immigrant parents are underrepresented (3.1/1000 children). Studies of child welfare workers perceptions of working with ethnic minority groups displays that communication is a major obstacle in meetings with ethnic minority groups (Kriz & Skivenes, 2009, 2010). They point out challenges with language, system-understanding, and cultural differences, and perhaps most importantly, a difference in how the child is viewed and considered as an independent person (Kriz & Skivenes, 2009, 2010). (Cf. KIM, 2009 and Holm-Hansen, 2007 for more information on immigrants.)

The expense for the child welfare system (state and municipalities) in 2008 was about 10.5 billion NOK (U.S. $1.6 billion), equal to about 1.2% of all public expenses.[7] On average, this means the Norwegian state spent about 238,000 NOK (U.S. $36,600) for each child receiving services in 2008.

Child Welfare Agencies and Child Welfare Workers

Each of the 430 Norwegian municipalities is required by law to have a responsible child welfare administration (interorganizational cooperation is possible and encouraged). As municipality sizes differ, there are huge size differences in their child welfare agencies. For instance, in Bergen, the second largest municipality in Norway, with a population of about 280,000, the child welfare agency has 180 full-time positions. In contrast, the municipality of Tysnes, only an hour's drive from Bergen, has a population of 2,800 and only 1.2 full-time positions. The responsibility for children at risk is the same in these municipalities, and the services and the quality of casework and decision making should be the same. The types of interventions and services implemented vary to a large degree in the various municipalities,[8] and this noncompliance with the principles of the rule of law is considered a problem for children and parents.

At the municipal level across Norway, there are 3,300 full-time positions—three positions per 1,000 children—and the number of child welfare workers has steadily increased since 1994. About half of child welfare workers hold a BA in child welfare/protection work, and the rest have either a BA in social work (circa 40%) or a higher degree (circa 10%).

Three Main Reasons for Intervention

There are three main reasons why the child welfare system intervenes.

- First, at the lowest level, the system intervenes when a child has special needs, according to the definition given in the child welfare act §4–4 (1). The agency will provide in-home services.
- Second, if the agency cannot help the child with in-home services, or if in-home services are inappropriate (if the child is maltreated or abused, for instance, as described in more detail in the child welfare act §4–12), an out-of-home placement will be sought.
- Third, if a youth is behaving destructively or violently (e.g., misuses substances), the child welfare agency can provide in-home services or an out-of-home placement, as stated in the child welfare acts §4–24 and §4–26.

Intervention can be voluntary or compulsory. Serious interventions, such as the use of force and out-of-home placements, must be decided by the court, a requirement that is being violated increasingly.

The Child Welfare Act of 1992

The Child Welfare Act (CWA) of 1992 set the legal criteria and thresholds for interventions and decision making. The legislation was gradually implemented with the help of an increase in resources and a development program that was launched as a result of a huge crisis in the child welfare system.[9] The CWA of 1992 focused on two major issues in the child welfare system. First, there was a problem related to the rule of law, because the child welfare system did not always secure due process for parents and children. Thus, decisions did not meet the standards of legal justice and reason. The second problem was a lack of sufficient prevention work in families, a trend that had started in the 1980s.

The CWA of 1992 introduced a county tribunal (a judge, two professionals, and two jurors) to decide all serious cases, such as those that involved mandatory action or out-of-home placements. Furthermore, the 1992 law lowered the threshold for providing services for children, following the assumption that providing services at an early stage would result in fewer incidents of serious maltreatment and thus fewer out-of-home placements. The law also tried to make the child welfare system more service oriented and to remove some of the stigma of being a service user by associating the child welfare system with the positive connotations of the welfare state.

Four Governing Principles of the Child Welfare System

Norwegian child welfare law (and hence the child welfare system) is based on four basic principles that should guide child welfare work and decision making in child welfare cases. First and foremost is the *best interest principle* as stated in the CWA of 1992:

> [D]ecisive importance shall be attached to framing measures which are in the child's best interest. Hereunder, that importance shall be attached to giving the child stable and good contact with adults and continuity in the care provided. (§4-1).

The act does not give decision makers much guidance about how to interpret the term "best interest," except for the stability consideration stated in the principle.

Second, the *stability principle,* which refers not only to stability in the child's relationships to adults and other important persons but also to stable surroundings, such as continuity in school and with friends.

The third principle, and undoubtedly the most influential of the four, is the *biological principle* (i.e., the blood-tie presumption, see Weyland, 1997). This principle is primarily understood to favor the child's biological parents as care providers but also includes the wider family, such as grandparents and siblings. Growing up with his or her biological parent(s) is presumed to be in the child's best interest, and parents and children are presumed to have a moral and legal right to each other. Finally, although this is not often mentioned, it is also presumed to be easier (and cheaper) for parents to take responsibility for their children rather than for the state to do this.

The fourth principle favors the *least intrusive form of intervention*. This means that interventions regarding a reported concern about a child in need or at risk should be reasonable, and services should not be more excessive than necessary.

In sum, the four basic principles underlying the Norwegian child welfare system represent different directions. It is possible to interpret each of them in many ways, depending upon one's perspective and position. For instance, a child's perspective and an adult's perspective can be very different. This freedom of interpretation leaves much room for discretion among decision makers and may potentially be unjust.

Children Performing Criminal Acts

The age of criminal responsibility in Norway is 15 years. The ambition is to provide help to young people and to avoid imprisoning them. By the middle of 2009, 11 children had been sentenced to prison. Since 1999, the number of children in prison has decreased from 161 (138 of whom were in prison while their cases were being prepared) to 75 in 2008 (51 of whom were in prison while their cases were being prepared) (Ministry of Justice, NOU, 2008, p. 15).

FROM PROTECTION TO PROMOTION

A major shift in the history of the Norwegian child welfare system occurred formally in 1992, when parliament passed the CWA of 1992. This law marked the beginning of a new era in child welfare. It introduced the idea of integrating child welfare into the general welfare state platform, as well as clearer rights-oriented thinking for both children and parents. It also established tribunals for decision making in child welfare cases, focusing on knowledge- and evidence-based practice, and it made legal changes to secure children's rights and dignity. Policy developments during the last 30 years can be divided into three phases: protection, prevention, and promotion of equal opportunities and access to welfare. These general trends reflect some of the basic thinking that can be identified in the child welfare system overall, but they are probably relevant for other social and health areas as well.

Protection

Until the mid-1980s, ending with the new CWA of 1992, the child welfare system largely focused on protecting children from harm and abuse. Thresholds for intervention were high, and the policy philosophy emphasized that harm should be significant before a child could be removed (NOU, 1985, p. 18). Even though in-home services were seen as important among professionals, few services were available for a family with a child at risk of harm. Basically, the child's family/parents were the focus of welfare state intervention, and normative values stressing "normal" (i.e., good) parenting and adult behavior were the much-used criteria for intervention.

Prevention

With the 1992 Act, prevention really came into focus. The policy aim was to reduce risk and to avoid maltreatment by commencing services at an early stage. This meant significantly lower thresholds for offering services provided by the child welfare agencies. The major slogan was that the child welfare system should primarily be a service institution, not an intervention institution. Through this change, the biological principle, which prioritizes biological family members as children's caregivers, was also given high priority. In practice, this meant that in-home services would have to be proven useless before a care order could be issued. A major goal was to reduce out-of-home placements. In-home services would be voluntarily accepted by parents, and only a few in-home services (e.g., monitoring) could be coercively enforced. Interestingly, the services often provided for children and families were "compensating" services, often day care, that did not aim to change the problems of a child's biological caregivers. The intention was to maintain rather than to change the family status quo, by keeping the child with the family. It is ironic, then, that many of the services used to implement the policy goal of maintaining the family status quo (day care and weekend homes), actually keep children away from their parents.

Promotion of Equal Opportunities

The next significant period in the Norwegian child welfare system started in 2000. This period emphasized the promotion of equal opportunities and welfare for children. Much of the foundation for these ideas was laid by an expert committee's report, called the Befring Report (NOU, 2000, p. 12), and by the implementation of new methods of front-line work with children and families at risk. However, because of political considerations, it took some years for this philosophy to manifest itself in policy programs and the child welfare system. The Befring Report focused on the potential for improvement present in children and parents. Its slogan was "change," a change for the better by using the positive forces in a person or a relationship. Many of the new methods subsequently implemented in the child welfare system were based on this approach, such as Multi-System Therapy (MST)[10] and Parent Management Training (PMT), Family Conferences, and general empowerment measures. The aim was to improve the quality of decisions and interactions with service users by focusing on change and development of parenting skills, communication skills, relations between adolescents and parents, and the like. As such, the programs had a holistic approach to neglect and abuse, looking at contextual factors for families and their struggles; if this also has manifested itself in front-line practice, we do not have a clear answer to yet. A related and even more fundamental issue for the child welfare system is how principles of family preservation may harm disadvantaged children. The principle is based on the biological nuclear family model, and as such is an obstacle for alternative family models that might provide better support and living conditions for the child.

CRITERIA THAT DEFINE CHILD MALTREATMENT

The ordinary understanding of maltreatment is treating "a person cruelly or with violence," and psychological maltreatment of children "occurs when a person conveys to a child that he or she is worthless, flawed, unloved, unwanted, endangered, or only of value in meeting another's needs" (Kairys & Johonson, 2002, p. 1). In Norway, three types of maltreatment are considered criminal acts: incest, sexual abuse, and physical abuse. A recently enacted act defined all sexual behavior toward children below the age of 14 as rape (criminal code §229). This marks quite an interesting turn in Norwegian thinking about sexual crimes in general and sexual abuse of minors in particular.

The CWA of 1992, §4–12, which defines the more serious maltreatment of children just described, states that care orders may be made if:

(a) there are serious deficiencies in the daily care received by the child, or serious deficiencies in terms of the personal contact and security needed by a child of his or her age and development,

(b) the parents fail to ensure that a child who is ill, disabled, or in special need of assistance receives the treatment and training required,

(c) the child is maltreated or subjected to other serious abuses at home, *or*

(d) there is every probability that the child's health or development may be seriously harmed because the parents are incapable of taking adequate responsibility for the child.

An order may only be made pursuant to the first paragraph when required by the child's current situation. Hence, such an order may not be made if satisfactory conditions can be created for the child by assistance measures pursuant to section 4-4 or by measures pursuant to section 4-10 or section 4-11.

An order pursuant to the first paragraph shall be made by the county social welfare board pursuant to the rules of chapter 7.

These criteria set the thresholds for undertaking a care order, which can only be decided by the court. In 2008, 5.8/1,000 children were formally under care by the end of the year. This is only a slight increase from 1994.

RESPONSIBILITY FOR REPORTING SUSPECTED CASES OF MALTREATMENT

Norway has a mandatory reporting system in place for suspected maltreatment of children. This system includes all public employees, including teachers, day care center workers, health services personnel, and the like, and some types of professionals, such as psychologists and general practitioners. In addition, citizens in general are expected, on moral grounds, to report neglect and abuse of children. The mandatory reporting system is primarily rooted in the legal obligation introduced in the CWA of 1992, article 6–4:

> Notwithstanding the duty of secrecy, public authorities shall on their own initiative disclose information to the municipal child welfare service when there is reason to believe that a child is being maltreated at home or is subjected to other serious deficit of parental care,…or when a child has shown persistent, serious behavioral problems.

The definition of public authorities includes agencies and employees that provide services for, or receive funding from, public agencies; for instance, employees working in a private-sector day care program. Several professional groups are required by law to report suspicions of abuse and neglect of children. However, few professions have regulated how to proceed in situations where maltreatment is suspected. As for laypersons' obligations, moral norms suggest that the general population ought to care for those who are not able to protect their own interests.

In 2008, 27,850 cases[11] were opened for investigation by the child welfare agency, which amounts to 25.3/1,000 children, close to twice the amount in 1994, when it was 13/1,000 children.[12] In more than half of the 2008 cases, the investigations were triggered by "conditions in the child's home," which is a broad category, often implying minor problems. Twenty-three percent of the reports were registered as "maltreatment/abuse," 19% as "other" (a category whose content is not specified), and 16% as a young person's "behavioral problems."[13] Half of all these investigations resulted in the provision of child welfare services, the most common of which were advise, economic support and weekend homes.

The statistics show that more than half of the registered reports come from public officials, and 25% come from the child and his or her family. Four percent of referrals are from day care, and 6% are from public health centers. If we examine the details of who reports, we see that at least two public agencies (day care programs and public health care centers) do very little reporting relative to the number of children they serve. This has lately raised concerns among professionals and politicians, as these two agencies meet a large number of young children on a regular basis and thus have the opportunity to report suspected maltreatment at an early stage.[14] Early intervention is important to prevent serious harm and to provide assistance to the family/parents, according to Norwegian child welfare policies.

PROCESSES FOR ENQUIRING INTO REFERRALS

The processing of referrals about suspected child abuse or neglect can be divided into three stages. First, upon receiving a referral, the child welfare agency must decide within 1 week whether an investigation is necessary. To make a decision, a child welfare worker has a right to visit the child's home and to speak with the child alone. Second, if there are reasonable grounds to believe that the referred child has special needs (as defined in the CWA of 1992, §4–4), a designation that meets the initial threshold for intervention, then the child welfare agency has 3 months to assess the situation and to decide either that services are needed or that the case should be dropped. Third, if the child welfare agency concludes that services are needed, it can then suggest either in-home services or an out-of-home placement, with the former being more common. If an out-of-home placement is suggested, the case must be brought to the court, which will make the decision about a care order (as well as other orders that the courts are empowered to make).

If the referral is about sexual or physical abuse, then the police will be involved, because these are criminal acts, and the child welfare agency will cooperate with the police. In response to criticisms from professionals that children often have a limited role to play in lengthy evidence-gathering procedures, several cities in Norway have established "children houses."[15] These houses provide a single place where children who may have been sexually or physically abused can receive help and give evidence to authorities. All the appropriate professionals who must gather evidence, solicit valid testimony, and provide help and comfort to the child are present in one location, so that child care and police activities can be coordinated.

On May 28, 2009, the mandatory reporting provision of the Criminal Code Act was changed. To make sure that police receive information about family violence, anyone who suspects that sexual or physical abuse of women or children has occurred is required to notify the police. If a citizen fails to comply with this requirement, she or he can be sentenced to prison for 1 year. This is a very interesting turn in the handling of domestic violence and child abuse, which traditionally have been hidden, in a literal as well as legal sense, by the private sphere of the family. This change in the law signals a major change in the balance between private and public responsibilities and the kinds of steps that the state can take to prevent harm against individuals.

Returning to the investigation process, the general critique of it is threefold. First, critics feel that 3 months is too long for an investigation, but there is no current initiative to change this. Second, they feel that the child welfare agency does not sufficiently inform other official agencies about, or involve them in, their investigations. Recently, the Ministry of Justice and the Ministry of Children presented guidelines to improve cooperation between day care programs and child welfare agencies.[16] They suggested that the child welfare agency has a duty to inform those who make referrals about the handling of the case, and in some cases, about the results of the investigation.[17] The third criticism of the investigation process is that it typically does not rest on evidence-based knowledge and systematically collected information but rather on the cultural norms of the agency and personal/professionals beliefs (Kvello, 2007). In some municipalities, programs for systematic investigations have been implemented based on risk assessment research and practice from the United States.

SUBSTANTIATION OF ALLEGATIONS OF MALTREATMENT

The Norwegian child welfare system does not have a unified approach to substantiating allegations of maltreatment. To a large degree, substantiation is handled by the child welfare worker who receives the referral, or according to local agency procedures. Hence, there can be myriad approaches to how a report of maltreatment is handled, depending in part upon the size of the child welfare agency and the workers' type and level of education and experience. Typically, in medium-sized and large child welfare agencies, child welfare workers (often two social workers are involved in investigations) will undertake the following procedure.

1. *Speak with the person or agency that made the referral.*
2. *Check their own system for information about the child and the family.*
3. *Provide orientation for, and send an invitation to, the family.* A letter is sent to the child's parents about the report, stating that the child welfare agency will investigate the case. The parents and the child (depending on his or her age) are asked to attend a meeting to discuss the report.
4. *Gather information.* Child welfare workers will collect information about the child and the maltreatment allegations. They will send letters to all public authorities that might have knowledge of the child (police, school, general practitioner, health visitor, etc.), and they will ask the parents about other relevant persons to interview. However, if the child welfare workers want to contact private individuals, such as neighbors or grandparents (assuming that these individuals want to speak to the agency), they must obtain permission from the child's parents.
5. *Analyze information.* Based on their analysis of the reported information and discussions with the parents and the child (age dependent) regarding how to resolve the alleged maltreatment, the child welfare workers identify possible outcomes.

6. *Draw a conclusion.* The process ends with one of three types of written conclusion.

   a) The case is dismissed because maltreatment is not substantiated, or because the parents do not accept the services and the child's situation is not considered (or proven) to be serious enough to undertake compulsory action.
   b) In-home services are provided, such as day care for the child, economic support, etc.
   c) An out-of-home placement is considered. The child welfare agency will explore the case further and present a care order case to the court, which makes the final decision.

A major critique of the Norwegian child welfare system is that it gives too much leeway to professionals and puts too little emphasis on scientific methods and knowledge, a practice that is contrary to child protection practices in other countries discussed in this book.

PATTERNS AND MAKEUP OF OUT-OF-HOME PLACEMENT RATES

An important goal of the CWA of 1992 was to lower the threshold for helping children at risk of neglect and abuse by increasing the provision of in-home services. Indeed, the number of children receiving services has steadily increased from 12.2/1,000 children in 1992 to 24.0/1,000 children in 2008. Obviously, in-home services do not work for all children, and the number of children with care orders has been rather stable during this period (5.4/1,000 children in 1994 vs. 5.8/1,000 children in 2008). This development shows that the use of early interventions to prevent out-of-home placements, as advocated in the CWA of 1992, has not prevailed. The total number of children in out-of-home accommodations has actually increased quite markedly since the implementation of the CWA of 1992. In addition to the children with a care order, many children are placed out of home on a voluntarily basis. In 2008, 2.4/1,000 children were placed on a voluntary basis, an increase from 0.6/1,000 children in 1994. In total, this means that 8/1,000 children were placed out of home in 2008.[18] This additional route to out-of-home placements stems from legislation that gives parents who need short-term help (because of sickness or hospitalization, for example) an opportunity to place children outside the home on a voluntary basis (CWA of 1992 §4–4 [5]). Although the legislature intended this option for a very small number of exceptional cases (Skivenes, 2002), the number of children involved tells us that this has not been the case. Many of these children remain in out-of-home placements for years (but exact numbers of how many and for how long are not available), effectively subverting the goal of keeping more families together by preventing permanent out-of home placements. Furthermore, because such short-term placements are voluntary, there is no court-ordered assurance that the out-of-home placement is stable, well-suited for the child involved, and in his or her best interest. According to informal interviews with child welfare workers, placing a child out of home under parental authority is done to maintain a positive relationship with the parents, to avoid the use of force, and to avoid expensive and time-consuming court cases. The downside is that children can be in these placements for years, due process and the rule of law are not guaranteed for the child or the parents, and out-of-home placements may be coerced rather than truly voluntary. In addition, the short- and long-term needs of the child may be overlooked.

Adoption

In Norway, in line with other Nordic countries, adoption is rarely used, even though the CWA of 1992 clearly states that a child can be adopted if it is in his or her best interest. Adoption numbers have steadily declined since 1992, and in 2007, only 27 children in the child welfare system were adopted (through voluntary or compulsory action). Adoption against a parent's will, a case that must be decided by the court, is not often suggested. In 2008, the child welfare system presented 12 cases to the courts, whereas in 1995 there were about 53 cases (Grinde, 2005). In addition to an obviously reluctant front-line child welfare practice, these numbers might very well reflect the courts' unwillingness to allow forced adoptions, perhaps because of the biological principle (Skivenes, 2010). The courts' restrictive practice might also be based on a 1996 European Court of Human Rights (ECHR) decision, in which the Norwegian child welfare system (the Norwegian state) was criticized for violations of Article 8 (protection of family life) in a case involving the forced adoption of a girl.[19] The interpretation of this decision has been very strict in Norway, both by the Supreme Court (Rt, 1997; Rt, 2001) and by the Ministry of Children and Family. In contrast, legal interpretations of the ECHR adoption rulings are different in England (Freeman, 2007), for example, and adoption practice is also quite different there. However, two recent changes have occurred regarding adoptions in Norway. In 2007, the Supreme Court decided an adoption case that is less restrictive on adoptions (Rt, 2007), and the Ministry of Children and Equality now explicitly encourages child welfare agencies to consider whether adoption might be in the best interests of the child.

SIGNIFICANT TRENDS AND CHANGES IN THE CHILD WELFARE AREA

Among the major changes and trends over the last 15–20 years, four prominent developments are likely to have influenced practice and thinking in the field: juridification, competencies, political orientation, and a child perspective. Before elaborating on these broader developments, I shall briefly address some of the specific measures and efforts that have been undertaken in the Norwegian child welfare system lately.

Changes to and Improvements in the Child Welfare System

There have been many changes since the CWA of 1992 was implemented. Important are new methods, such as the family-oriented and evidence-based programs MST and PMT, which the government encouraged to prevent serious harm and out-of-home placements. Helping children when they grow out of the child welfare system at age 18 has been a constant worry, and the government has steadily increased services to young persons (18- to 22-year-olds; see Table 8.1 in Conclusion section). The role of professionals in court cases and as assessors of, and advisors to, the child welfare system, has been a recurring issue, first in 1995 (NOU, 1995, p. 23) and then again in 2006 (NOU, 2006, p. 9). Furthermore, a major status report on the knowledge base for the Norwegian child welfare system was published in 2000 (NOU, 2000, p. 12, mentioned above). The court process has also been examined (NOU, 2005, p. 9), resulting in a simplified process for some cases. One historical issue that has created much debate and concern in Norway was the maltreatment of children who stayed in residential units from 1945 to 1980. Municipalities (as well as the national government) have investigated what happened (NOU, 2004, p. 23), and they have often paid compensation for the damage done to those harmed. Finally, in 2004, a major organizational reform of the child welfare system was implemented, which deserves to be described in some detail.

On January 1, 2004, a large-scale organizational reform of the Norwegian child welfare system was implemented, moving the responsibility for out-of-home accommodations from the county to the state level. Only 2 years earlier, in a proposal for new legislation (Ot. Prp. Nr. 9, 2002–2003), the government suggested that the child welfare system be reorganized to provide high-quality services (in particular, out-of-home accommodations) on an equal basis throughout the country (Bogen, Grønningsæter, & Jensen, 2007). This goal was to be met by taking all the tasks and responsibilities that were handled by county municipalities and giving them to the state. The reform took effect on January 1, 2004, and a five-region organizational model was established with the Norwegian Directorate for Children, Youth, and Family Affairs as the system's headquarters.[20] In the current organizational model, the regions are responsible for (a) residential units, including the quality of programs offered and the professionalism of the staff; (b) recruiting and training of foster home staff; and (c) assisting and supervising front-line child welfare workers in the process of identifying the best out-of-home placements for children.

The success of the reform lies in its explicit criteria for quality and professionalism that private and public residential units must meet, and in the willingness of the government to shut down any units that do not do so. At the same time, two major criticisms have been leveled at this reform. The first concerns poor cooperation and communication between regions and front-line agencies. Reports from child welfare workers indicate that state-level teams, which should be professional advisors and discussion partners, are controlling, arrogant, uncoordinated, inefficient, and not helpful in finding the best accommodation for the child (Karlson, 2007; Staveng et al., 2008). Second, child welfare workers feel that they are being pushed to use public rather than private residential units without good reason. They also report that they now have less flexibility in finding the most suitable place for a young person in need (Karlson, 2007).

Juridification

The Norwegian child welfare system has clearly experienced increased juridification in the last 15 years. Juridification is a process that has implications for several different aspects of legal issues. Blichner and Molander (2005) distinguish among five different meanings for juridification, which involve an increase in (a) the use of constitutional norms to regulate political order, (b) the use of legislation to regulate social matters, (c) the use of courts to resolve conflicts, (d) power for legal professions and the legal system, and (e) thinking about relations in legal terms. The CWA of 1992 introduced; a clear focus on the rule of law, stronger rights for both parent and child, certain legal procedures, and the court as a decision-making institution. This development has very likely improved due process in child welfare work (although there is not much research to support this assessment). However, more child welfare cases are now appealed (Grinde, 2000) and hence spend more time in the judicial system, which is usually bad for children and parents. In general, little is known about the impact of juridification on the child welfare system, decision making, and the children and parents involved.

Skills and Education for Child Welfare Workers

Various complaints about education and skills among child welfare workers have been ongoing since the 1990s. I distinguish between issues raised about the daily practice of child welfare and the larger question of what constitutes a proper education for child welfare workers. The latter issue is, in this author's opinion, among the most important challenges facing the Norwegian child welfare system today.

Day-to-Day Knowledge

Between 1992 and 2009, demands for new knowledge and skills for child welfare workers emanated from several sources. After the CWA of 1992, a need for two types of knowledge emerged. First, and most evidently, child welfare workers needed legal skills and understanding, because the new system demanded that all serious cases be presented for the court to decide, making legal concerns more important. Child welfare workers considered this a huge challenge throughout the 1990s, and it was a recurring topic in the most prominent journal for the child welfare system. Second, the transformation of the child welfare system into a service institution with lower thresholds for service and a greater emphasis on prevention demanded interprofessional cooperation and knowledge about how to prevent maltreatment of children. The former has been an issue for the welfare services in general since the mid-1980s (NOU, 1985, p. 18), and it is still an issue in the Norwegian welfare system overall (Fimreite, 2008). After 2000, three other topics have been on the agenda: evidence-based practice, communication with children, and how to work with ethnic minorities. All of these new demands for workers' knowledge have been met with day or weekend courses arranged by the municipalities and increasingly more courses offered by universities and private organizations.

Basic Education of Child Welfare Workers
Lately, a more overarching issue has come to the fore—the basic education provided to child welfare workers, which was raised by the interest organization Barnevernsambandet in 1998.[21] One major question is how well the courses offered in today's university colleges meet the needs of prospective child welfare workers. The majority of the 3,000 frontline child welfare workers in Norway today hold bachelor's degrees (3 years) in either social work or child welfare. In 2009, many workers took additional courses. The question remains whether a 3-year BA in social work or child welfare is sufficient to train workers in handling the tasks and challenges of child welfare work. This issue was raised at a ministry conference on May 10, 2006, but the discussion was limited because it met with serious protests from the established university/university college educators, who argued that a BA-level education with practice periods was sufficient. Hence, the conference never led to other solutions.

In the wake of this meeting, an expert group was established to work on the issue. They delivered their report in April 2009, which suggested that the established 3-year programs should be upheld, and that an arrangement for certification should be established. Workers would be obliged to obtain further education to keep their certificate. The suggested changes, however, do not provide any opportunities for workers to gain in-depth knowledge about all the important topics that are involved in child welfare work. In addition, workers have little chance of developing analytical skills and understanding. The expert group identified no less than 14 subjects from many different disciplines in which a child welfare worker must be skilled (see NOU, 2009, p. 8, p. 103 ff.). With a 3-year track, this means that topics will be studied for less than 2 months each (assuming equal time devoted to each topic). The main problem is that the required subjects are conceptually very different (e.g., legal studies and psychological studies), leaving students little time for an in-depth understanding of any given subject. In addition, the most important union representing workers in this sector, the Norwegian Union of Social Educators and Social Workers (FO),[22] advocates that many other subjects must be included in a child welfare worker's education, such as minority perspectives, poverty, substance abuse, sexual abuse, housing, and unemployment, to mention just a few.[23] The Ministry is processing the expert report and its suggestions, and university educators and members of various interest organizations are doubtless perusing the document as well.

Policies and Normative Orientation

Much scholarship about the child welfare system concerns how to interpret and balance parents' and children's rights, especially with respect to normative issues, which depend upon how one views the responsibilities of the state and the family. In Norway, there are clear political demarcation lines between left- and right-wing political parties regarding how much state intervention can be allowed, and this in turn is often reflected in views on the blood-tie principle. Analyses of child welfare policy documents from 1990 until today have shown that the Labor party, which governed from 1990 to 1997, had a relatively balanced approach to children's and parents' rights (Report to Parliament no. 39, 1995–96). This is quite different from the Christian-Democratic party, which governed for most of the period from 1997 to 2005 (except from March 2000 until October 2001). They had a rather strong emphasis on parents' rights and the autonomy of the family (Report to Parliament no. 40, 2001–2001). An often-mentioned result has been family-oriented measures, such as the MST and PMT, which aim to prevent out-of-home placements by using a comprehensive program in which professionals are available for the family 24/7. The normative orientation changed again when the Labor party (together with the Socialist party and the Center party) regained control. This has been particularly evident during the last few years, with changes in both political signals and the law, such as more restrictive criteria for reunification and a greater use of adoptions.[24]

Even though fluctuations have occurred in the normative policy foundations of the child welfare system, an overarching trend toward a child-centric perspective has emerged. This approach has also developed in other areas, such as school, family, politics, health, and welfare.

A Child-Centric Perspective in the Norwegian Child Welfare System

The main characteristic of a child-centric perspective is that children are seen as individuals with opinions, interests, and viewpoints that they should have an opportunity to express. Even though this perspective is interpreted in different ways by scholars and laypersons (Halldén, 2003; Sommer, 2003), a common ground is the belief that a child-centric perspective is valuable and that it deserves recognition from society at large. A way of conceptualizing the child-centric perspective is to distinguish between three aspects: (1) children's legal rights and organizational procedures, (2) adults' recognition of children as individuals with particular interests and needs in interactions with adults, and (3) the use of the individual child's viewpoint as a way of interpreting what the world means to children.

There are many indications that a child-centric perspective has emerged in the Norwegian child welfare system. First, with respect to rights and procedures, children obtained extensive rights by the ratification of the United Nations (UN) Convention of Children's Rights (CRC) in 1991. This was followed by the Norwegian Human Rights Act of 2003, which ensured that all Norwegian legislation was in accord with human rights conventions (Søvig, 2009). The strong standing of children's rights is particularly evident in the right to participate, understood as children's active input and involvement in decisions that concern their lives. In 2003, the government took its longstanding focus on promoting children's interests one step further by giving children aged 7 years or older a right to be heard in child welfare cases (CWA of 1992, §6–3). Hence, those who work on the front lines of Norway's child welfare system are legally obliged to both hear children and "weight" their views according to age and maturity.

Second, child welfare workers in Norway increasingly[25] seem to view children as individuals and as the main person in a child welfare case. In recent comparative, qualitative studies of child welfare workers' views on children's participation in Norway and England, more than half of the Norwegian workers stated that the participation of children was important, because the children's lives were what their work was all about (Archard & Skivenes, 2009a; Skivenes, 2009).

Third, there are indications that decision makers and policy makers view welfare cases from the child's point of view, not simply regarding the child as a future adult (Lister, 2004, 2006). For instance, this is evident in the Supreme Court's positive decision about adoption in 2007 (Rt, 2007), and in the subsequent changes in the CWA of 1992, making it clear that children's need for permanent care trumps parental rights and the biological principle (Skivenes, 2010).

These three developments, and most clearly the change in age level, symbolize the right of children to participate qua individuals who can form opinions. The presumption is that children who can form opinions have a right to express them. Although this right is more than a right to be consulted, it does not translate into an entitlement for the child's views to guide adults or child welfare workers regarding interventions, nor is it simply a right to show that children are mature enough to be self-determining agents. The best way to interpret this change in participation rights for children in Norway, and for children in the child welfare system in particular, is to think of it as:

> [A] basic right of individuals who have their own views (who are capable of forming them) to express those views. It is a right of all individuals to be involved in a process whereby their own future is determined even if their view of that future has no weight in any final determination of matters, and even if they cannot hope to persuade others of their ability to make their own decisions. (Archard & Skivenes, 2009)

CONCLUSION

What does this chapter tell us about the Norwegian child welfare system? Perhaps the most obvious conclusion that can be drawn from this analysis is that the Norwegian child welfare system has high ambitions for children who might be at risk, and that many resources are used to provide services and to keep families together. The trend in child welfare work in Norway since the beginning of the 1990s is characterized by a steady increase in the child welfare system's responsibilities and the services provided. More children receive services, more children are placed out of home, and more workers are employed by the system. In Table 8.1 the numerical developments are presented.

Topics related to knowledge have consistently been an issue over the last 20 years in the child welfare system, although with different focuses, such as evidence-based practice, knowledge about different types of issues, and child welfare workers' competencies and skills. The latter focus is perhaps the most pressing one, and it was also an area of political concern in 2009. If politicians want to change the child welfare system markedly, they will need to upgrade the education (and hence, the wages) of child welfare workers.

Finally, the Norwegian government is in many ways clearly addressing children as individuals who deserve respect and dignity, not only as future adults. This trend is in opposition to the social investment approach, which primarily sees children as future workers (Lister, 2004). However, the identification of a child-centric approach is not clear cut, because it challenges the biological presumption of the traditional family-centered approach that has dominated Norwegian child welfare thinking for a long time. There is no consistent political stream that puts a child-centric perspective above a family approach, but rather the evidence suggests that the child welfare system embraces both approaches. The outcome of an eventual conflict between these approaches is not yet clear, and the child-centric perspective might well be abandoned. Which of these two approaches prevails is primarily a political issue, and so far, the Norwegian way has been to embrace conflicting values and principles without indicating how to balance them in practice. This leaves it up to child welfare workers and the courts to interpret and prioritize, with all the pitfalls that such a system implies.

Table 8.1: Overview of Basic Child Welfare Statistics

	1992	1994	1995	2000	2005	2007	2008
Referrals investigated, per 1,000 children	.	13.2	14.0	16.5	19.5	22.8	25.2
Children receiving services (all types), end of year, per 1,000 children	18.4	19.9	20.2	21.8	25.2	27.5	28.4
Children receiving in-home services, end of year, per 1,000 children	11.0	14.6	15.1	16.9	19.7	21.8	22.6
Children placed out of home (with and without a care order), end of year, per 1,000 children	.	5.9	5.9	6.7	7.4	8.0	8.2
Children with a formal care order decision, end of year, per 1,000 children	.	5.3	5.0	4.8	5.5	5.7	5.8
Children placed out of home without a formal care order decision, end of year, per 1,000 children	.	0.6	0.9	1.9	1.9	2.3	2.4
Adoption cases presented for court, N = cases	.	.	53	27	11	7	12*
Workers in the child welfare system, 100% position, end of year, per 1,000 children	.	2.3	2.3	2.4	2.7	2.9	3.0
Young persons (18–22) receiving child welfare services, end of year, N = persons	.	.	.	1,722	2,348	2,472	2,570
Children receiving services (all types), through year, per 1,000 children	24.1	27.3	28.1	30.3	36.0	39.0	40.2
New children in the system, N = children**	.	.	.	8,583	10,045	11,731	11,760
Child population, end of year, N = children	988,760	1,003,203	1,012,924	1,060,857	1,092,728	1,099,279	1,103,481

Source: www.ssb.no
. = statistics not available/reliable
* An additional two cases were withdrawn before court proceedings
** Might include a few young adults (18–22 years old).

NOTES

1   I owe great thanks to E. Backe-Hansen, to the co-authors of this book, and to N. Gilbert and N. Parton for important comments and fruitful discussions. My work is founded by the Norwegian Research Council.

2 Retrieved from http://www.regjeringen.no/nb/dep/bld/pressesenter/press emeldinger/2009/bedre-vern-av-barn-og-unges-rettigheter-.html ?id=557585). Translation by the author.

3 Preceded by the Child Welfare Act of 1953 and the Child Protection Act of 1896 (Vergerådsloven). An English translation of the CWA of 1992 is available at: http://www.regjeringen.no/en/doc/Laws/Acts/The-Child-Welfare-Act. html?id=448398. For an in-depth analysis of the making of the CWA of 1992, see Skivenes (2002), and for general information about the child welfare system provided by the Ministry of Children and Family, see http://www. regjeringen.no/en/dep/bld/Topics/Child-welfare.html?id=1058.

4 I use the term "child welfare agency/system" as it reflects the Norwegian approach to children at risk. However, in some circumstances, it is just as appropriate to call it "child protection," and empirically, comparative studies show that there can be difficulties in differentiating between the child welfare and child protection parts of a system (Hetherington et al., 1997; Gilbert, 1997).

5 Retrieved from http://www.regjeringen.no/en/dep/bld/BLD-arbeider-for-at/ Offices-and-agencies-associated-with-the-Ministry-of-Children-and-Equality/County-social-welfare-boards.html?id=418110.

6 An overview of the statistics in this chapter is outlined in the Concluding section, Table 8.1.

7 Information retrieved from the Ministry of Children and Equality by the journalist Pål Mæland in *Bergens Tidende–BT* (regional newspaper), published in BT, November 1, 2008.

8 See http://www.ssb.no/english/subjects/03/03/barneverng_en/.

9 By the end of the 1980s and the beginning of the 1990s, it was revealed that, in many municipalities, referrals of maltreatment were not investigated, and that children in need did not receive help. The children's Ombudsman reported several municipalities to the police for neglecting their duty. By the end of 1993, the Ministry of Children and Family declared the crisis in the child welfare system to be over (*Journal of the Norwegian Child Welfare System* 4/1993).

10 A relation-based method to treat youths' antisocial behavior. For additional information, see http://www.mstservices.com/text/treatment.html.

11 The child welfare agencies do not keep track of their total number of referrals. Only those referrals that are investigated are included in the official statistics.

12 These numbers are very uncertain, as the statistic does not register how many children are included in each case, and we cannot know whether the same child was investigated several times.

13 Several incidents can be registered, and thus the total number exceeds 100%.

14 These two agencies are expected to have higher reporting rates because public health centers are in contact with all newborns in their first year on a regular basis. Seven out of ten 1-year-olds attend day care programs, and about 90% of all children aged 1–6 years attend day care. Day care programs are available for all children in Norway, and it is affordable for most parents. The maximum price is NOK 2,600 (~$US 450) and lower for low-income parents.

15 For information about children houses, see: http://no.wikipedia.org/wiki/Barnehus (the information is in Norwegian).

16 Retrieved from http://www.regjeringen.no/upload/BLD/Til%20barnets-%20beste%20-%20samarbeid%20mellom%20barnehagen%20og%20barne verntjenesten.pdf.

17 A change in the CWA of 1992; by Act of June 19, 2009, no. 45.

18 According to National Statistics, there have been no huge changes in children's age composition for out-of-home placements in the last 20 years.

19 Retrieved from http://cmiskp.echr.coe.int/tkp197/view.asp?action=html&documentId=695936&portal=hbkm&source=externalbydocnumber&table=1132746FF1FE2A468ACCBCD1763D4D8149.

20 The Norwegian Directorate for Children, Youth and Family Affairs (Bufdir) is the Norwegian governmental office responsible for the welfare and protection of children and families. Its main objective is to provide high-quality services to children, young people, and families in need of assistance and support, regardless of where they live in Norway.

21 *Journal of the Child Welfare System*, 1998, number 4. It demanded a national plan for strengthening the competencies of child welfare workers, because the high turnover rate meant that many child welfare workers were inexperienced.

22 Retrieved from http://www.fo.no/english/category28.html.

23 Retrieved from http://www.fo.no/politikk/om-kompetanseutvikling-i-barnevernet-befring-utvalget-article2095-114.html.

24 A change in the CWA of 1992; by Act of June 19, 2009, no. 45.

25 I write "increasingly" because research published in 2000 and earlier on participation in the child welfare area often concluded that children do not participate (Amundsen, 2008). At the same time, reviews of this scholarship show that many different concepts of participation are used, and thus how participation is measured differs across studies.

REFERENCES

Archard, D., & M. Skivenes (2009). Balancing a child's best interest and a child's views. *International Journal of Children's Rights*, 17, 1–21.

Archard, D., & M. Skivenes. (2009a). Hearing the child. *Child & Family Social Work*, 14(4): 391–399.

Backe-Hansen, E. (2002). *Rettferdiggjøring av omsorgsovertakelse: En beslutning-steoretisk analyse av barneverntjenestens argumentasjon i en serie typiske saker om små barn* [Justification of care orders–an analysis of decisions-making processes]. Oslo: Norsk institutt for forskning om oppvekst, velferd og aldring. (In Norwegian.)

Blichner, L., & Molander, A. (2005). What is juridification? Arena Working Paper, No.14, March.

Bogen, H., Grønningsæter, A., & Jensen, A. (2007). *The child welfare systems in Oslo and Bergen. A comparative evaluation of the organisations reform of 2004.* Oslo: Fafo rapport 2007:11. (In Norwegian.)

Child Welfare Act (Norway). (1992). English translation retrieved from http://www.regjeringen.no/en/doc/Laws/Acts/The-Child-Welfare-Act.html?id=448398.

Children's report to Parliament no. 1. (2008–2009). *Barnas St. meld. nr. 1 (2008–2009) Om vold og overgrep mot barn. Justis- og politidepartmentet* [About violence and abuse against children.]. Oslo: Ministry of Justice. (In Norwegian.)

Clausen, S. (2004). Har barn som mishandles større risiko for å bli kriminelle?[Do mistreated children become criminals?]. *Tidsskrift for Norsk psykologforening*, 41, 971–78. (In Norwegian.)

Esping-Andersen, G. (1999). *Social foundations of post-industrial economies.* Oxford: Oxford University Press.

Esping-Andersen, G. (1990). *The three worlds of welfare capitalism.* Oxford: Polity Press.

Felitti, V. J. (2002). The relationship of adverse childhood experiences to adult health: Turning gold into lead. *Z Psychosom Med Psychother*, 48(4), 359–369.

Felitti, V. J., Williamson, D. F., Koss, M. P., Spitz, A. M., Anda, R. F., & Nordenberg, D. (1998). Relationship of childhood abuse and household dysfunction to many of the leading causes of death in adults. (ACE) Study. *American Journal of Preventive Medicine*, 14(4), 245–258.

Fimreite, A.L. (2008). *Mission impossible made possible? - Tenkning og argumentasjon bak partnerskapet mellom stat og kommune.* [Mission impossible made possible? - The philosophy of the co-operation between municipalities and state in the welfare reform.) Rokkan paper no. 14.i NAV. (In Norwegian.)

Freeman, M. (2007). *Article 3: The best interests of the child. A Commentary on the United Nations Convention on the Rights of the Child.* Leiden: Martinus Nijhoff Publishers.

Gilbert, N. (1997). *Combatting child abuse: International perspectives and trends.* New York: Oxford University Press.

Grinde, T. V. (2005): Adoption practice in Norway. Paper presented at Childhood conference. Oslo 2005.

Grinde, T. V. (2000). *Rettslig overprøving av fylkesnemndsvedtak* [Appeal cases in the child welfare system]. In S. Falck & T. Havik (Eds.), Barnevern og fylkesnemnd [*Child welfare and the court*], pp. 205–238. Oslo: Kommuneforlaget. (In Norwegian.)

Halldén, G. (2003). *Barnperspektiv som ideologisk och/eller metodologisk begrep* [A child's perspective as ideology and/or methodological concept?]. *Pedagogisk Forskning i Sverige 8*(1–2), 12–23. (In Swedish.)

Hetherington, R., Cooper, A., Smith, P., & Wilford, G. (1997). *Protecting children: Messages from Europe.* Lyme Regis, Dorset: Russel House.

Holm-Hansen, J., Haaland, T., & Myrvold, T. (2007). A multi cultural child welfare–an overview of research and knowledge. Oslo. NIBR-Report. (In Norwegian.)

Journal of the Norwegian Child Welfare System, for the period of 1992–2008, four issues each year. (*Tidsskriftet Norges Barnevern* 1/1992–4/2008). Published by Barnevernsambandet. (In Norwegian.)

Karlson, S. (2007). *Samarbeid mellom profesjonelle aktører i velferdstjenesten: hva hemmer og hva fremmer et godt samarbeid* [Co-operation between professionals in the welfare services. An analysis of co-operation between state level and municipality level in the child welfare system]. MA thesis, university of Bergen, Norway. (In Norwegian.)

KIM. (2008) European Commission against racism and intolerance–KIMs contribution to the 4th report on Norway. Retrieved June 22, 2009 from http://www.kim.no.

Kriz, K., & M. Skivenes. (2010). We have very different positions on some issues: Communication challenges in child welfare work with ethnic minority families in Norway and England. *European Journal of Social Work.*Vol. 13. No. 1, pp. 3–18.

Kriz, K., & M. Skivenes. (March 27, 2009). Lost in translation: How child welfare workers in Norway and England experience language differences when working with minority ethnic families. *British Journal of Social Work.* doi:10.1093/bjsw/bcp036.

Kristofersen, L. B. (2005). *Barnevernbarnas helse: Uførhet og dødelighet i perioden 1990–2002* [The health of child welfare clients: Disability and mortality]. Oslo: NIBR. (In Norwegian.)

Clausen, S-E., & Kristofersen, L. (2008). *Barnevernsklienter i Norge 1990–2005 - En longitudinell studie* [Child welfare clients in Norway 1990–2005: A longitudinal study]. Oslo: NOVA Report 03. (In Norwegian.)

Kvello, Ø. (2007). *Utredning av atferdsvansker, omsorgssvikt og mishandling* [Investigations about maltreatment, neglect and behavioral problems]. Oslo: Universitetsforlaget. (In Norwegian.)

Lister, R. (2004). The third way's social investment state. In J. Lewis & R. Surender (Eds.), *Welfare state change: Towards a third way?* New York: Oxford University Press.

Lister, J. (2006). An agenda for children: Investing in the future or promoting well-being in the present? In J. Lewis (Ed.), *Children, changing families and welfare states.* Cheltenham, Northampton: Edward Elgar.

NOU. 1985: 18. Law panel paper on a Act of Social Services and more. Official Norwegian Reports conducted by a working group reporting on different aspects of society. (In Norwegian.)

NOU. 1995: 23. *Barnefaglige sakkyndighetsoppgaver* [Expert committee report]. (In Norwegian.)

NOU. 2000: 12. *Barnevernet i Norge* [The Norwegian child welfare system. Expert committee report]. (In Norwegian.)

NOU. 2004: 23. *Barnehjem og spesialskoler under lupen* [Residential units and special schools. Expert committee report]. (In Norwegian.)

NOU. 2005: 09. *Ressursbruk og rettssikkerhet i fylkesnemndene for sosiale saker* [Use of resources and rule of law in county social welfare boards (court). Expert committee report]. (In Norwegian.)

NOU. 2006: 9. *Kvalitetssikring av sakkyndige rapporter i barnevernsaker* [Control of the quality of professionals' assessments in child welfare cases. Expert committee report]. (In Norwegian.)

NOU. 2008: 15. *Barn og straff* [Children and punishment. Expert committee report]. (In Norwegian.)

NOU. 2009: 8. *Kompetanseutvikling i barnevernet* [Expert committee report on education, knowledge and skills in the child welfare service]. (In Norwegian.)

Ot. Prp. No. 44 1991–1992. (1992) The government's suggestion for the Child Welfare Act of 1992. White paper suggestion about new law to be decided by the Parliament. (In Norwegian.)

Ot. Prp. Nr. 9. (2002–2003). *Om lov om endringer i barnevernloven og familievernkontorloven* [Government suggestion for new legislation. About changes in the CWA of 1992 and Family Office Act of 1997]. (In Norwegian.)

Report to Parliament no. 39. Child Welfare Report from the Government. (St meld nr 39 1995–96, Barnevernmeldingen.) (In Norwegian.)

Report to Parliament no. 40. Child Welfare Report from the Government. (St. meld nr. 40 2001–2001, Barnevernmeldingen.) (In Norwegian.)

Rt 1997–534 (150–97). Norwegian Supreme Court decision about adoption of children from foster care. Retrieved from www.lovdata.no. (In Norwegian.)

Rt 2001–14 (7–2001). Norwegian Supreme Court decision about adoption of children from foster care. Retrieved from www.lovdata.no. (In Norwegian.)

Rt 2007–00732-A. Norwegian Supreme Court decision about adoption of children from foster care. Retrieved from www.lovdata.no. (In Norwegian.)

Skivenes, M. (2010). Judging the best interests of children under care order–rational reasoning or subjective presumptions? *Acta Sociologica.* Vol. 53. No. 4.

Skivenes, M. (2009). Children as participants and service users in child welfare cases. In H. Sinding (Ed.), *Human rights, dignity and autonomy in health care and social services: Nordic perspectives.* Belgium: Intersentia.

Skivenes, M. (2002). *Legislation and legitimacy: An evaluation of the Child Welfare Act of 1992.* Bergen: University of Bergen, Department of Administration & Organization Science. (In Norwegian.)

Sommer, D. (2003). *Børnesyn i udviklingspsykologien. Er et børneperspektiv muligt?* [Children's point of view. Is a child perspective possible?]. *Pedagogisk Forskning i Sverige 8*(1–2), 85–100. (In Swedish.)

Stavseng, G., Aspelund, G., Skutlaberg, L., & Larsen, E. (2008). *Vurdering og videreutvikling av fagteam* [Assessment and development of professional teams at state level]. Report. Oslo: Rambøll Management AS. (In Norwegian.)

St. Meld. Nr. 39 (1995–1996). *Om barne- og ungdomsvernet* [About the child welfare system]. Report to Parliament. (In Norwegian.)

St. Meld. Nr. 39 (2001–2002). *Oppvekst- og levekår for barn og ungdom i Norge* [Living and growing up conditions for children in Norway]. Report to Parliament. (In Norwegian.)

St. Meld. Nr. 40. (2002). *Om barnevernet* [About the child welfare system]. Report to Parliament. (In Norwegian.)

Søvig, K. (2009). *Barnets rettigheter på barents premisser - utfordringer i møtet mellom FNs barnekonvensjon og norsk rett* [Children's rights on children's terms–challenges when Norwegian legislation meets UN Convention of Children's Rights]. Report made for the Ministry of Children and Equality. (In Norwegian.)

Weyland, I. (1997). The blood tie: Raised to the status of a presumption. *Journal of Social Welfare and Family Law, 19*(2), 173–188.

PART III

CONTINENTAL SYSTEMS

9

CHILD PROTECTION IN AN AGE OF UNCERTAINTY: GERMANY'S RESPONSE

REINHART WOLFF, KAY BIESEL, AND STEFAN HEINITZ

SYSTEM DEVELOPMENTS

Since the beginnings of modern child welfare services at the end of the 19th century, child protection in Germany has always been a major task of, at first, nongovernmental charitable agencies and then local government services. This bipartite and mostly state-funded service structure of voluntary and public agencies has always characterized the German child and youth welfare system (*Kinder- und Jugendhilfe*), in which, since the early days of the Weimar Republic, the local Youth Office (*Jugendamt*) in every municipality and county played a leading and coordinating role. Together with the local Health Office (*Gesundheitsamt*), the child and youth welfare departments and voluntary agencies provided early health services (including counselling, home visiting, and help for women during pregnancy and around the birth of a child), as well as a wide array of youth and family welfare and day care services. The Youth Office intervened when the well-being of a child or an adolescent—mostly in working-class or lower-class contexts—was endangered. The predominant response to such cases of child maltreatment was out-of-home placement of "difficult" and "dangerous" children, as abused and neglected minors were mainly called. In Germany, as in many other countries, with the huge expansion of the whole social welfare system came a new awareness and understanding regarding child maltreatment, and a new child protection practice developed in the course of the 1960s and 1970s, the major historical trends of which have been outlined in an earlier work on combatting child abuse (Wolff, 1997).

The first stage of the development of modern child protection work in Germany occurred in the early 1970s and was characterized by the foundation of nongovernmental multidisciplinary child protection centers in the major cities of the country. These centers provided comprehensive nonpunitive services and steered clients away from police investigations and criminal court procedures. This new approach of combining family-based and out-of-home services with preventive and crisis intervention programs that furthered interagency coopera- tion not only tremendously influenced the innovative transformation of the field of family counselling, pedagogical services in families, and residential care, but also the entire public sector of child welfare. This trend finally, in 1990/91, led to a new federal Child and Youth Welfare Act (*Kinder- und Jugendhilfegesetz*), which granted parents concrete entitlements to receive a wide array of services, and established the obligation of the democratic social welfare state to further the well-being of children and to provide services for children and their parents in need. The Act also emphasized the concept of partnership between service recip- ients and professional providers, and laid down that parents and children should fully participate in the planning and monitoring of the helping process.

However, the German unification process, which included rebuilding the infrastructure and public administration system of the Eastern Laender and merging the social security systems of the East and the West, was an enormous financial strain for federal government in the 1990s. Under this burden, the process of expanding and reforming this broad and locally organized child and family welfare system (with about 600 municipal or county Youth Offices and about 80,000 nongovernmental social work agencies, among them Catholic, Protestant, and Jewish or other nonreligious charitable organizations) came to a halt—while social problems increased.

At the same time, extensive media coverage of fatal child abuse cases ("Lydia" in Osnabrueck, "Jessica" in Hamburg, "Kevin" in Bremen, "Lea-Sophie" in Schwerin), child abuse errors, and systemic failures drew widespread public attention. Child protection systems were suddenly regarded as being "risky systems" that did not contribute to safeguarding children. Social workers in child protection were harshly criticized for having neglected their duties and were made responsible for the harm and even death of children. Moreover, it was alleged that, in some cases, they had done too little or acted too late, and in others had intervened too early or for no reason at all. Therefore, many child protection workers increasingly came to believe that they were already "standing with one foot in the jug." However, only few of them were prosecuted and convicted (see also Moersberger & Restemeier, 1997).

These events caused a massive child protection panic in the public sector, political arena, and also in the professional field that led to a refocusing of child and family welfare services on child protection, with an emphasis on early risk assessment, crisis intervention, and quick out-of-home placements. This trend became even more pronounced in 2005, when the Child and Youth Welfare Act was amended with a new paragraph (§ 8a Social Code VIII) that reformulated the role of social workers as guardians and guarantors of the well-being of children. It made close cooperation and formal procedures obligatory in child protection work and underlined the central role of the public Youth Offices. More recently, since 2008, there have been heated debates over the unsuccessful introduction of a new Child Protection Act (*Bundeskinderschutzgesetz*) calling for a further formalization of child protection practices (e.g., obligatory home visits) and the introduction of mandatory reporting procedures (for an overview see Ziegenhain & Fegert, 2008; Wolff, 2008).

In 2005, when the Christian Democratic Party and the Social Democratic Party formed the federal grand coalition government, a special section of the coalition agreement on "the family-friendly society" highlighted "the development of early social warning systems and the advancement and support of early services for endangered parents and their children." On this basis the new government—with a budget of €10 million for the next five fiscal years (2005–2010)—created the National Center for Early Services (*Nationales Zentrum Fruehe Hilfen*–NZFH), the agenda of which ambivalently strengthened both a statutory control approach and a marked commitment to prevention and cooperation in child welfare. This program emphasized:

> The duty as a guardian and the mission of the state to protect children has to be strengthened and early warning systems have to be developed. Child welfare and preventive health care together with the active involvement of civil society shall be linked to bring about a new quality of early support services for families. Especially for socially deprived families, the classical "demand orientation" (*Komm-Struktur*) of many programs has to be improved with regard to the target groups, and new "outreach program structures" (*Geh-Struktur*) have to be developed (BMFSFJ 2005; our translation).

The federal family ministry declared when the program was launched:

> The federal government will initiate, support, monitor, and evaluate several national model programs, set up a competence center that will encourage the realization of such programs in the Laender and municipalities, and secure the transfer of experiences. Besides the strengthening of the direct responsibility of parents, this requires a stronger joint responsibility of the state for the process of growing up in early childhood. The child's need for and right to positive conditions to develop and to grow must increasingly be a focal point (BMFSFJ 2006; our translation).

The same strategic orientation became apparent when, for the first time in the modern history of child protection and under tremendous pressure from the media—and after another fatal child abuse case in the fall of 2006—the chancellor convened a conference of all prime ministers of the Laender in 2007 (later called the "Child Protection Summit") that was solely concerned with how to cope with the pervasive child protection crisis. Without parliamentary consultation, the conference concluded that a federal law should be implemented to establish a new framework for cooperation in child protection, to install a close-meshed system of early health check-ups, to identify and close the gaps in prevention in federal law, and to enhance networking among and exchange between the Laender. These promised for their part to improve program coordination, provide resources for networking, develop standards for quality assurance, and design elaborate programs and guidelines for early services, risk assessments, and early warning systems in child protection. They moreover pledged to further education and training and to get special state child protection laws passed. This last point has so far been realized by the Laender parliaments of Schleswig-Holstein, Mecklenburg-Western Pommerania, Baden-Wuerttemberg, Saxony-Anhalt, Thuringia, Hesse, Bavaria, Rhineland-Palatinate, and Saxony. In particular, the new child protection laws in Rhineland-Palatinate, Schleswig-Holstein, and Saxony-Anhalt go far beyond obligatory early assessments and screenings and aim at installing comprehensive early support programs for families through local networks, using the Youth Office in a steering role. The primary aim of getting these child protection laws passed is to invite or oblige all parents with small children to use early medical check-ups. If they do not show up, most Laender child protection laws now also include provisions that medical professionals in private practices, clinics, and the local health departments must—even without the consent of the involved parents and their children—report nonusers of these early health services to the local Youth Office in order to better keep track of potential cases of child abuse and neglect. In Bavaria and Thuringia, parents have to attend early medical check-ups or run the risk of no longer receiving parents' grants (see also Nothhafft, 2008).

Until now, these measures have not been fully evaluated with regard to whether they contribute to the increasing awareness of cases in which the well-being of children is endangered. Child welfare professionals have argued that obligatory medical control systems and, most of all, sanctions, probably do not help families to more easily access child welfare and medical services. They moreover entail considerable bureaucratic and financial efforts, and the question remains whether they actually contribute to identifying child maltreatment. In addition to these steps to restructure the legal framework of child protection and early childhood services, by implementing the respective paragraphs of the family law (e.g. §§ 1631, 1666 and 1696 of the Civil Code), the threshold for intervention in cases of child abuse and neglect was lowered. More power was given to the family courts to restrict the rights of parents and minors: for example, to lock up minors in closed residential or clinical institutions "to safeguard the well-being of children if the endangerment of the child could not be averted in other ways"; to take the necessary measures "to avert the endangerment of the well-being of a minor"; to compel parents to use public child welfare and health services, ensure school attendance, leave the family home, or not contact the child; and to suspend or restrict parental rights in various other ways.

The goal of all these political and legal initiatives, which were paralleled by activities of the local (municipal or county) Youth Offices, sometimes in partnership with local nongovernmental child welfare agencies, was to formalize, restructure, develop, and strengthen their child protection practice. The outcome, however, is an ambivalent system that oscillates between, on the one hand, strengthening and qualifying comprehensive child and family welfare services early on and, on the other, opting for more investigatory risk control, reactive interventions, and surveillance of "deviant populations," the installation of mandatory reporting systems (which German social work professionals had up to now successfully resisted), and the introduction of forms of so-called "new public management" (NPM) that, mainly in the public sector of child welfare, dramatically changed the overall character of social work and child protection practice. It has since become much more formalized, with preregulated procedures in the helping process that are often narrowed down to a bureaucratic concept of "case management," and that generally produce standardization and procedural rigidity in social work practice.

Taking into account these trends and the developments of the last decades, the marked family orientation of the whole child welfare service system that has been promoted by the "new child protection movement," with nonpunitive child protection centers as its driving force (Beiderwieden, Windaus & Wolff, 1999), it becomes evident that the German child protection system has arrived at a crossroads. The system must choose to go either

- toward a postmodern security society, embracing an expertocratic and interventionist tendency to surveillance and conflict control, and at the same time cutting back support services and conceptually moving away from furthering "child and family well-being" to assessing and managing maltreatment, or
- toward a postmodern democratic civil society based on social and political justice, providing open and participatory comprehensive services that are of good quality and that enable all citizens (adults *and* children) to develop their capabilities to act freely and responsibly, thus receiving the chance to become "artisans of democracy" (Rosenfeld & Tardieu, 2000).

Where to go, of course, depends on a clear understanding of how, in late modern societies, child maltreatment and child protection have become key sociopolitical issues that far transcend the issues per se. They have become metaphors

(Lakoff & Johnson, 1980; Lakoff & Wehling, 2007) that thematize, address, and focus on much larger societal, political, and cultural issue that are at stake. These include:

- Shifts in the relationship between the state and the individual/citizen in modern societies that are increasingly being understood as "risk societies" (Beck, 1986, 2007): The autonomy of the private sphere becomes increasingly supervised and monitored. "Reduced to a formula: Individualization in the second modernity means 'dis-embedding *without* re-embedding.' For the first time in history, the individual becomes an element of social reproduction. In other words: Individualization becomes a paradoxical social structure of the second modernity. Individuals are set free from national industrial capitalism and the welfare state as a matter of course and find themselves in the middle of the turbulences of the world risk society" (Beck 1994, our translation).

- Changes in the relationship between the family and the meso- and macro-systemic ecological contexts: These occur, above all, between the family and the workplace where—with diminishing family institu-tional strength and power—parents, and not least of all single parents, and children become more and more involved with the environmental systems on which they increasingly depend. In such a situation, not autonomy but rather the capability and competence for bridge-build-ing from the micro- to the meso- and macro-systems are of major importance.

- Irritations concerning major changes in generation and gender rela-tionships, and the changing significance of cultural norms: Especially within ethnic groups, these changes are structurally threatening the entire family system. Equal rights for women and children, as well as the distribution of authority and power, have to be rebalanced and continuously negotiated.

- Anxieties arising from increasingly pressing social problems and crises in the life histories of a growing number of poor, deprived, unqualified, marginalized, and politically, economically, and culturally excluded people, so that social justice becomes an issue of high priority.

- Fervent debates about sociocultural changes, the relativizing of moral standards, and the validity of normative systems: These challenge abso-lute value judgments that have always played a role in child protection work and that have greatly contributed to one-sided assessments and decisions. Parents often resented these decisions, based as they were on a differing sociocultural norm, but were in no position to negotiate; these families were forced, therefore, to accept the mainstream class and culture-oriented value judgments.

- Finally, controversies about the relativist and constructivist epistemologies of modern science, which also arise in our reasoning about child abuse and its causes: These represent complex issues that can only fully be understood by applying a multidisciplinary, multifaceted theoretical framework and a constructivist epistemology.

All these issues contribute to the complexity of processes within the child protection system. In order to deal with them, we need complex systemic strategies of understanding and practice.

SYSTEM STRUCTURE AND PRACTICE

Theoretically, child protection work in Germany has profited from a multifaceted and multidisciplinary approach. Child maltreatment (including physical abuse, emotional abuse, sexual abuse, and neglect) is basically—and above all legally—understood as the "endangerment of the well-being of a child" (*Kindeswohlgefaehrdung*). (Endangerment in this context mainly concerns the relationship between parents/guardians and children.) Thus, there is a semantic change from the action-oriented term of "maltreatment" (as a commission or omission that causes harm) to a much vaguer notion of "danger." Endangerment of a child's well-being is the guiding concept that the family court uses to assess and judge whether a parent or guardian is competent, willing, and fit to adequately care for a child, and if not, to intervene in or restrict the constitutional rights of parents as guardians of their children (art. 6 of Basic Law, the German constitution). Moreover, it is also a central conceptual principle for all the human services (social work, health services, and education) available to help parents cope with situations in which the well-being of a child is endangered and to provide a wide array of home-based or out-of-home services (when, in severe crisis situations, a secure out-of-home placement of the child is advisable). "Endangerment" has long been defined by the German High Court (NJW, 1956) as "an actually existing danger to such a degree as to be able to foresee with a considerable degree of certainty a serious impairment (or harm) in the further development of the child."

At the same time, social work practitioners and researchers have developed a more contextual and relativist concept of child maltreatment. This views maltreatment as a harmful social practice and interaction process that is embedded in a structure of "societal and systemic violence" (Bast et al., 1975, 1985). For social workers in Germany, the concept of conflict (and not so much of crime) has become important: Child maltreatment is an expression of a conflict in which an attempt is made to maintain a threatened relationship by force, and by defence and denial. To maltreat a child is basically a helpless and inarticulate attempt to overcome or contain relationship conflicts, or a desperate effort to cope with stress and crisis when one is overwhelmed (Bernecker et al., 1985). Social deprivation, cultural exclusion, poverty, and below-average living conditions considerably increase the risk of child abuse and neglect. Already in 1975, one of the leading agencies in child protection in Germany, the Berlin Child Protection Center (*Kinderschutz-Zentrum Berlin*), outlined a broad sociopolitical concept that defined child maltreatment as "not just an isolated violent act of injury. Child abuse encompasses the entire system constituted by the living conditions and the actions and omissions that restrict the rights of a child, that endanger his or her development, education, and well-being. The discrepancy between these rights and the child's actual [endangered] living conditions constitutes the totality of child maltreatment" (Kinderschutz-Zentrum Berlin, 1975; our translation).

In more recent publications, the construction of "endangerment of the well-being of a child/child maltreatment" came to be understood as "a harming behavior or action or an omission of adequate care that—according to prevailing societal norms and professionally substantiated assessments—infringe upon the well-being and the rights of a child, committed by parents or other persons in families and institutions (e.g., residential homes, day care centers, schools, clinics, or certain therapies), that result in nonaccidental injuries and/or impairments in the development of a child. In these situations, in order to safeguard the needs and the well-being of the child, helping services or ultimately interventions of child welfare agencies or family courts into the rights of the legally responsible parental guardians are necessary" (Kinderschutz-Zentrum Berlin, 2009; our translation; see also Beiderwieden, Windaus & Wolff, 1986; Wolff, 2007).

Even though child protection is the legal duty of the local public child and youth welfare department (the Youth Office) and of nongovernmental child and youth welfare agencies that provide child protection services, comprehensive and valid national data on child maltreatment reports, substantiated reports, and service delivery do not exist in Germany. "The real incidence of child neglect and child abuse can only be estimated since the few existing older estimates are only based on nonreliable research results, and newer representative evidence-based results on the basis of valid research instruments are lacking" (13. Kinder- und Jugendbericht, 2009; our translation). However, the most severe forms of offences against children, such as murder, assault, physical and sexual abuse, and neglect, are nationally documented by the *Bundeskriminalamt* (the German equivalent of the U.S. Federal Bureau of Investigation). The number of registered (but not substantiated) cases of criminal offences against children known to the police has increased considerably from 43,815 in 1994 to 67,140 in 2008. With a steadily declining number of children under 18 years of age among the overall population (from 15,871,943 in 1994 to 13,683,557 in 2008), the per thousand rates of registered criminal offences against children and adolescents that are known to the police have nearly doubled, rising from 2.7/1,000 minors (1994) to 4.9 (in 2008), with a peak of 5/1,000 in 2007 (Table 9.1). There are no valid data in Germany on how many child maltreatment perpetrators are actually convicted.

Table 9.1: Criminal Offences Against Children (Number of Victims <18) Germany, 1994–2008

Offences	1994	1995	1996	1997	1998	1999	2000	2001	2002	2003	2004	2005	2006	2007	2008
Murder	174	132	152	103	116	89	109	105	113	101	103	97	92	72	99
Second-degree murder	-	-	-	-	-	185	183	182	188	179	185	171	176	209	191
Infanticide	26	32	31	24	20	-	-	-	-	-	-	-	-	-	-
Homicide through neglect	-	127	161	162	138	161	157	159	127	132	129	122	147	111	102
Aggravated assault	16,975	19,586	22,368	24,696	26,273	28,296	29,511	31,377	31,632	33,258	35,393	36,372	38,071	40,062	37,467
Fatal assault	78	102	106	86	80	54	76	46	40	42	45	34	23	17	13
Rape	1,493	1,570	1,592	1,812	2,130	1,927	2,068	2,309	2,489	2,508	2,556	2,276	2,209	2,040	1,970
Child sexual abuse	18,414	19,644	19,526	21,130	20,992	19,431	19,716	19,196	20,385	19,477	19,090	17,534	15,995	15,933	15,098
Sexual abuse of wards	1,791	1,979	1,942	1,988	2,077	2,228	1,906	1,937	1,886	1,828	1,787	1,531	1,628	1,517	1,599
Maltreatment	2,165	2,094	2,237	2,359	2,419	2,629	2,416	2,843	3,071	3,370	3,409	3,377	3,639	3,926	4,102
Maltreatment of wards	2,675	2,645	2,817	2,946	3,025	3,341	3,094	3,596	3,906	4302	4,414	4,340	4,589	4,837	4,985
Kidnapping	-	1,201	1,482	1,499	1,524	1,547	1,621	1,648	1,636	1,606	1,619	1,589	1,684	1,451	1,502
Hostage-taking	24	55	35	18	17	19	17	20	23	13	12	14	19	8	12
Total	43,815	49,167	52,449	56,823	58,811	59,907	60,874	63,418	65,496	66,816	68,742	67,457	68,272	70,183	67,140
Per 1,000 of all children <18	2.7	3.09	3.2	3.57	3.7	3.8	3.9	4.1	4.2	4.4	4.6	4.6	4.7	5.0	4.9

Source: Police Crime Statistics, Federal Republic of Germany, Federal Criminal Police Office. Wiesbaden. 1987–2008.
The data have been especially compiled for this study by the authors.

If one compares severe injuries or fatalities of children caused by traffic accidents with those caused by child abuse and neglect, a substantially higher number of children is still injured in traffic accidents (55,549 in 2008) than because of child maltreatment (41,569 in 2008). However, the numbers of child fatalities related to abuse (290 out of 13,683,557 children or 0,021/1,000 children in 2008) or to traffic accidents (276 or 0,020/1,000 children in 2008) are approximately the same (Table 9.2).

The available data from the child welfare field show that the number of children receiving child and youth welfare services has steadily increased over the last decade: for educational counselling from 229,867 (in 1995) to 309,357 (in 2005), and for social-pedagogical family services from 93,722 (in 1995) to 187,088 (in 2005). But the real number of out-of-home placements (the most expensive service the German child welfare system has to offer) has decreased from 152,487 in 1995 to 145,397 in 2005. However, the per thousand rate of out-of-home placements for minors under 18 (including all forms of residential and family foster care, but not including adoptions, which are of minor importance in Germany) has increased from 9.5/1,000 (in 1995) to 9.9/1,000 (in 2005) (Table 9.3).

As a reaction to intense public debates about child abuse and neglect and the campaigns to report child maltreatment cases, the most remarkable change is an overall increase in temporary (crisis) placements of children and adolescents.

Table 9.2: Comparison of Traffic Accidents and Criminal Offences Against Children (Number of Victims Under 18) Germany, 2005–2008

	2005	2006	2007	2008
Injured in traffic accidents	65,332	61,131	60,457	55,540
Aggravated assault	36,372	38,071	40,062	37,467
Maltreatment	3,377	3,639	3,926	4,102
Fatal traffic accidents	383	309	287	276
Murder	97	92	72	99
Second-degree murder	171	176	209	191

Source: Federal Statistical Office. Police Crime Statistics, Federal Republic of Germany.
The data have been especially compiled for this study by the authors.

Table 9.3: Development of Cases/Services for Children and Their Families, Federal Republic of Germany, 1995–2005

Kind of Cases/Year	1995	2000	2005
Educational counselling	229,867	274,573	309,357
Social educational family support	93,722	143,773	187,088
Placements	152,487	152,932	145,397

Source: Federal Statistical Office: Statistics of the Child and Youth Welfare Services; calculations by Jens Pothmann and Sandra Fendrich; Dortmund Agency for the Statistics of Child and Youth Welfare [Dortmunder Arbeitsstelle Kinder- u. Jugendhilfestatistik]

Although fewer children and adolescents have asked to be taken out of their families voluntarily, at the same time out-of-home-placements demanded by the child and youth welfare departments rose dramatically, and those that were demanded by parents themselves nearly doubled. Most of all short-term—crisis or temporary—placements of children under the age of 18, after a decline from 2000 to 2005, now have risen by 25.7% from 25,664 (in 2005) to 32,253 (in 2008). After the changes in the Child and Youth Welfare Act in 2005 (which according to the new §8a Social Code VIII) underlined the role of child and youth welfare professionals to act as "guarantors of the well-being of children"), child and youth welfare practitioners have more often opted for crisis placements in order to be on the "safe side." Whereas in 2000, 2/1,000 children and adolescents were taken into "short-term custody" (*Inobhutnahme*), in 2008, this number rose to 2.3/1,000 minors under the age of 18. Most strikingly, there was a considerable change in the age structure of the placed children and adolescents. The proportion of children under the age of 3 doubled from 5% of all children placed in 2000 to 10% in 2008, which shows that child and youth welfare departments and family courts have increasingly come to focus on protecting very young children by taking them into care in short-term residential homes and crisis shelters (see Tables 9.4, 9.5, and 9.6).

After 2005, another marked trend has been the steady rise of the number of family court rulings (care orders) to restrict or withdraw parental rights because of an "endangerment of the well-being of a child," with a sharp increase of 18.5% (from 12,752 cases in 2007 to 14,906 in 2008). In Germany, child welfare agencies and family courts obviously have become more control-oriented and tend to intervene earlier. Assessing the risk of possible future child maltreatment, social workers more often opt for higher risk rate estimates and then choose the option of out-of-home services more readily—not least of all in order to protect themselves against the allocation of blame in case child maltreatment should, in fact, occur or continue. At the same time, following the enactment of a new family law in 2008 (*Gesetz zur "Erleichterung familiengerichtlicher Massnahmen bei Gefaehrdung des Kindeswohls"*) that facilitates earlier interventions of the family courts in cases of child maltreatment, family court judges—similar to the French *juges d'enfant*—have become much more active in giving advice to parents and ordering them to use obligatory child and family welfare services (BMFSFJ–Federal Ministry for Families, the Elderly, Women, and Youth, 2009).

Germany has undoubtedly become an immigration country in recent decades. Approximately every fifth resident has an immigrant background (Bericht der Beauftragten der Bundesregierung für Migration, 2005), and the proportion of immigrant children and adolescents in some urban areas is up to 40% (Stuewe, 2004). However, these children are clearly underrepresented in preventive services, but overproportionately represented in crisis and risk situations (cf. Kinder- und Jugendbericht). At the same time, no data are available on the specific challenges faced by children and adolescents from immigrant milieus. Thus, many open questions concerning the special situation of families with

Table 9.4: Short-Term Placements of Children <18 With Parental Consent in Germany, 1995–2007

Temporary placements	1995	1996	1997	1998	1999	2000	2001	2002	2003	2004	2005	2006	2007
Because of endangerment	15,389	18,192	20,116	20,248	20,588	20,449	20,830	19,477	18,508	17,674	17,758	18,728	20,729
At one's own desire	7,882 (33.9%)	9,630 (34.6%)	11,448 (36.3%)	11,029 (35.3%)	10,843 (34.5%)	10,565 (34.1%)	10,504 (33.5%)	9,250 (32.2%)	8,701 (32.0%)	8,056 (31.3%)	7,684 (30.2%)	7,119 (27.5%)	7,028 (25.3%)
Total	23,271	27,822	31,564	31,277	31,431	31,014	31,334	28,727	27,209	25,730	25,442	25,847	27,757

Source: Federal Statistical Office: Statistics of the Child and Youth Welfare Services–short-term placements, various yearly issues; calculations by Jens Pothmann

Table 9.5: Short-Term Placements of Children Under 18 Without Parental Consent in Germany, 1995–2007

	1995	1996	1997	1998	1999	2000	2001	2002	2003	2004	2005	2006	2007
Temporary placements	161	230	243	138	214	110	104	160	169	186	222	151	435

Source: Federal Statistical Office: Statistics of the Child and Youth Welfare Services–short-term placements; calculations by Jens Pothmann; Dortmund Agency for the Statistics of Child and Youth Welfare [*Dortmunder Arbeitstelle Kinder- u. Jugendhilfestatistik*]

Table 9.6: Overview of the Persons and Services/Short-Term Placements of Children Under 18 With and Without Parental Consent in Germany, 1997–2008

	1997	1998	1999	2000	2001	2002	2003	2004	2005	2006	2007	2008
Placements suggested by the police	8,676	8,301	8,128	7,787	7,603	6,790	6,640	6,302	6,243	6,221	6,751	7,263
Placements suggested by the Youth Office	6,750	6,730	7,201	7,083	7,414	7,335	6,519	6,264	6,296	6,982	7,748	9,634
Placements suggested by children <18	11,475	11,042	10,862	10,580	10,516	9,267	8,734	8,089	7,723	7,130	7,064	7,807
Placements suggested by parents	2,201	2,563	2,731	3,016	3,135	2,987	2,992	2,909	2,998	3,150	3,843	4,136
Placements suggested by physicians	304	352	359	328	363	311	326	314	365	398	446	561
Placements suggested by schoolteachers and educators	524	569	517	536	553	580	644	563	542	606	692	825
Placements suggested by neighbors	766	752	760	746	641	531	611	557	545	502	582	603
Placements suggested by other persons	1,111	1,106	1,087	1,048	1,213	1,086	912	918	952	1,009	1,075	1,424
Total	31,807	31,415	31,645	31,124	31,438	28,887	27,378	25,916	25,664	25,998	28,192	32,253

Source: Federal Statistical Office: Statistics of the Child and Youth Welfare Services–short-term placements; calculations by Jens Pothmann; Dortmund Agency for the Statistics of Child and Youth Welfare [Dortmunder Arbeitstelle Kinder- u. Jugendhilfestatistik]

immigrant backgrounds and their interactions with the German child welfare system warrant further consideration and research. These include questions of specific risk factors in these families, as well as questions concerning potential "cultural clashes" between clients from other cultures and countries and the German child welfare system. A detailed investigation of these questions is highly relevant, but is beyond the scope of this chapter (see also Pluto, Gragert, van Santen & Seckinger, 2007).

Yet, the overall structure of the family and child welfare system has not changed. It is still characterized by a bipolar design of local government services (with the Youth Office as its major institution) and nongovernmental agencies (most of them nonprofit organizations), both of which are monitored by a local Youth Welfare Council (*Jugendhilfeausschuss*), in which all the stakeholders in the family and the child and youth welfare field are represented. 67% of the residential child welfare institutions (with 61% of all available places) are run by nongovernmental agencies, employing 61% of the family and child welfare workforce. The for-profit sector in Germany is only of minor importance (encompassing only 1.5% of the residential child welfare institutions, 2.8% of all places, and 5.8% of the employed workforce). As Table 9.7 shows, the overall number of about 618,500 employed professionals in about 80,000 agencies (2006) that have mixed qualifications (graduates from professional training schools, professional universities, and universities) is still growing, but in different directions: Although the number of employed professionals has declined in most fields of child and youth welfare, in the field of child and youth work, this change has been more marked, decreasing between 2002 and 2006 by 28.1%, in the residential care sector by 12.5%, and, for example, in agencies for the handicapped by 17.7%. Only in the day care sector has the number of employed personnel increased (by 1.9%), and it is still growing.

In the last decades, expenses in child and youth welfare have risen continuously, keeping pace with the growth of services offered—although with the mounting public debts accumulated in the course of the last decade and with a worldwide crisis in financial markets, the era of growth may be a thing of the past. The major part of the national child and youth welfare budget goes to the day care sector (€11.6 billion), with educational services (family and child welfare educational services and residential care) at second place (€5.6 billion) in 2006. Table 9.8 offers a detailed picture of public expenditures for child and youth welfare services in Germany from 1992 to 2006 (Kinder- und Jugendbericht, 2009).

However, child protection is still only one among many other obligations of child and youth welfare services. Day care provided both by public and nongovernmental agencies continues to represent the major part of child and youth welfare services: In 2008, in eastern Germany 94% and in western Germany 89% of all 3- to 6-year-old children were in day care, while a growing number of infants and young children (up to 31% of children <3) attend different early day care programs (day nurseries, family day nurseries, parents' cooperatives, or day care centers with mixed age groups). The German child and youth welfare system

Table 9.7: Development of Full-Time Professionals in Child and Youth Welfare in Different Work Sectors (Germany; 2002 and 2006/Absolute Numbers and %)

	Dec. 31, 2002	Dec. 31, 2006	Change 2002–2006	
	No.	No.	No.	In %
Total				
Day care agencies	285,341	290,842	+5,501	+1.9
Child and youth work	27,541	19,814	−7,727	−28.1
Youth social work	4,739	4,448	−292	−6.2
Educational services (children and families)	17,435	15,261	−2,174	−12.5
Residential educational services	33,604	31,687	−1,917	−5.7
Services for handicapped minors	10,953	9,013	−1,940	−17.7
Other	26,453	25,520	−933	−3.5
Administration	15,251	14,900	−351	−2.3

Source: 13. Kinder- und Jugendbericht. (2009). Statistical Federal Office and Calculations Dortmund Agency for the Statistics of Child and Youth Welfare [Dortmunder Arbeitsstelle Kinder- u. Jugendhilfestatistik]

includes early counselling and home visiting services, educational in-home services to provide respite care, and parental education and training, a wide array of day care programs, and youth work and group work services for adolescents, as well as out-of-home residential care, foster family care, and adoption services. Moreover, special child protection center programs help families early on in crisis situations and when children are threatened or endangered by child maltreatment. The current debate basically concerns where the threshold should be drawn between the need for a broad system of helping services and the necessity of child protection interventions, and whether the whole system should be structured in response to a worst-case child protection scenario of fatal child abuse cases—which are indeed very rare incidents—or whether child protection should rather be embedded in a broader concept of a universal and comprehensive democratic child and youth welfare service. Figure 9.1 shows where this threshold could be drawn, and where the child protection function can be split up, thus undermining a comprehensive child and youth welfare system.

SYSTEM CHALLENGES: CAN THE CHILD PROTECTION SYSTEM LEARN?

Since child maltreatment and child protection, in Germany as in many other countries, have become top issues of national public and professional social

Table 9.8: Public Expenses (+ Revenues) for Child and Youth Welfare Services in Selected Service Fields–Social Law Viii/Germany/Euro (1992–2006)

	Total expenditure in 1,000 Euro	Youth Work	Youth Social Work	Education-al Services in Families	Day Care	Pedagogical and Residential Serv,	Administrative Services in Child Welfare	Other Expenses
1992	14,284,341	1,116,804	193,066	70,469	8,490,895	2,968,614	592,323	852,170
1993	16,291,525	1,206,876	187,099	58,797	10,011,514	3,567,125	641,520	618,594
1994	16,631,045	1,238,695	169,879	67,155	9,979,929	3,822,083	704,148	649,157
1995	17,020,311	1,301,845	184,440	60,135	9,796,698	3,811,116	726,979	1,139,100
1996	17,517,213	1,254,208	248,911	65,156	10,037,736	3,966,150	733,793	1,211,258
1997	17,512,851	1,263,318	218,304	65,077	9,872,174	4,364,471	697,344	1,032,162
1998	17,709,618	1,297,277	211,102	65,423	9,892,003	4,436,775	707,778	1,099,261
1999	18,077,611	1,356,972	213,422	69,095	9,956,635	4,613,564	717,635	1,150,288
2000	18,464,958	1,411,459	219,067	72,430	10,035,690	4,857,443	773,471	1,095,398
2001	19,210,662	1,432,060	237,870	74,385	10,427,626	5,124,549	767,532	1,146,640
2002	20,176,896	1,459,099	253,236	121,959	10,951,366	5,476,958	705,232	1,209,046
2003	20,612,447	1,387,142	270,778	89,175	11,290,788	5,636,946	720,644	1,216,976
2004	20,671,147	1,349,776	260,582	76,965	11,430,891	5,634,389	708,391	1,210,154
2005	20,865,232	1,377,591	251,960	79,563	11,542,452	5,668,067	668,088	1,277,510
2006	20,924,286	1,400,846	241,923	85,104	11,638,762	5,650,389	635,935	1,271,327

Source: Statistisches Bundesamt. Statistics of Child and Youth Welfare–Expenses and Revenues, 1992–2006. Wiesbaden; Kinder- und Jugendbericht. (2009); Dortmunder Arbeitsstelle Kinder- und Jugendhilfestatistik (2008).

Figure 9.1: System structure child and youth welfare and child protection

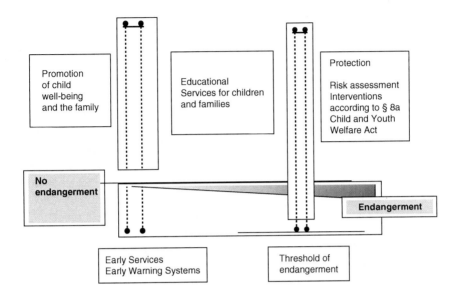

policy and social work debates, the child and youth welfare system faces a number of major challenges concerning how the system can be responsibly managed and reformed. Child welfare is increasingly confronted with growing expectations and concerns that "every child matters," and that safeguarding children should be guaranteed. At the same time, welfare state support for child protection agencies is dwindling (with declining budgets, high staff turnover, and a negative professional image), and these agencies have come under fierce attack as inefficient and underachieving organizations. Therefore, "new directions," organizational reforms, and new approaches in designing programs and methods have become necessary.

Child welfare is at a crossroads. It may move toward integrating the task of responsibly protecting children into a comprehensive, universal child and family welfare system with a broad set of services (from early family services and day care programs to crisis intervention and residential and family foster care services), or toward a gradual transformation into a statutory, interventionist, last-resort system, in which involuntary clients are supervised and controlled by involuntary professionals who do not like what they do and therefore, caught in their defensive stances, cannot become change agents. The direction taken depends in part upon whether it is possible to both cope with risks and errors in daily child protection practice and simultaneously avoid a highly bureaucratized system with formalized risk assessment technologies and proceduralized performance management methods. The essential issue is: Can child welfare systems— continuously confronted with insecurities, unexpected developments, and organized impermanence (Weick, 2009), with real "messes" in a complex, "unknowable world" (Schön, 1983; Weick, 2009)—become High Reliability Organizations (HRO) that are able to learn and develop in spite of a widespread withdrawal of recognition and appreciation?

Germany may move further toward a mainly protection-based service, or foster a broad family service orientation within the context of a universal welfare state policy, which was the basis of the very well-accepted Child and Youth Welfare Act. In this direction, there are increasing initiatives to integrate child protection into a comprehensive context of early support services, a trend that is highlighted by the creation of the influential National Center for Early Services (*Nationales Zentrum Fruehe Hilfen*) in 2007. This institution seeks to promote better cooperation between the social work, health, and education sectors, and to help develop a new philosophy of working together to better safeguard childhood. Furthermore, the public, political leaders, and professionals are eager to initiate quality development programs (such as the national project Learning from Mistakes: Quality Management in Child Protection) that help to avoid developments that have led, among other things, to the "bankruptcy of the prevailing child protection system in the English-speaking industrialized countries of Oceania, North America, and Europe" (Melton, cited in Lonne et al., 2009). In spite of the current overall tendency of drifting into a system of surveillance and control of "deviant" and poor populations that are forced to live at the margins of late modern societies, a new democratic child welfare movement (see also outside of Germany: Naves, 2007; Renoux, 2008; Lonne et al., 2009) is not committed to resignation, but to acting courageously in partnership with parents and children, with professionals inside and outside of the child welfare system, with local and state administrations, and with the wider public. The activists in this movement—practitioners, researchers, and service participants—strive for a voice and to be recognized as "artisans of democracy," working to create a culture of understanding, support, solidarity, and social justice to further the well-being of children. Their program includes:

- A commitment to overcoming the traditional negative image of child protection and to developing a tri-polar child welfare and child protection concept (furthering and protecting children, parents and families, and the community), true to the self-confident motto: "We are furthering and protecting children—jointly and gladly!" (*"Wir foerdern und schuetzen Kinder—gemeinsam und gern!"*)
- A nonauthoritarian quality development program that combines middle-up-down management approaches with dialogical communication strategies
- A quality assurance method that promotes learning from both mistakes and successes

- An effort to qualify the workforce using new reflexive theory-into-practice-models (e.g., the "practice university") and in-service training programs, and to enlarge the research base and the theoretical understanding of an evidence-informed practice in child welfare
- A focus on cooperation with all stakeholders in order to overcome the many frictions in the system
And, last but not least,
- A readiness to invite the community—young and old, politicians and professionals, the media and the wider public—to join forces, to create a sustainable development ecology for all children (Wolff 2008).

Whether this approach will prevail remains to be seen.

REFERENCES

Bast, H., Bernecker, A., Kastien, I., Schmitt, G. & Wolff, R. (Eds.). (1975; 1985). *Gewalt gegen Kinder* [Violence against children]. Reinbek bei Hamburg: Rowohlt Taschenbuchverlag.

Beck, U. (1986). *Die Risikogesellschaft* [The risk society]. Auf dem Weg in eine andere Moderne. Frankfurt am Main: Suhrkamp.

Beck, U. (1994). Bindungsverlust und Zukunftsangst. Leben in der Risikogesellschaft. In: H.H. Hartwich (Ed.), *Bindungsverlust und Zukunftsangst. Leben in der Risikogesellschaft* [Loss of bonds and anxieties for the future. Life in the risk society], pp. 25–35, 73–78. Eine Disputation. Opladen: Leske + Budrich.

Beck, U. (2007). *Weltrisikogesellschaft. Auf der Suche nach der verlorenen Sicherheit* [Global risk society. In search of forlorn security]. Frankfurt am Main: Suhrkamp.

Beiderwieden, J., Windaus, E. & Wolff, R. (1986; 1999). *Jenseits der Gewalt. Hilfen fuer mißhandelte Kinder* [Beyond violence. Services for abused children]. Basel, Frankfurt am Main: Stroemfeld/Roter Stern.

Bernecker, A., Merten, W. & Wolff, R. (Eds.). (1985). *Ohnmaechtige Gewalt* [Powerless violence]. Reinbek bei Hamburg: Rowohlt Taschenbuchverlag.

Bundesministerium fuer Familien, Senioren, Frauen und Jugend (BMFSFJ). (2005). *Nationaler Aktionsplan* [National action plan]. Berlin: BMFSFJ.

Bundesministerium fuer Familien, Senioren, Frauen und Jugend (BMFSFJ). (2006). *Presseerklaerung zum Nationalen Aktionsplan* [Press release]. Berlin: BMFSFJ.

Bundesministerium fuer Familien, Senioren, Frauen und Jugend (BMFSFJ) (Ed.). (2009). *Bericht ueber die Lebenssituation junger Menschen und die Leistungen der Kinder- und Jugendhilfe in Deutschland–13. Kinder- und Jugendbericht. Deutscher Bundestag* [Report on the living conditions of young people and child and youth welfare provisions. 13th child and youth welfare report to the German parliament] 16.Wahlperiode. Drucksache 16/12860.

Bundesministerium fuer Familien, Senioren, Frauen und Jugend (BMFSFJ). (2009a). *Aktiver Kinderschutz–Entwicklung und Perspektiven* [Active child protection–Developments and perspectives]. Berlin: BMFSFJ.

Jacob, M. (2006). *Soziale Arbeit zwischen Hilfe und Kontrolle–Moegliche Auswirkungen des § 8a SGB VIII auf die Traeger der Jugendhilfe* [Social work in between helping and control–Possible consequences of §8a of the Social Law VIII for child and youth welfare agencies]. Diplomarbeit an der FH Muenster (unpublished).

Kinderschutz-Zentrum Berlin. (1975). *Plan und Begruendung* [Child Protection Center. Concept and reasons]. Berlin: KSZ Berlin.

Lakoff, G. & Johnson, M. (1980). *Metaphors we live by.* Chicago: The University of Chicago Press.

Lakoff, G. & Wehling, E. (2008). *Auf leisen Sohlen ins Gehirn. Politische Sprache und ihre heimliche Macht* [On soft sneakers into the brain. Political language and its hidden power]. Heidelberg: Carl-Auer-Systeme.

Lonne, B., Parton, N., Thomson, J. & Harries, M. (2009). *Reforming child protection.* London; New York: Routledge.

Moersberger, T. & Restemeier, J. (Eds.). (1997). *Helfen mit Risiko* [Helping services at risk]. Neuwied: Luchterhand.

Naves, P. (2007). *La réforme de la protection de l'enfance. Une politique publique en mouvement* [The reform of child protection. Public politics in transition]. Paris: Dunod.

Neue Juristische Wochenschrift (NJW) (1956): Heft 39, Muenchen: Beck

Nothafft, S. (2008). *Landesgesetzliche Regelungen im Bereich des Kinderschutzes bzw der Gesundheitsversorgung* [Laender–state- laws/regulations in the field of child protection and public health]. Koeln: NZFH. Retrieved from www. nzfh.de

Pluto, L., Gragert, N., van Santen, E. & Seckinger, M. (2007). *Kinder- und Jugendhilfe im Wandel. Eine empirische Studie* [Changing child and youth welfare]. Muenchen: Verlag Dt. Jugendinstitut.

Renoux, M.-C. (2008). *Réussir la protection de l'enfance. Avec les familles an précarité* [Creating success in child protection. Together with families living in poverty]. Paris: Les Éditions de l'Atelier/Éditions Ouvrières.

Rosenfeld, J. & Tardieu, B. (2000). *Artisans of democracy.* Lanham, MD: University Press of America.

Schone, R. (2008). *Kontrolle als Element von Fachlichkeit in den sozialpaedagogischen Diensten der Kinder- und Jugendhilfe* [Control as a professional element in social pedagogical services in child and youth welfare]. Expertise im Auftrag der AGJ. Berlin: AGJ.

Schön, D.A. (1983). *The reflective practitioner.* New York: Basic Books.

Weick, K.E. (1995). *Sensemaking in organizations.* Thousand Oaks, CA: Sage.

Weick, K.E. (2009). *Making sense of the organization*. Vol. 2, The Impermanent Organization. Chichester: Wiley.

Wolff, R. (1997). Germany: A nonpunitive model. In: N. Gilbert (Ed.), *Combatting child abuse: International perspectives and trends*, pp. 212–231. New York: Oxford University Press.

Wolff, R. (2007). Demokratische Kinderschutzarbeit–Zwischen Risiko und Gefahr [Democratic child protection work–in between risk and danger]. *Forum Erziehungshilfen*, 3(13), 132–139.

Wolff, R. (2008). Die strategische Herausforderung–oekologisch-systemische Entwicklungsperspektiven der Kinderschutzarbeit [Strategic challenges - Ecological systemic development perspectives in child protection]. In: U. Ziegenhain & Fegert, J.M. (Eds.). *Kindeswohlgefaehrdung und Vernachlaessigung*, pp. 37–51. Muenchen, Basel: Ernst Reinhardt Verlag.

Ziegenhain, U. & Fegert, J.M. (Eds.). (2008). *Kindeswohlgefaehrdung und Vernachlaessigung* [Endangerment of child well-being and neglect]. Muenchen, Basel: Ernst Reinhardt Verlag.

10

POLICY TOWARD CHILD ABUSE AND NEGLECT IN BELGIUM: SHARED RESPONSIBILITY, DIFFERENTIATED RESPONSE

KRISTOF DESAIR AND PETER ADRIAENSSENS

THE BELGIAN SYSTEM AND ITS BACKGROUND

Child abuse and neglect is a complex social problem that is tackled in Belgium with a set of direct and indirect measures. To understand Belgian[1] policy on child abuse and neglect, it is essential to consider the Confidential Centres for Child Abuse and Neglect in Flanders and the Centres SOS-Enfants in the Walloon Region. Since the mid-1980s, these centers have been implemented to deal with reported cases of child abuse and neglect. In addition, to understand Belgium's approach to this problem, two other factors should be taken into account. First, seen from a broader social perspective, measures to combat child abuse in Belgium include policies that address general social risk factors, such as poverty, teenage parenthood, unemployment, and neighborhood deterioration. Second, in Belgium, as in other mainland European countries, preventing and dealing with child abuse and neglect is commonly considered a social responsibility shared by public and private partners and not only residing with governmental institutions. For example, on the one hand, there is a child protection system that operates under governmental authority; on the other hand, there are also private services, funded with public money, which are active in this field.

The view of child abuse as an individual, intrapsychic problem has been superseded and replaced by a consensus that child abuse and neglect is a multifaceted problem that must be addressed from a comprehensive perspective, taking into account the rights and needs of the children and others involved. Many pathways lead to child abuse and neglect, including a variety of risk factors (such as parent/child characteristics and social conditions) that outweigh protective factors (Belsky, 1993). Accordingly, there is no single solution to the problem. Interventions can have many different targets, ranging from parental behavior to the social conditions that prevent parents from being emotionally sensitive or available for their offspring. Protecting children from maltreatment cannot be separated from policies to improve children's lives as a whole. Thus, insight into the measures addressing child abuse and neglect can best be gained by taking different policy levels and dimensions into account.

From this perspective, we can think in the Belgian context of a comprehensive array of policies that form a pyramid. At the base, we find all the efforts necessary for the reinforcement of the position of children in general (Nationale Commissie tegen Seksuele Uitbuiting van Kinderen, 1997; Cappelaere & Willems, 1998). This involves an approach aimed at preserving and improving the well-being of children in society. Often this is achieved through indirect measures not specifically targeting child abuse and neglect, but of a more preventive nature, like home visits by a nurse for every newborn. The higher one climbs on the pyramid, the more specific, specialized, and reactive the policy interventions become. At the apex, we find procedures and interventions designed and implemented specifically to target child abuse and neglect. Between the base and the apex, a wide range of policies and services (welfare, health, and other) can be listed that contribute to the welfare of children, to the prevention of all kinds of abuse, and to the care of victimized children. Although services in this area have a general mandate, they sometimes also deal with child abuse and neglect. An important principle here is *subsidiarity*, which basically refers to the idea that more investments at the base will reduce the need for interventions at the apex. Overall, this means that only a residual group of cases of child abuse and neglect are dealt with by services that have the sole task of improving the safety and well-being of abused and neglected children.

In this chapter, when dealing with the Belgian response system toward child abuse and neglect, we will mainly focus on the apex; that is, on those facilities that have an official and specific mandate in the area of child abuse and neglect, and only in this area. However, to fully understand the apex, it is imperative that we also consider the other parts of the pyramid. If we ask ourselves who works with child abuse and neglect, then, according to the pyramid structure, there are services such as the Confidential Centres for Child Abuse and Neglect and the Centres SOS–Enfants, which only deal with child abuse and neglect. However, many other services also are confronted with cases involving child abuse and neglect, in addition to other child welfare issues (such as the Committees for Special Youth Care or Mental Health Services). Finally, the justice system includes specific criminal laws regarding child abuse and neglect, as well as child protection legislation with a broader perspective, so it also deals with cases of child abuse and neglect.

In conclusion, we can make a distinction between broadly focused social policy that, in general, reduces risk factors linked to child abuse and neglect, and policy that is more narrowly focused on intervening once child abuse and neglect occur. This chapter mainly looks at the narrow focus in Belgium. Policies addressing issues such as poverty and deprivation, teenage motherhood, substance abuse, and unemployment remain important in combatting child abuse and neglect, but they will not be considered here. Finally, we will address the influence of societal change on this system. In this respect, the changes that occur in the broader policy areas, due to the process of globalization, new risks in society, and the emergence of a more neo-liberal governmental system, can be regarded as among the most compelling developments. These changes also affect the apex of the pyramid and thus put into question its sustainability.

The Belgian approach can be located on a continuum between a disciplinary or criminalizing and an emancipatory or caring system. The evolution of this approach and its implementation are strongly related to the development of the Belgian Welfare State and the history of youth care in Belgium. In principle (if not always in practice), the Belgian approach meets the requirements of the United Nations (UN) Convention on the Rights of the Child. This convention provides the basic tenets for the educational duties of a government, especially the duty to prevent, intervene, and repair in cases of child abuse and neglect (Willems, 2005b). Judicial intervention is regarded as a last resort in systematic prevention (Willems, 2005a).

PROBLEM SIZE

In 2008, the size of the Belgian population was 10,666,866 people, of which 2,194,507 were minors. How big is the problem of child abuse and neglect in Belgium? There is no national registration of cases of child abuse and neglect, nor are there any national incidence or prevalence studies about child abuse and neglect. Nevertheless, several indicators give an idea about the size of the problem in Belgium. First, the data from registration systems of the Confidential Centres for Child Abuse and Neglect and the Centres SOS–Enfants and the Justice Department provide valuable information. Next, several survey studies have been undertaken that give a useful estimate of the situation of children in Belgium.

Registration Data

Figure 10.1 and Table 10.1 illustrate a steady growth in the number of reports made at the Confidential Centres in Flanders up to 2005, after which the number of reports levelled or showed a slight decline. A similar pattern of growth in the Walloon region is shown in Figure 10.2, although without a decline after 2005. The number of reports at the Justice Department also increased slightly over this period. Nevertheless, in both regions, this number always remained well below

Figure 10.1: Number of reports and reported children at Confidential Centres and the Department of Justice in Flanders 1991–2007

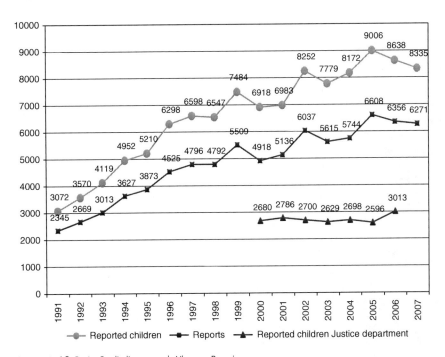

Source: Kind & Gezin, Studiedienst van de Vlaamse Regering.

Table 10.1: Report Ratio in Flanders: Number of Reported Minors Per 1,000 Minors at Confidential Centres 2000–2008

Year	Number of Reported Minors Per 1,000
2000	3.66
2001	3.64
2002	4.33
2003	4.04
2004	4.51
2005	4.96
2006	4.90
2007	4.82
2008	4.25

Source: Kind & Gezin.

Figure 10.2: Number of reports and reported children at Confidential Centres and the Department of Justice in the Walloon Region 1991–2007

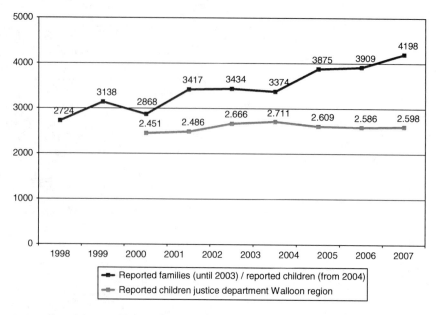

Source: Bulletin de l'Action Enfance Maltraitée n° 59 & n° 69, Studiedienst van de Vlaamse Regering.

the number of reports made at the Confidential Centres and the Centres SOS–Enfants, which confirms the subsidiarity principle and the view that intrafamilial child abuse should be dealt with by welfare services, rather than by law enforcement agencies. It is commonly assumed that the rise in reporting can be attributed to greater public awareness and concern about child maltreatment, along with the breaking of the taboo that surrounded this problem. Over the last decade, families and professionals have increasingly turned to Confidential Centres and Centres SOS–Enfants.

Survey Children in Flanders

Focusing on the living situation of young people (10–18 years) in Flanders, Van den Bergh, Ackaert, and De Rijcke's (2003) survey was not explicitly designed to map intrafamilial child abuse and neglect, but investigated certain topics that give insight into this problem. The researchers measured negative interaction between mother and child and between father and child, as experienced by the child or youngster. The results indicate that .8%–1.8% of Flemish children (10–18 years of age) are often or almost always beaten (as a form of negative interaction) by their mothers, and .9%–1.9% by their fathers. Between .3% and .9% are often or almost always beaten by both parents. Regarding negative verbal communication, this study shows that 2.2%–3.8% of Flemish 10- to 18-year-olds are cursed often or almost all the time by their mothers and 3.1%–4.9% by their fathers. Between .4% and 1.2% are often or almost always cursed by both parents.

Analyzing the self-reports of maltreatment, Bal and colleagues (Bal, Crombez, et al., 2003; Bal, Van Oost, et al., 2003) found that, in one sample of 820 Flemish children aged 11–19 years, about 4% reported having experienced some kind of sexual abuse, intrafamilial or extrafamilial, committed by peers or adults. In a second sample of 970 children in the same age range, the researchers found that 10% reported experiences of sexual abuse. They also found reports of physical neglect in these samples around 1%.[2]

DEFINING CHILD MALTREATMENT

Runyan, Cox, Dubowitz, et al. (2005) found that definitions of child abuse and neglect varied in time and in space, between cultures and between professional disciplines. Even within a single professional discipline, the definition is subject to debate. It is difficult to reach a general agreement because of differences across disciplines in the way that definitions of maltreatment are utilized: those that are based on research criteria are often not useful for child protection practice. Hence, the definitions of maltreatment often differ according to whether they are employed for research purposes, for criminal procedures, or for child welfare services. This complexity is also prevalent in Belgium.

The legislation that constitutes the Confidential Centres in Flanders defines child abuse and neglect as "any situation in which a child is harmed physically or psychologically, in an active way by means of harmful action, or in a passive way, as a consequence of negligence of adults who are responsible for taking care of the child" (Ministerie van de Vlaamse Gemeenschap 17.05.2002, art. 1).

The definition used in practice by the Confidential Centres emphasizes the importance of early detection of child abuse and neglect. The position of the child/victim takes a central place. The Confidential Centres state that child abuse and neglect is any situation in which a child is a victim of violence of a physical, psychological, or sexual nature, whether in a passive or active way. The Confidential Centres refer to the definitions prescribed by the International Society for Prevention of Child Abuse and Neglect and the World Health Organization. As for the equivalent centers in the French-speaking community, similar definitions are employed.

The definition of child maltreatment in Belgium varies depending upon the context in which the problem is being addressed. In the legal context, the Justice Department describes child maltreatment as it is designated in the Penal Code. In this code, there is not just one article that states what should be regarded as child abuse; rather, the issue is taken up in different articles throughout the Penal Code. In 2000, the criminal protection of minors was increased, modernized, and made more coherent (Vermeulen, 2001). The articles related to criminal protection of minors are about indecent assault and rape of minors, juvenile prostitution, abduction of minors, family abandonment, beating and inflicting injury, child pornography, sexual/genital mutilation, coercion to indecent sexual behavior, and deliberately withholding food and care. In criminal law, these articles describe certain behaviors that are eligible for criminal prosecution. Currently, there is, however, no article of criminal law that specifically targets emotional forms of abuse or neglect.

In the context of Child Protection and Special Youth Care, the concept of "problematic situations for raising a child," viz. POS (*Problematische Opvoedingssituatie*) is used. Special Youth Care can intervene "when minors find themselves in situations in which their physical integrity or opportunities for affective, moral, intellectual, or social development suffer due to incidents, relational conflicts, or because of the special conditions in which they live" (Ministerie van de Vlaamse Gemeenschap 04.04.1990).

Every form of child abuse and neglect can be considered as POS. But not every POS case is about child abuse and neglect. Similarly, the Youth Help Act in the French-speaking community defines its scope as "every youngster in difficulties" and "every child whose health or security is in danger or whose conditions in which to be raised are compromised by his or her behaviour or the behaviour of his or her family" (Ministère de la Communauté Française 04.03.1991, art. 2).

In the Flemish-speaking community, the concept of "social exigency" is introduced (Beleidsondersteuningsteam Integrale Jeugdhulp, 2007). To deal with social exigency means coping with alarming situations or environments. A situation is considered as alarming when, at a certain moment, someone feels the need or formulates the expectation that youth care is exigent for a minor and/or his or her family environment. This can then be grounded in a concern, a suspicion, or an assessment of a socially unacceptable condition. Such situations threaten the development of the minor and/or affect the integrity of the minor. Examples are situations in which a minor runs away from home, child abuse, domestic violence, suicidal tendencies, truancy, prostitution, substance abuse, and parental psychiatric disorders.

Definitions for youth care purposes follow criteria related to the context of providing help and assistance. An example is the very broad definition used at the Confidential Centre in Leuven: "child maltreatment is any form of injustice that a child experiences" (Adriaenssens et al., 1998). This definition lacks conceptual clarity or subtypes, which is why it would not serve well for instance research purposes. However, in child care, this degree of generality is exactly what the definition requires in order to limit the exclusion of potential victims. This definition provides an expansive safety net for children and young people who recognize themselves in such situations and feel validated in their decision to contact Confidential Centres or other child care services. Although such a general definition may be well suited to the child care arena, within the criminal justice system it would be problematic. In criminal procedures, it is necessary that clear descriptions are formulated about what kind of behavior is not allowed and is eligible for prosecution.

The definitions used in practice often share common elements and overlap. In practice, they can be considered as different attempts to guarantee the right to intervention laid down in the Convention on the Rights of the Child and to open up the eligibility criteria for children and young people to be taken into care and to be protected. They express a democratic concern to avoid a "one problem one door" policy.

REPORTING: AN ACT OF MORAL RESPONSIBILITY

In Belgium, it is not mandatory to report a suspected or observed instance of child abuse and neglect. Nevertheless, it is considered as a moral responsibility of every member of society to ensure children's well-being. This applies specifically to child maltreatment: If someone is confronted with a situation of child abuse and neglect, he or she has to do something by providing help or by contacting others who are able to help. The absence of mandatory reporting of child abuse and neglect to the judicial authorities can be understood in the light of two principles: subsidiarity and the interest of the child. The subsidiarity principle has two important meanings. Firstly, intrafamilial child abuse and neglect is considered to be a health and welfare problem for the minor and his or her family (Adriaenssens, 2009) and should, according to the Convention on the Rights of the Child, initially be dealt with by the extrajudicial system. Second, when equivalent alternatives are available in the field of assistance, preference should be given to the least radical alternative. The "interest of the child" principle means that care should be demand-based: It should start from and fit in with the demands and the needs of the minor. The minor is an equal partner in the care process and in the dialogue about the intervention and its goals.

Although there is no mandatory reporting, every citizen, including the professional, is free to report instances of child abuse (Adriaenssens, 2009). Moreover, everyone is obliged by law to provide help to a person in need. The latter obligation and the right to free speech are laid down in Belgian legislation, and are in agreement with the law on professional confidentiality. Regarding the right to free speech, two considerations are important. The first one is about reporting to the judicial authorities, the second about reporting to those services holding a specific mandate in the area of child abuse and neglect, namely the Confidential Centres and the Centres SOS–Enfants. This distinction is important because it matters to whom a professional talks. In the judicial system, article 458 of the Belgian Penal Code stipulates the requirement of confidentiality for many professions. Confidentiality has a private/individual importance, as it serves to protect people's privacy. However, confidentiality also has a social importance: It ensures that those in need have the opportunity to seek and find the care they require, irrespective of the cause for that need. The importance of professional confidentiality is underlined by the fact that violations are penalized (Broeckx, Dumarey, & Fock, 2001). Certain cases of emergency stipulated in the criminal code—child abuse is always considered an emergency—can be invoked to break professional confidentiality. Nevertheless, in 2000, the legislature introduced the additional article 458*bis* in the Penal Code, stating the following (Broeckx, Dumarey, & Fock, 2001):

> Everyone who by reason of his status or occupation is confronted with confidential information and as a result has knowledge of a felony... committed to a minor is allowed, without prejudice to the obligations imposed by art. 422*bis*, to bring the felony to the attention of the public prosecutor, on the condition that he has examined the victim or that the victim has taken him into confidence, that there is serious and imminent danger for the psychological and physical integrity of the person involved, and that he cannot protect this integrity himself or with the help of others.

As stipulated by this article, it is the professional's own decision, made in good faith, whether or not to disclose any confidential information. The legislation deliberately did not make reporting mandatory in light of the importance of confidentiality mentioned earlier, thus striving to avoid situations in which people would choose not to seek help for a child because professional secrecy was not guaranteed. In addition, the conditions set out in the Penal Code aim to hold professionals fully accountable for the assistance they provide, in accordance to article 422*bis* of the Criminal Law (Belgische Senaat 24.05.2000). This points to the importance of the subsidiarity principle.

As far as reporting cases to child abuse centers is concerned, there is no violation of the law regarding professional secrecy. If a professional discusses the case with another professional from a confidential center, the concept of "shared professional secrecy" is applicable, because both are bound by article 458 of the Penal Code (Broeckx, Dumarey, & Fock, 2001). This facilitates reporting to and consulting with the Confidential Centres and the Centres SOS–Enfants.

Finally, article 422*bis* declares that everyone is obliged to provide help to a person who is in danger. To begin with, health and welfare professionals are required to do something about a child in a situation of child abuse and neglect, either by themselves or with the help of others (for instance Confidential Centres). When this is not possible or sufficient, the public prosecutor must be informed. Article 422*bis* transposes a moral responsibility into a social responsibility because it sanctions those who neglect to provide help in cases where a child is in danger (Broeckx, Dumarey, & Fock, 2001). A general obligation to solidarity is enforced. According to this article, anyone bound by professional secrecy (and every citizen in general) is compelled to consider whether or not it is ethically justifiable to report an instance of child abuse and neglect (Broeckx, Dumarey, & Fock, 2001).

RESPONSES AT THE APEX

Confidential Centres for Child Abuse and Neglect and Centres SOS–Enfants

In 1987, the Confidential Centres for Child Abuse and Neglect and the Centres SOS–Enfants, were created specifically to handle child abuse reports, assess concerns, and offer assistance in cases of intrafamilial child abuse (Marneffe & Broos, 1997; Adriaenssens, 2009). These centers are specialized in the following tasks (Ministerie van de Vlaamse Gemeenschap, 17.05.2002):

- Providing expert support for professionals who work with cases of child abuse and neglect
- Providing assessment, coordination, intervention, care, and in some cases, therapy
- Raising awareness among professionals and laypeople regarding child abuse and neglect, in order to optimize detection

At these centers, multidisciplinary teams receive reports of child abuse and neglect, and work through some initial phases including assessment, confrontation, and motivation for further assistance. These activities are guided by the following principles:

- The care provided corresponds with the needs of the child or youngster. Establishing a safe environment is the primary goal.
- Care is voluntary and provided through collaboration and dialogue with different stakeholders on different levels (child, parents, siblings, other professionals, family members).
- The care offered attempts to restore safe relationships between children and parents and safe parenting.

What is the rationale behind these centers? In the development of the Confidential Centres and the Centres SOS–Enfants, several (implicit) choices have been made regarding their mission of tackling child abuse and neglect. First, the mission is to stop child abuse and neglect and help the child. The processes employed for this are reporting and assessment. Second, the best results are achieved when parents are able to name and face the problem. The process to achieve this involves encouraging self-reporting by victims and their parents and providing discreet assistance in a setting of accountable care. Third, the aim is to reduce the impact of the violence experienced by children through early detection and collaboration. The instrument for this is not forensic evaluation, but rather easily accessible help and care.

The model does not focus on forms of abuse. Categories such as sexual abuse, emotional neglect, or physical abuse can be useful for professionals or research, but for the child, there is only one form of abuse: the one that he or she endures. Most of the victims suffer a complex of mutually related forms of violence and neglect. This insight can be lost when a system is organized around categories.

The child plays a leading role in the Confidential Centres' efforts to define the problem and point out the direction for change. Diagnostic work and assessment are considered supportive rather than leading. The aim of assessment is to perform an analysis of the strengths and vulnerabilities of the child, the parents, and the family, in order to lay the foundation for care and assistance.

The Confidential Centres and the Centres SOS–Enfants try to integrate an intervening and leading approach with a voluntary and empowering approach. The view is that help is possible without exact knowledge of the facts. The centers are also family-oriented, in trying to maintain family bonds and working with children while they remain with their family. They legitimize their views with knowledge from attachment research, but also consider the limits when attachment to the birth family can be severely damaged.

The model of the Confidential Centres combines an interventionist with an empowering approach. On the one hand, children need protection because they are vulnerable in their development. On the other hand, the competencies of children and families need to be recognized and treated respectfully. Confidential Centres operate primarily on the basis of voluntary care, respecting children's rights, instead of enforcing criminal law. Early detection is encouraged, not from a judicial standpoint, but from the view that it is important for the victim's recovery. The model shows strong similarities with empowerment, but does not impose it. The model stands for a deliberation of best practices, in which the preferential solutions of children are taken into account and facilitated, whether or not in collaboration with the parents. The final responsibility in establishing a safe environment remains with the Confidential Centre. Confidential Centres carry a mandated responsibility to stop child abuse and neglect, using an appreciative and questioning model to motivate and move families toward change in favor of the children. One can question in practice to what degree the Confidential Centres and the Centres SOS–Enfants operate on a voluntary base. In principle, there is no discussion about this qualification since these centers have no authority to enforce any kind of measure on a family, unlike juvenile judges. Nevertheless, people are intensively approached by the centers for help. Many efforts are made to motivate people to understand why help may be necessary and to participate in help. This is a different starting point from when the first response is enforced on the family or is mandatory for the family. When the family and social worker do not find an agreement, they can call for a referral to the juvenile court. Over the last 5–10 years, research has been done in Belgium and the Netherlands around the issue of "care on voluntary basis, but not free of commitment" (see Ministerie van Volkshuisvesting, 2010). There seems to be growing understanding that "voluntary" is a continuum concept.

The Judicial System Role in Child Abuse Interventions

Reports of child abuse and neglect can also be made to the judicial authorities. Most cases of extrafamilial child abuse are preferentially referred to the judicial authorities. The safety of children is established by prosecuting offenders. Over the past decade, the response in this system has become more victim-friendly and more specialized and professionalized. Thus, in police departments, special interrogation teams are trained in forensic interviewing of children and youngsters. Houses of Justice (*Justitiehuizen*) and Services for Victim Support have been put in place to provide information and to support children and parents who go through the criminal procedure. Specialized law courses are provided for lawyers who wish to act as a youth lawyer. Over the past years, a more collaborative attitude appears to have developed between welfare services and judicial services.

OUT-OF-HOME PLACEMENT

In this section, figures for out-of-home placement are presented. In some countries, these figures serve as an indicator of the response to child maltreatment; however, in Belgium we cannot assume that this is the case because of the different pathways that children may take to end up in placement outside the family, as in residential facilities and foster families. First, we can make a distinction between directly and indirectly accessible care. Families, mental health workers, hospitals, home nurses, school social workers, and other professionals can make use of certain placement services to provide residential care. In addition, there are placement services that can only can be accessed through a juvenile court decision, an investigation by the Committee for Special Youth Care, or an assessment of a specialized service for persons with disabilities. Second, most of the residential care (directly and indirectly accessible) is provided by private subsidized organizations; only a few institutions are state-run. Finally, and importantly, one cannot conclude that placed children are always the victim of child abuse and neglect, although this may be the case in many placements. The reasons for out-of-home placement are diverse and include problematic child rearing, disability, child maltreatment, and juvenile delinquency. Nevertheless, the rationale behind placement of minors remains the provision of care. With some caveats, we could explain this by the idea that placement is need-based (what does this child/family need?) rather than problem-based (what has happened to the child?). French-speaking Belgium has a similar system, using the same logic. Different pathways and different administrations also make it difficult to arrive at a single figure for out-of-home placement rates. For comparative reasons, we

Table 10.2: Number of Minors Per 1,000 in Residential Forms of Special Youth Care in Flanders (Placed by the Committee for Special Youth Care or Juvenile Court)

Year	Number of Minors Per 1,000 Placed Out-of-Home Through the Year
2004	7.91
2005	7.99
2006	8.12
2007	8.37
2008	8.64

display in Table 10.2 the annual out-of-home placement rates of children per 1,000 in the system of Special Youthcare (leaving out the directly accessible services and the facilities for children with disabilities). Although these figures show a small increase, investment in ambulatory services (the child remains at home and the family receives help in-home or at centers) is increasing at a greater rate than is investment in residential care outside the family. Increasingly, more subsidy policy efforts are made toward ambulatory service provision in comparison to (semi-) residential services. This exemplifies the attempts to put the principle of subsidiarity into practice. In Special Youth Care, an emphasis is placed on ambulatory forms of assistance. In addition to traditional arrangements for care provided through residential centers and foster families, more recently, alternative types of support are being adopted, such as day centers, home visiting services, and services that support an older child living alone. In the past 5 years, services for home visits during crisis situations have been put in place. The main objective of this form of home visiting is to avoid out-of-home placement in serious cases. It requires very intensive follow-up and is time limited.

CURRENT ISSUES AND TRENDS

The Dutroux Case: A Traumatic Experience for Belgium

In 1996, Belgium was shocked by the consecutive disappearances of six young girls. When Marc Dutroux was arrested, on August 13, 1996, four of these girls had already died. Only Sabine (13) and Laetitia (14) were rescued in time from the basement of this child molester and murderer. An (18) and Eefje (19) had been chained, sexually abused, drugged, and buried alive. Julie (7) and Mélissa (8) possibly died of starvation. These horrifying acts led to a public outrage, magnified by the fact that blunders by the police and judicial authorities seemed to have hindered a timely solution to these disappearances. Dutroux, who had a previous conviction for pedophilia, was the prime suspect in the early stage of the investigation and was being carefully monitored. During the time when the girls were held captive in his basement, the police had searched the house on several occasions. The police officers even heard the children knocking on the wall, but were duped by Dutroux, who explained that the knocking sound came from his central-heating boiler.

On October 20, 1996, in what has gone into history as "the White March," 300,000 people walked the streets of Brussels to express their indignation. Everybody carried something white: a balloon, a coat or their face painted white, as a symbol of hope. The message was that changes were needed in Belgium and that judicial authorities and the police should pay more attention to "the child." The parents of the missing children led the protest and were united in their efforts to give voice to the injustice that was committed on them and their children. Demanding change from the national government, they questioned everybody's authority and expertise, including human service professionals, judicial authorities, and the political bodies in power. Without them, the Dutroux case would have ended silently. Today, most are still active in the promotion of children's rights and have become a symbol of the flawed and insufficient approach to injustice for children.

In response to public outrage, the government established a national group of experts assigned to propose legislation that would initiate remedial and preventive measures to improve the fight against sexual exploitation of children in Belgium. In October 1997, the National Commission against the Sexual Exploitation of Children published its final report, which contained 63 proposals (Nationale Commissie tegen Seksuele Uitbuiting van Kinderen, 1997). It would take 10 years to implement the majority of these proposals, which introduced a number of measures to strengthen the penal code's protection of children against sexual exploitation, prostitution, and child pornography. Thus, for example, the time limit on criminal proceedings in cases of sexual abuse of minors was extended to 10 years after the victim attains the age of majority. Furthermore, the introduction of the extraterritoriality principle made it possible to prosecute sex tourism. The prohibition against employing people convicted of indecency in the youth sector was formulated more precisely and made more effective. In addition, parole of convicted offenders was made dependent on preliminary advice of specialized services in the field of offender assessment and treatment. At the very least, the opinion of the victims involved would also be taken into account before granting a convict parole. Improvements were made in the treatment and follow-up of sexual offenders. Genital mutilation became liable to punishment. Specialized centers for offender assessment and treatment were set up. Beyond all this, public opinion has changed in favor of the detection of child abuse. Since the Dutroux case, parents are more inclined to accept being called upon by youth care services to discuss concerns about child abuse and neglect in their family.

Even though the Dutroux case was horrible and traumatic for the whole country, it did not lead to a witch hunt or a moral panic. Thanks to the worthy responses of the parents of the missing children and the symbolic power of the White March, the case led to constructive changes that favor the protection and well-being of children in Belgian society.

Strengthening the Coordination of Child and Youth Care: The Development of Integrated Youth Assistance

This chapter began by pointing out that combatting child abuse in Belgium is part of a broad spectrum of policies in which roles are played by many different organizations. In 1999, the Flemish Parliament came to the conclusion that something was fundamentally wrong with the way in which youth assistance provision in Flanders was organized and implemented (Vlaams Parlement, 1999). Youth assistance was too compartmentalized: the different sectors and services were insufficiently familiar with each other's provisions, children and families did not always see the forest for the trees, and there were lacunae in the provision of care for children and youngsters. In May 2004, the Flemish parliament approved two decrees for Integrated Youth Assistance, which formed the legal framework for a far-reaching reform of child and youth care in Flanders. Integrated Youth Assistance aims at improving the collaboration and exchange of information between organizations, and at providing a solid legal position for minors taken into child care. Article 3 of the decree on Integrated Youth Assistance stipulates that youth assistance intends to safeguard children's and youngsters' scope to develop, to watch over their families and living conditions, and to improve their health and well-being. The sectors involved are welfare organizations, mental health services, services for infants and their families, social assistance provided by schools, special youth care, and services for persons with disabilities.

Six basis principles underlie the Integrated Youth Assistance (Bedert, 2007):

- Accessibility: Youth assistance is known, accessible, available, comprehensible, and affordable to a maximum extent.
- Demand-orientation: Youth assistance starts from and meets the demands and the needs of the client.
- Subsidiarity: When equivalent alternatives are available in the field of assistance, the least radical alternative is to be preferred.
- Client participation: The client is an equal partner in youth assistance and the dialogue on that matter.
- Acceptance: Youth assistance is only provided if the client agrees with it, unless the family judge decides otherwise.
- Emancipation: Youth assistance is aimed at increasing the possibilities of the client to act independently.

Working on these objectives, the various child welfare sectors and facilities now think and act not only at their own discretion, but also with an intersectoral perspective. The core objective of Integrated Youth Assistance is to realize cross-sectoral cooperation and intersectoral harmonization, so that requests for assistance receive rapid and appropriate support (Bedert, 2007). In Integrated Youth Assistance, modalities exist in which child abuse and neglect are considered as a social exigency. Special procedures are established to make sure that help on a voluntary basis is made possible or that protection is coerced. The decrees related to Integrated Youth Assistance clarify the legal position of minors in the system and pursue a policy of increased participation of children and youngsters.

CONCLUSION

Challenges for the Future

The Belgian system to promote child welfare and protect against child maltreatment is nested within the broader context of social protection provided by the Belgian welfare state, as illustrated by the pyramid system. The message in this chapter is that the premises on which the system rests are put under pressure by global and societal changes, and a possible shift toward a more neo-liberal and risk-adverse policy.

The current system has evolved through a growing awareness of vulnerability in a risk society, in which people are disconnected from traditional ways of living, supported by family and community, and re-embedded in new ways of life, in which life becomes a "do-it-yourself project" (Beck, 1992). *Re-embedding* refers to living outside of traditional bonds, but within the new standards of the market and the state, in a globalized world where market conditions generate new risks for people. These risks, however, do not appear as social events or natural circumstances that happen to the individual, but as the result of individual choices.

The welfare state's role in protecting citizens from these effects is dependent on the political regime in power. In a neo-liberal context, the management of these risks is seen as the responsibility of the individual. For instance, problems with children are regarded as consequences of parental behavior. Risk societies impose new forms of responsibility on young people and their families. In the current incarnation of the welfare state, people are viewed as free, entrepreneurial, competitive, and rational. This also means that they are judged as responsible for their problems—and for their solutions (Kelly, 2001). These transformations are structured by the continuous efforts of a variety of experts who problematize and monitor families and children (Furedi, 2002). Thus, the family has become responsible for making the right choices for the well-being of their children—regardless of larger social forces that impinge on family life. Families that do not live up to these expectations are labelled at-risk. From this perspective, many collective risks are individualized. Hasenfeld (2010) points out that, most importantly, the political and institutional environments of child care and protection are changing from welfare regimes that emphasize social protection to regimes that insist on individual responsibility.

Accordingly, problem definitions are also shifting. Although 20 years ago, youth problems were defined in terms of exclusion, poverty, and deprivation, now they are formulated in terms of inadequate parenting skills and incompetent parental behavior, or in terms of the nuisance caused by the children. For example,

Belgium has experienced a boom in projects for educational support, specifically targeting families living in poverty. In this way, poverty is defined as an individual's problem, rather than as a side effect of changing political and economic circumstances. Poverty becomes an individual risk that needs to be solved by individual behavioral changes. Similarly, child abuse is mainly considered an individual problem.

Over the past decades of practice and research, the social causes of child abuse and neglect have been increasingly acknowledged, but due to the current reshaping of the welfare state and the process of individualization in a globalizing society, it has become increasingly difficult to collectively address these social factors. Thus, care for children is valued highly, but also increasingly reduced to individual responsibility, rather than being dealt with on a collective level. As mentioned at the beginning of this chapter, the Belgian system requires a broad focus to improve the well-being of children. However, social changes have challenged this broad focus, leading to the question of how well the Belgian model can be sustained in the future.

NOTES

1   Today, Belgium is a federal state, composed of communities and regions (Belgian Constitution, article 1).There are several reasons to keep the structure of the Belgian State in mind when we try to understand the policies that inform current approaches to child abuse. First, child abuse is a matter that relates to the individual. Hence, it resides within the competence of the communities, leading to different systems in each community. Second, child abuse also relates to illegal or criminal practices, which makes it an issue for justice. Justice is a federal department. Finally, child abuse prevention policy involves a mosaic of parts of other more general policies, like social protection, welfare services, education, health care, etc. The regions, communities, and the federal state play a role in different aspects of these more general policies. This mosaic is not limited to state institutions. The welfare system in Belgium can be characterized as a mixed social order in which private and public stakeholders, such welfare organizations, professions, local and regional authorities, and clients, shape the welfare landscape. Nevertheless, there is little divergence between the different parts of the country. One can see difference in the kind of executive services, but there is a common ground that shapes the policy behind specific services. As in a mosaic, the different parts result in one picture.

2   Bal et al. (2003) remark that some evidence suggests that prevalence rates might vary depending on differences in definitions. The use of a more elaborated definition, as was the case in the second study, often leads to higher prevalence rates.

REFERENCES

Adriaenssens, P. (2009). From protected object to lawful subject. Practical applications of the Belgian model of child protection in case of child abuse. *International Journal on Child Health and Human Development, 2*(3).

Adriaenssens, P., Ivens, C., Smeyers, L., & Vanbeckevoort, B. (1998). *In vertrouwen genomen* [Taken into confidence]. Tielt: Lannoo. (In Dutch.)

Bal, S., Crombez, G., Van Oost, P., & Debourdeaudhuij, I. (2003). The role of social support in well-being and coping with self-reported stressful events in adolescents. *Child Abuse & Neglect, 27*, 1377–1395.

Bal, S., Van Oost, P., De Bourdeaudhuij, I., & Crombez, G. (2003). Avoidant coping as a mediator between self-reported sexual abuse and stress-related symptoms in adolescents. *Child Abuse & Neglect, 27*, 883–897.

Beck, U. (1992). *Risk society. Towards a new modernity.* London: Sage.

Bedert, P. (2007). *Integrated youth assistance in Flanders.* Brussel: Integrale Jeugdhulp.

Beleidsondersteuningsteam Integrale Jeugdhulp. (2007). *Nota Maatschappelijk noodzaak* [Memorandum on social exigency]. Brussel: Integrale Jeugdhulp (in Dutch).

Belgische Senaat. 24.05. (2000). *Wetsontwerp betreffende de strafrechtelijke bescherming van minderjarigen. Verslag namens de commissie voor de justitie uitgebracht door mevrouw Nathalie de t'Serclaes* [Bill on criminal protection of minors]. (In Dutch.)

Belsky, J. (1993). Etiology of child maltreatment: A developmental-ecological analysis. *Psychological Bulletin, 114*(3), 413–434.

Broeckx, P., Dumarey, M., & Fock, R. (2001). Schuldig verzuim en beroepsgeheim in de context van strafrechtelijke bescherming van minderjarigen [Illegal omission and professional secrecy in the context of criminal protection of minors]. In G. Vermeulen (Ed.), *Strafrechtelijke bescherming van minderjarigen.* Antwerpen/Apeldoorn: Maklu. (In Dutch.)

Cappelaere, G., & Willems, G. (1998). Child sexual abuse policy in Belgium: Special focus on Flanders. In R. Wazir and N. van Oudenhoven (Eds.), *Child sexual abuse: What can governments do? A comparative investigation into policy instruments used in Belgium, Britain, Germany, the Netherlands and Norway.* The Hague: Kluwer Law International.

Furedi, F. (2002). *Paranoid parenting. Why ignoring the experts may be the best for your child* Chicago: Chicago Review Press.

Hasenfeld, Y. (2010). *Human services as complex organizations.* Los Angeles: Sage.

Kelly, P. (2001). Youth at risk: Processes of individualisation and responsabilisation in the risk society. *Discourse, 22*(1), 23–33.

Marneffe, C., & Broos, P. (1997). Belgium. An alternative approach to child abuse reporting and treatment. In N. Gilbert (Ed.), *Combatting child abuse. International perspectives and Trends.* New York/Oxford: Oxford University Press.

Ministère de la Communauté Française. 04.03. (1991). Décret relatif à l'Aide à la Jeunesse [Decree on youth care]. *Moniteur Belge*, 12.06.1991. (In French.)

Ministerie van de Vlaamse Gemeenschap. 04.04.(1990). Besluit van de Vlaamse Regering tot coördinatie van de decreten inzake bijzondere jeugdbijstand [Decree of the Flemish Government on the coordination of the decrees on Special Youth Care]. *Belgisch Staatsblad*, 08.05.1990. (In Dutch.)

____. 17.05. (2002). Besluit van de Vlaamse regering betreffende erkenning en subsidiëring van de vertrouwenscentra kindermishandeling [Decree of the Flemish Government regarding the Confidential Centres for Child Abuse and Neglect]. *Belgisch Staatsblad*, 19.06.2002, 28130–28133. (In Dutch.)

Ministerie van Volkshuisvesting, Ruimtelijke Ordingen en Milieubeheer. (2010). *Eerste hulp bij sociale stijging. Literatuuronderzoek naar de "Achter de Voordeur" aanpakken van NICIS Institute* [First aid at social rise. Literature review in "Behind the frontdoor" approaches from NICIS Institute]. De Haag: Ministerie van VROM. (In Dutch.)

Nationale Commissie tegen Seksuele Uitbuiting van Kinderen. (1997). *Kinderen stellen ons vragen... Eindrapport van de nationale commissie tegen seksuele uitbuiting van kinderen* [Children ask us questions... Report of the national commission against sexual exploitation of children]. Brussel: Federale Voorlichtingsdienst. (In Dutch.)

Runyan, D., Cox, C., Dubowitz, H., Newton, R. Upadhyaya, M., Kotch, J., et al. (2005). Describing matreatment: Do child protective service reports and research definitions agree? *Child Abuse & Neglect, 29*(5), 461–477.

Van den Bergh, B., Ackaert, L., & De Rijcke, L. (Eds.). (2003). *Tienertijd. Communicatie, opvoeding en welzijn in context: 10- tot 18-jarigen, ouders en leerkrachten bevraagd.* [Youth: Communication, Child Rearing and Welfare in Context: 10- to 18-year-olds, Parent and Teachers Questioned] Antwerpen-Apeldoorn: Garant.

Vermeulen, G. (Ed.), (2001). *Strafrechtelijke bescherming van minderjarigen* [Criminal protection of minors]. Antwerpen/Apeldoorn: Maklu. (In Dutch.)

Vlaams Parlement. (1999). *Maatschappelijke Beleidsnota Bijzondere Jeugdzorg* [Policy document Special Youth Care]. Brussel: Vlaams Parlement. (In Dutch.)

Willems, J.C.M. (2005a). Het kindbeeld in het Verdrag inzake de Rechten van het Kind [The image of the child in the Children's Rights Convention]. *Justitiële verkenningen, 31*(5), 94–112. (In Dutch.)

____. (2005b). Children's rights and the prevention of child abuse and neglect: The quest for a trias pedagogica of children, parents and society. In I. Westendorp and R. Wolleswinkel (Eds.), *Violence in the domestic sphere*. Antwerpen - Oxford: Intersentia.

11

CHILD WELFARE IN THE NETHERLANDS: BETWEEN PRIVACY AND PROTECTION

TRUDIE KNIJN AND CAROLUS VAN NIJNATTEN

On May 19, 2009, two items concerning care for children reached the Dutch media. A ten-line story on page two of the well-regarded newspaper *NRC Handelsblad* reported "The quality of child care centres again decreased." The Dutch Consortium Childcare Research (Nederlands Consortium Kinderopvang Onderzoek/NCKO), evaluating the quality of child care on behalf of the Governmental Department of Education, Culture, and Science once again (as in 2005) came to the conclusion that the liberalization and commercialization of child care has had devastating effects on the quality of child care. The reasons given for this increasingly poor quality of care were a low level of professionalism among child care workers and a too-high child-to-worker ratio (Vermeer et al., 2005; De Kruif et al., 2008). Recruiting underqualified (and therefore cheap) child care workers to take care of too many children seems to be the only way for commercial child care centers to become profitable. The results of this research did not reach mainstream news magazines or television, in contrast to the second item, which revived an issue that almost had disappeared from collective memory.

A young woman, Elise Wats, announced that she was bringing a legal case against the Dutch state for having destroyed her life because of the "Bolderkar Affaire" (see also Roelofs & Baartman, 1997). Elise, now 23 years old, was only 4 years old when the staff of her child care center investigated the children there using a new but contested method to detect child abuse. The staff asked the children to comment on several parts of the bodies of dolls prepared specifically for the purpose of detecting sexual abuse. On the basis of the results of that investigation, the staff concluded that Elise and 14 other children had been sexually abused by their fathers. Elise was placed into a protected children's home and did not see her father again for quite a while. After months, during which time she was taken care of by an aunt and uncle, her father was proven innocent. He, however, was so exhausted by the affair that he could not bear the responsibility for his daughter again and emigrated to Great Britain. Although their lives had been turned upside down and they have lost each other to despair, neither father nor daughter received any apology from the state. Elise now requires an official acknowledgment of the state's failure, a *mea culpa* that recognizes her lost father and her lost youth.

This story can be read in many ways: as a cry for recognition by the unintended victims of an overprotecting state, a search for justice by a wounded daughter who feels still guilty about giving the "wrong" answers to questions about a doll's body parts, or as a complaint against the failures of professionals' efforts to do their best. Irrespectively, the unbalanced media attention given to both cases is striking. Individual drama, particularly if it concerns child abuse, apparently is worth more attention than the collective drama of very low-quality child care provisions afforded daily to thousands of children. In such a context, framed by the media, developing an appropriate balance between family support and child welfare versus child protection interventions is a challenging policy issue.

This media attention to severe incidents has resulted in a public debate on the protection of children against the risks of abuse and maltreatment by their families and the legitimacy and timing of professional interventions. During the past few years, several ghastly cases have drawn public attention: The body of a 12-year-old girl was found dismembered in the river Maas; this child, called "Maas-girl," was murdered by her father. Another very young girl, Savannah, was found in the boot of her mother's car; this 3-year-old was killed by her mother and stepfather after years of neglect, maltreatment, and starvation. A young girl's severed head and body were found in lake Nulde; this 4-year-old, Rowena Rikkers, called the "Nulde girl," appeared to have been murdered by her mother and her mother's new partner. Finally, a wide range of professional social and care workers have not been able to prevent a series of family tragedies in which fathers, and sometimes both parents, have killed their entire family.

The main issues of public debate center on the questions of why professionals have not intervened in time, and why sometimes more than ten welfare agencies were involved in these families' lives, but none took final responsibility. The Dutch inspectorate on child welfare conducted an inquiry on these issues; their report gives a shocking picture of middle managers not taking responsibility, agencies talking at cross-purposes, and professional child welfare workers led down the garden path, working without plan and not calling on co-professional expertise (Inspectie Jeugdzorg, 2005). Since hardly any Dutch child welfare workers are members of a professional organization, complaints against them could not be dealt with by an internal professional disciplinary committee.

Instead, the family supervisor was held responsible by the state prosecutor for not having intervened in time in Savannah's case, and a penal procedure was started against her. Although, in the end, the court declared the supervisor not guilty, child welfare workers were in shock. At a protest meeting, they reacted in disbelief to the general disapproval of their professional quality, blamed the government for imposing workloads that were too high, and asked for more money for child welfare.

This chapter examines developments in child protection practices in the Netherlands since the 1990s, analyzing changes in both law and policy. We will describe the institutional relationship between child protection agencies and overall child welfare agencies, as this setting forms the foundation of the triangulate system of family support, youth care (and prevention), and child protection. It is also the main characteristic of the Dutch policy approach to child protection as a last resort. This analysis will focus on two key issues. First, the challenge of balancing privacy and protection, as reflected in the legal and professional guidelines for protecting children, which has fostered a debate on the legitimacy of professional intervention. Second, we will focus on professional intervention for child welfare itself: What are the conditions of adequate child protection? Do current policy reforms contribute to these conditions? Since 2007, the Dutch coalition government involves a combination of social-democratic and Christian-democratic parties. The political coalitions from 2001 to 2007 were unstable, following a period of 8 years of social-democratic and liberal (Purple) governments in the 1990s.

INSTITUTIONAL SETTING OF CHILD PROTECTION AND CHILD WELFARE

The Netherlands is a small and densely populated country, with about 16.5 million inhabitants (400 per square kilometer) of whom 4 million are children below the age of 20. Since the start of state involvement in the beginning of the 20th century, Dutch activities in child welfare have been a mixture of governmental and nongovernmental interventions, making child welfare a psycho-juridical complex (Van Nijnatten, 1988) at state, county, and municipality levels. The basic child welfare provisions exist in public health care (local baby clinics, advisory centers, and school doctors) and public welfare (sport, play grounds, etc.) that are organized at the municipal level. A new phenomenon involves local centers for Youth and Family (*Centra voor Jeugd en Gezin* /CJG) initiated by the Programme Minister of Youth and Family that should be in operation in every municipality by 2011 (Programmaministerie Jeugd en Gezin, 2008a). These centers are an attempt to organize child welfare at the level of the local community and to bring basic provisions closer to families. Although the new Ministry of Youth and Family coordinates initiatives in this field, the tension between care and control in child welfare is manifest in the provisions and orientations of two governmental departments: the Ministry of Justice on one side and the Ministry of Health, Welfare, and Sports on the other, and the corresponding flows of money.

The second layer exists in the Youth Care Agency that functions as a gate-keeper to child welfare providers, which for the most part is organized on a provincial level. In addition to all kinds of voluntary preventive and supportive services for family and children (such as psychological and social support, pedagogical advice, and divorce mediation), this Agency identifies children at risk and delivers early intervention services to combat problems in child development. It is this Youth Care Agency that brings child protection cases to the Child Protection Board. Although prevention in child welfare is more than 100 years old, the policy of the last few decades dictates that family intervention should be as short, as light, and delivered by units as close to the family as possible. These provincially organized institutions[1] include the *Advies en Meldpunt Kindermishandeling* (AMK/Advice and Report point Child maltreatment), to which everybody may report suspicions of child abuse. If the Youth Care Agency evaluates a family situation as being at high risk,[2] it may bring this case to the attention of the Child Protection Board. The same case may then, after a court order, return to the Youth Care Agency, namely to the department of family supervision and guardianship.

Hence, the third layer of the child welfare system is the Child Protection Board, which is part of the Ministry of Justice and operates at the national level. It has an exclusive position in informing the court of situations in which intervention in the family is warranted. Social workers execute a social inquiry by interviewing family members and important bystanders and professionals involved. Social workers, together with the Board's lawyers, formulate a request for the family court. If the Child Protection Board assumes that the child is in real and immediate danger, it can ask the juvenile court for a temporary Emergency Protection Order (EPO; *Onder Toezicht Stelling/OTS*) that gives the Youth Care Agency immediate supervision over parental authority. The juvenile court judges cases within the frame of family law, and may order family supervision, which restricts parental authority.

CHILD PROTECTION AND CHILD WELFARE POLICIES

Child welfare has a long history in the Netherlands. Since the last decade of the 20th century, many new initiatives have emerged to advance legal regulation of child protection while at the same time offer better support to families at the local level. These initiatives have been developed in reaction to concerns about children in multiproblem families, estimated to be about 5% of all families with children (Zeijl et al., 2005). In particular, poverty, low parental educational levels, single mothers, and a non-Western cultural background are indicated as risk factors for children. The new policy initiatives seek to enhance prevention and protection of children against maltreatment and abuse by parents and/or other relatives. However, it was not only endogenous concerns that led to these policies. Since the 1990s, Dutch governments received comments and suggestions from the grassroots organization (NGO) Kinderrechtencollectief[3] and from the United Nations (UN) Committee for the Rights of Children. Both organizations are not yet satisfied with the government's child welfare initiatives. The particular sources of concern focus on the implementation of the National Action Plan against child maltreatment, the rights of child refugees, the waiting lists of the AMK, the tendency toward more repressive instead of pedagogical interventions, and poor coordination of child welfare agencies (Kinderrechtencollectief, 2008).

Initiatives to alleviate the risks of children's poor development and maltreatment include new legislation, reforms of the institutional relations between layers of child welfare, and new guidelines for professionals dealing with child protection. A major political change is that, for the first time in Dutch history, a coalition of social-democrats and Christian-democrats has created a new "programmatic" governmental department for Youth and Family in 2007. New legislation includes laws on Care for Youth (2001 and 2005), and the introduction of an income-related child benefit (2008). Also with regard to child protection, new legislation has been introduced, such as the ratification of the UN Rights of Children declaration (1995), the legal foundation of the Advice and Report Centre Child Maltreatment (Staatsblad, 2004), the redefinition of child maltreatment in both the Civil Code and in the law on Care for Youth, a National Action Plan for combatting child maltreatment (2007), and a governmental proposal for the introduction of an Electronic Child Dossier for all Dutch children (Programmaministerie van Jeugd en Gezin, 2008b). Additional legislation on reporting child maltreatment is currently under discussion.

Concerning child protection, the Dutch government took more than 10 years to implement the UN rights of children into new law. First, in 2001, the Youth Care Act extended the definition of child maltreatment to include psychical violence and humiliation:

The passive or active thrust to infants of each form of physical, psychical, or sexual interaction that is threatening or violating an infant, by parents or any other person to whom the infant has a dependent or involuntary relationship, that occasions or may occasion severe physical or psychical damage to the infant. (TK 2001–2002, 28168)

Finally, in 2007, discussions on child maltreatment in the Netherlands have resulted in an adjustment of the Civil Code, per April 25, 2007, which states:

Caring and raising children also includes the care about and the responsibility for the psychical and physical well-being of the child and its safety, plus the stimulation of its personal development. In taking care and raising children parents do not apply psychical or physical violence or any other humiliating treatment. (Burgerlijk Wetboek, art. 247, Boek 1).

At the same time, several forms of maltreatment are distinguished in the Actieplan Aanpak Kindermishandeling (*Action Plan Child Maltreatment*) of the Dutch Government: sexual abuse, physical abuse and maltreatment, emotional/psychical abuse and maltreatment, and witnessing partner violence. This Action Plan dates from 2004 and is a reaction to the demand to implement the UN program "A World Fit for Children."

The redefinition of child maltreatment sets a new norm for parenthood: parents should be aware that they not only have the obligation to care for their children without using violence or humiliation, they also are held responsible for the child's personal development. The new Civil Code not only offers an instrument for protecting children against the risk of living with offensive parents, it also redefines parental responsibilities as explicitly avoiding humiliation and as stimulating a child's personal development.

However, the language of the Code is somewhat ambiguous, leaving much room for political, juridical, and professional interpretations of what is assumed to be appropriate parental behavior. Since these interpretations must encompass the diverse cultural habits of the country's population, courts, child welfare, and other social professionals are involved in a dynamic process of interpreting the best interests of the child. That process reflects a tendency to assume that not only the 5% of families at risk, but "the family" as such is no longer a protective haven for children, for which parents hold final responsibility. This has generated considerable public debates, public inquiries, and professional considerations on the rights of children and on appropriate parental behavior. Are parents crossing the borders of the Civil Code if they harshly criticize their children (in front of their friends) for stealing in a supermarket? Do they misbehave if they slap their children for throwing a tantrum if they do not get an ice-cream cone while shopping? Are parents still allowed to criticize their teenage children who tend to drop-out from school about the consequences of that "decision," or is this confrontation interpreted as humiliating? Also, are parents still allowed to take a bath together with their children, or will this be interpreted as sexually abusive? Hazy borders separate parental responsibility to raise children well from the state's responsibility to protect children against the risk of being subjected to the aggression of their angry and aggressive or fragile and instable parents. Since the political and cultural climate influences norms and values regarding appropriate parental behavior, the borderlines are not just vague but shifting as well.

Child welfare work is a delicate business that seeks to balance between the parental right to raise children according to one's own insights, beliefs, and hopes, and the children's right to healthy development in a safe environment, free of aggression and humiliation. Traditionally, in the Netherlands, state intervention in family life is associated with state control. For that very reason, the promotion of health and welfare is contracted out to social agencies.

CHILD PROTECTION: IN PRACTICE

Until 2005, no empirical evidence on child maltreatment was available in the Netherlands, with the exception of some estimations based on the reports of Confidential Doctor offices. On basis of these reports, Roelofs and Baartman (1997: 203–204) identified 13,220 cases concerning 18,404 children that had been reported in 1993. The first prevalence study of child maltreatment was conducted in 2005, by IJzendoorn et al. (2007). This study drew on interviews with 1,100 professionals across the country who worked with children. In addition, the researchers analyzed the registrations of the AMK. IJzendoorn and his colleagues concluded that about 3% of all children between 0 and 18 years old (110,000 out of 3.5 million children) have experienced maltreatment, such as physical or emotional neglect and neglect of education. Although, on basis of this study, no conclusions could be drawn on the actual prevalence of child maltreatment, the findings revealed that reported cases contained seven times more children of parents with very limited education and five times more children in families where both parents were unemployed. The researchers estimate the number of sexually abused children at about 4,700, and another 19,000 children who were physically abused. The finding that 3% of the children in the Netherlands were maltreated came as an unexpected shock.

Generalizing on the basis of a (according to the researchers) representative study, Lamers-Winkelman, Slot, Bijl, and Vijlbrief (2007) concluded that 7% of Dutch children suffered during the past 12 months from a combination of different kinds of maltreatment, and as many as 20% of children below the age of 15 had experienced at least one kind of maltreatment. Moreover, a third of Dutch children at some time had experienced serious psychical aggression by their parents, physical violence at home, sexual abuse, or serious neglect, or was aware of physical conflicts between their parents. This study is based upon self-reporting by young people (N = 1,845 high school students at 14 randomly chosen schools throughout the country). Whether this method resulted in more reliable data is open to question.

In addition to the high, and unexpected, number of children at risk found in both studies, a comparison of both studies makes clear that many cases of child maltreatment never reach professional youth workers and are not reported to the AMKs. The literature offers several explanations for such underreporting of child maltreatment. First, despite the policy rhetoric in support of prevention, serious cutbacks in preventive child care have reduced professional capacity.

The "neighborhood nurse" disappeared, school doctors have less intensive check-ups with children, and, since the beginning of the 21st century, highly rated "consultation offices" for babies and young children have suffered financial cut-backs. The Dutch Inspector of Health, Van der Wal (2009), writes in a letter to the Minister of Youth and Family that the foundation of the new local Centres for Family and Youth will probably go at the cost of already existing and well-func-tioning youth health care offices, and that local authorities had already proposed to reduce the number of contacts between professionals and children. These con-cerns, however, seem to be exaggerated according to a recent report (MOgroep, 2009) of the MO Group that monitors developments in Youth Care. This report shows that, in 2008, 7% more children (95,000 vs. 70,000) received support from the Youth Care Agency than in 2007, and that these children had a shorter wait-ing time (12.5 vs. 16 weeks) to receive support. The kind of support that these children received includes ambulatory care, foster care, and juvenile care. The report praises the increasing effectiveness of the Youth Care Agency, noting a decrease in the average length of ambulatory as well as of juvenile care per child.

Underreporting of child abuse may also reflect the fact that, until recently, professional child care workers, teachers, youth workers, and family doctors had no obligation to report child maltreatment. Based on past practice, it may be that most professionals tend to give priority to supporting families rather than intervening and reporting maltreatment. From that perspective, being confronted with signs of child abuse does not automatically have to result in a punishing attitude toward or sanctions against the parents. It is assumed that they have problems themselves and need help. A sanctioning approach is seen by many professional child and youth workers as too-severe and unhelpful an intervention into private family life (Baeten, 2001).

This tendency toward supporting rather than sanctioning families coincides with other child welfare practices during the last decade, such as the preference of provincial administrations for ambulatory programs for families and juve-niles at risk, even in cases where serious problems exist. Moreover, less far-reaching arrangements, such as family support programs or temporary fos-ter care, are preferred over institutional placements for children who can no longer live with their original families. From 2000, the number of children liv-ing in foster families has almost doubled from 5 to 10/1,000 Dutch children below the age of 20. In 2008, more than 22,243 children live in foster care; the number of children entering foster care for the first time more than doubled to 8,122 children and adolescents.

In spite of the policy emphasis on organizing child welfare interventions as light-handedly and as close to family life as possible, repressive solutions for problematic youth have become more common. Since 1998, the capacity of Judicial Youth Centres increased from 1,581 to 2,758 in 2007. In these centers, juveniles are received with different judicial backgrounds, either penal or civic placements. The so-called penal placements include juveniles with detention on demand, detention, and juveniles with a placement order because of a violent or vice-related incident (these juveniles are assessed with a developmental disturbance). Civic placements include juveniles who are placed by the court "in the best interest of their development." From 2010, these two categories of juveniles will no longer stay together in the same center. The Minister of Youth and Family recently announced that the capacity for closed placements will be increased from around 1,150 in 2009 to 1,590 in 2013 (Rouvoet, 2009).

If a child is in real and immediate danger, the Child Protection Board asks the juvenile court for a temporary EPO (*Onder Toezicht Stelling/OTS*), which gives the Youth Care Agency immediate supervision of parental authority. No figures are available on the number of children who are placed out of home for reasons of child maltreatment. The Child Protection Board, as Roelofs and Baartman (1997) indicated, did not register child abuse cases, nor decisions taken in those cases in 1997, and they still do not. The main reason for this absence of hard data is that the Child Protection Board does not have to legally prove maltreatment as the reason for children's outplacement. Their judgment for outplacement is typically based on "social evidence"; that is, the conviction that several "risk factors" undeniably exist and present strong reasons for intervention. In order to recommend a family intervention that might limit parental authority, child welfare workers need not prove that the parents have abused their children. Rather, they have to make a reasonable case that a family intervention would be in the child's best interest (Van Nijnatten, 2007). Separately, each observation may be insufficient to convince judicial authorities, but the sequence and accumulation of events suggestive of a relationship among them makes this social evidence hard to dispute. Or, as Dingwall says, "Many of these observations relate to deviations from a model of normality whose finer details are so woven into a front-line worker's framing of a particular event as to be almost impossible to formulate separately in the manner that the construction of a legally manageable case would require" (1983, pp. 150–151). Research organizations related to the Ministry of Justice (such as the Scientific Research and Documentation Centre/WODC) and Dutch Statistics do not keep records of child maltreatment–related out-of-home placement rates. The only data available at Dutch Statistics concern family supervision orders. Table 11.1 shows that the number of EPOs, which gives the Youth Care Agency immediate supervision of parental authority, increases steadily (after a drop in the 1970s and 1980s) from 2% to more than 3% of all children aged 12–18.

There are several reasons for putting children under supervision of the Youth Care Agency. In addition to protecting them from maltreatment, children with severe behavioral and educational problems and criminal young adolescents can be put under supervision. Given these different reasons, data on EPO provide at best tentative insights into child maltreatment trends in the Netherlands. It is

Table 11.1: Emergency Protection Order (Epo) Per Year; New Pupils, Finished Epo, Pupils Per 31 December

Year	New Pupils	Finished OTS	Pupils Per 31–12
1998	5,447	4,838	19,445
1999	5,598	5,246	20,441
2000	5,513	5,203	20,955
2001	4,957	5,442	20,605
2002	5,378	5,890	20,429
2003	6,670	5,243	21,415
2004	6,745	5,594	22,243
2005	7,701	5,865	23,979
2006	8,279	6,009	26,379
2007			29,503
2008			31,820

Source: Dutch Statistics, Voorburg/Heerlen 14-08-2008.

plausible that the rise in coercive family interventions illustrated in Table 11.1 stems in part from the increasing public attention to child abuse.

The length of an EPO is 1 year at maximum, although the court can decide to prolong the measure every year until the child reaches the age of 18. If a child is put under supervision of the Youth Care Agency for reasons of child abuse or maltreatment, the court can also decide to place the child with a foster family or in a residential home. This out-of-home placement can be made without parental consent, but can last for only 3 months. During that period, the Child Protection Board has to investigate whether a child protection measure is needed. In cases that require a family supervision order, a family supervisor is appointed who monitors the family and starts negotiations with the family members in order to deal with the social factors that put the child in danger. Dutch Family Law has two other family orders, one in which parents voluntarily consent to relinquish parental authority, and another in which the court abrogates their authority. Only a minimal number of children (on average 15) are adopted annually from the child welfare system. Under these two orders, parental authority is completely severed and the child is placed under the guardianship of a private agency that is authorized and paid by the government. In most cases, the child is (temporarily) placed in an environment different from that of the family of origin. The case-worker of the Child Protection Board tries to understand how parents and children view and experience their predicament, and may also get information from professionals who are involved with the family. Although parents have the right to employ their own professional experts, in practice they rarely take advantage of this right.

DUTCH CHILD PROTECTION: A NEW AGENDA FOR THE 21ST CENTURY

During the last decades of the 20th century, combatting child abuse became a major part of Dutch child welfare policy. In this period, the new Confidential Doctors agency drew public attention to child abuse as a problem with an unprecedented number of victims. Yet exact figures were hard to come by, especially because of the difficulty in distinguishing between child maltreatment and other child protection cases. Actually, the term "child abuse" has broadened during the past decade, and now includes cases in which parents are assumed to be incapable of socializing their children properly. When he came into power, Rouvoet, the minister of Youth and Family, introduced several important policies to the domain of child maltreatment. Two new policy initiatives aimed at changing the child protection system involved the Electronic Child Dossier (ECD; Programmaministerie Jeugd en Gezin, 2008b) and the *Actieplan Aanpak Kindermishandeling* (Action Plan Tackling Child Maltreatment) (TK 2006–2007, 31 015, nr. 16).

The ECD and the additional *Verwijsindex risicojongeren* (Youth at Risk Index) aim to coordinate signals from all societal domains in which children participate voluntarily or involuntarily: (youth) care, labor market, and social assistance, as well as juvenile agencies. If professional staff in one of these domains signals a risk for a young person and a second risk signal is registered that offers a "match" to the initial reporting professional staff, these signals are taken as an indication that the agencies must coordinate their activities. In this way, a comprehensive network of surveillance is created to identify young people at risk. The Youth at Risk index is based on a national ICT system because, as the minister explains: "Coordination above the local level is important because the life world of young people includes several municipalities, and some social agencies work in several municipalities too. In addition, the index can follow young people if they move from one municipality to another" (Programmaministerie Jeugd en Gezin, 2008b, p. 24).

The ECD, which was implemented in 2008, contains all the paperwork available in the local youth health care centers. Since nearly all parents of newborn Dutch children visit the youth health care centers for advice, vaccination, health control, and the like, this dossier will cover almost the entire population of Dutch youth within a few decades. The intention is to link these data with information about prenatal care, birth, and later, information from school and family doctors (general practitioners).

The minister of Youth and Family also intended to implement the ECD on a national level and to record all the ECD data centrally. This has been contested for several reasons. First, the ECD still has to be adjusted to meet the criteria of Dutch privacy law. Various professional organizations hesitate to cooperate with the ECD process because they are not convinced (yet) that the privacy of their young clients and their parents are guaranteed. Professionals criticize this control-oriented policy based exclusively on information, which replaced former policies that were based more on trust and negotiation-oriented. The national organization of medical specialists refuses for reasons of confidentiality to share its data with the police and the Ministry of Justice.

Second, many citizens, and in particular liberal political parties, object to the ECD because of its intrusiveness. The ECD, as proposed by the government, not only includes medical information, but also contains a number of questions that many people think should not be made public information. For instance, the ECD questionnaire asks parents of newborn children if they have made love without having coitus: The possible answers are no, never; yes, we did once; yes, a few times; yes, often. Another question that has surprised some members of parliament refers to the parents' private parts, in particular the characteristics of their pubic hair. Parents can choose, among other answers: (a) dark curled hair, (b) dispersed to the thigh-bones, or (c) nonpigmented hair along labia. In response to these severe objections to a national electronic system by many professional organizations and citizens alike, minister Rouvoet withdrew the proposal for a centralized ECD archive in 2009. Instead, all youth healthcare organizations will be obliged to record data on every child, his or her family situation, and the child's environment electronically from June 2010 onward.

The Action Plan (*Actieplan Aanpak Kindermishandeling*) policy initiative intends to: (a) prevent child maltreatment; (b) signal it in an early stage; (c) stop it as soon as it happens by an active intervention of youth care, youth protection, penal law, and combinations of these interventions; and (d) limit the damaging effects of child maltreatment (TK, 2006–2007, 31 015, nr. 16). A main objective is to reduce the waiting lists of the AMK, for which additional money (a part of the 10–20 million that is budgeted to support this strategy) is reserved in 2007 and 2008.

Confidential doctors and social workers are the main professional groups working at the AMKs, which are part of the Youth Care Agency. A variety of professionals and their organizations can, and some must, report suspected cases of maltreatment. Importantly, professionals working in Youth Care Agencies are obliged to report any suspicion of child maltreatment by their colleagues, and the organization itself has to report to the AMK immediately. However, this reporting obligation only extends to colleagues within the organization. Professionals are not obliged to report suspicion of child maltreatment outside their organization, nor by parents. In addition, the Ministry of Health, Welfare, and Sports developed a Reporting Code for professionals who work with children (family doctors, confidential doctors, child care workers, teachers, sporting coaches, etc.), which was implemented in 2006. This Reporting Code includes directives for professionals on how and to whom they can report if they suspect maltreatment, but it remains on a voluntary basis.

The Reporting Code has a rather long history in the Netherlands, in contrast to many other European countries that have implemented a compulsory reporting code only in the 1990s. Since 1998, the National Youth Council (at that time an Advisory board of the Dutch government) recommended the development of a code on child maltreatment. At first, the Ministry of Health, Welfare, and Sport agreed, but it did not take any initiative until the end of the 1990s. The NGO *Werkgroep Meldpunt Kindermishandeling* (Working Group Report Centre on Child Maltreatment) again strongly recommended the establishment of a reporting code, but it took another 5 years before the Ministry developed the current Reporting Code. The arguments against introducing compulsory reporting were (a) fear that too many false reports would be made, (b) compulsory reporting does not improve signals of maltreatment, (c) compulsory reporting can be a risk for the relationship between professionals and their clients, and (d) it would be hard to maintain the obligation to report (Baeten, 2001). Although it is difficult to prove empirically, we assume that the decision not to introduce a compulsory reporting code was inspired to some extent by the "moral panic" in reaction to false reports in the 1990s (for instance, in the Bolderkar affair, as described by Roelofs and Baartman [1997]) and in combination with cutbacks in the youth care sector. The issue, however, remains on the table, since both the UN committee and the NGO Kinderrechtencollectief insist on a compulsory code.

The Netherlands Institute for Care and Welfare has developed a guideline including a five-step procedure for professionals to follow in cases of suspected child maltreatment: (1) the suspicion phase, (2) deliberations with colleagues, (3) more investigations, (4) start of support, and (5) after-care (Baeten, 2001, 2002). For steps 2 through 5, the professional who suspects maltreatment can be supervised, at his own request by the AMK; the AMK, however, does not offer direct support to the child. This reporting code is mainly based on the assumption of professional support for the child and his or her parents, in which case the professional can manage the whole process. However, this approach depends on parental cooperation and approval. For instance, step 3 demands more investigations, which could include medical expertise. This step cannot be taken without parental consent. In cases in which parents do not cooperate or refuse to approve further investigations, the professional can report the case to the AMK, which in turn reports the case to the Child Protection Board. Then the case shifts from the domain and service orientation of family support to a penal/criminal domain, and from the jurisdiction of the Ministry of Health, Welfare, and Sports to the Ministry of Justice.

Thus far, fewer than half of these organizations have introduced the code. In a web-based survey of about 1,500 professionals, 83% answered that they had encountered suspected cases of maltreatment, and 80% were in favor of a reporting code (Dekker en Volaart, 2008). On the basis of this survey, minister Rouvoet is considering to oblige professional organizations to introduce the code. In 2009, a public debate on the obligation of professionals to report signs of child abuse was ongoing in relation to the introduction of the code for ambulance staff. These professionals hesitated to accept the code because they perceived it as contradictory to and even undermining of their efforts to offer direct help in cases of emergency. They argued that if citizens realize that the ambulance staff might report "inappropriate" behavior behind the front door, people might avoid calling for help. In addition, criteria for inappropriate behavior are contested: What exactly should be reported, and what are the limits of private autonomy?

To stimulate a more active professional approach to child abuse, a new strategy labelled RAAK (named after the NGO that developed the strategy) has been implemented on a national scale (Programmaministerie Jeugd en Gezin, 2008b). Initiated by psychiatrist Von Dantzig and advanced by developmental psychologists Hermanns and Ter Meulen (2007), this strategy focuses on the integration of professional support for children and young people by using child maltreatment as a "spotlight and a crowbar" for analyzing and filling the existing gaps in youth care work. From 2003 to 2006, the strategy was tested in four Dutch regions by Hermanns and Ter Meulen, as well as by the programming department of Youth and Family. The Dutch parliament concluded that the results of these experiments were promising enough to implement the strategy on a national scale (Hermanns & Ter Meulen, 2007). By 2011, the strategy is expected to be implemented throughout the country under the direction of the National Youth Institute (TK, 2006–2007, 31 015, nr. 16). The application of this strategy will involve financial supports for prevention and low-threshold Centres for Youth and Family (CJG), dissemination of a RAAK handbook for professionals who work with children, a public opinion campaign financed by the government, the implementation of the Reporting Code in all organizations that work with children, the dispersal of and a website on a *Manual Domestic Violence and Professional Confidence* for professional workers, and an ECD containing a wealth of information on each child from birth, based on his or her contacts with professional youth health care professionals.

ASSESSMENT OF THE NEW AGENDA: TWO PERSPECTIVES

This chapter shows how child maltreatment legislation has broadened the definition of maltreatment by including humiliation and the parents' duty to stimulate child development, therefore explicitly including more (although vaguely defined) causes of parental failure. At the same time, the number of children and adolescents in foster care has doubled since 2000, and there has been a steady increase of young people in Juvenile Centres and under EPOs (in absolute numbers as well as in percentages). From one perspective, the increasing numbers of children in care might be seen as a reflection of the increasing effectiveness of the Dutch system of child protection. Over the last decade, reporting procedures were improved through the introduction of the Reporting Code and AMKs, and efforts were made to better coordinate responsibilities among the three layers of the child welfare system. The limited data available indicate that while more children are at risk than previously had been assumed, the Youth Care Agencies seem, for the first time in the recent history, to provide better support to those children and to need less time to do so. From this perspective, one might conclude that good progress has been made over the last decade in the protection of children at risk in the Netherlands. In addition, one might see the growth of the number of children in foster families as evidence that more children at risk are being identified and that the support for these children has been provided in the sphere of (another) family, rather than in institutional settings. Also, the new centers for Family and Youth point to the direction of providing community family supports.

However, in assessing these developments, another, more critical perspective bears consideration. The current tendency to put more children under state control (either in foster families or in juvenile centers) also reflects a tendency toward repressive interventions rather than services that support family life. These repressive measures strike at some types of families more than others. As indicated by van Zeijl (2005) and van IJzendoorn (2007), children are mainly at risk in unemployed, low-income families in which both parents have low levels of education. Also, children in large families, stepfamilies, and single-parent families are more at risk than average.

A critical perspective on developments over the last decade also questions how well the new policy agenda is able to balance support for the privacy of family life with protection of the best interests of the child. It has taken a long time for successive Dutch governments to succeed in implementing legal rules for child protection according to the international criteria. These new laws however, are open to interpretation in both the courts and in professional practices. And that is where confusion and even arbitrariness come to the fore: Open-ended and vague concepts such as "stimulating child development" create a growing tendency to assume that parents a priori do not know what is best for their children, or how to behave in their best interests. In addition to severe and deadly incidents of maltreatment (as in the cases of Savannah, "Mass-girl," and "Nulde girl," described in the introduction), an increasing number of other problems, such as school drop-outs and children suffering from attention-deficit hyperactivity disorder (ADHD) and obesity, are seen as indications of malfunctioning families. Such broadening of the definition of malfunctioning creates a playing field for intervening "behind the front door" of any family, as with the ECD. Yet, this has not led to a total imputation of family responsibility, since at the same time, family-like and noninstitutional out-of-home care for children has become more popular in Dutch child welfare.

Professionals appear to be rather insecure about how to interpret child protection, and also how to interpret the family conditions of children at risk. In the severe and deadly cases mentioned above, professionals in a dozen social work organizations were involved for years in supervising these families. The new and stricter laws do not solve the problem of clearly interpreting the conditions of risk. The introduction of the RAAK method and the professional obligation to report signs of child maltreatment aim to intervene in an earlier stage of maltreatment, in the hope of avoiding serious harm. These new instruments are contested, however, because some professional groups fear that troubled families will no longer ask for help if they are aware that the professionals are obliged to report their misbehavior. So, in the end, child and youth care workers are left with the task of balancing pedagogical autonomy of the family on the one hand and child protection on the other—a task as old as child protection itself. New procedures to prevent child abuse or to deal correctively with abusive families may then be considered as efforts to redefine criteria for intervening in families (in order to protect children's rights), while avoiding strict criteria for appropriate parental behavior (in order to recognize cultural and social diversity and to maintain room for professional negotiation with parents).

Finally, the current political context is one in which the Dutch government leans toward a liberal paternalistic approach, which implies a strong focus on moral policies without offering much support for preventive measures, such as good-quality child care, the once very effective children's consultation offices, or temporary homes for young adolescents. Child maltreatment is only a small part of the agenda of the new department for Youth and Family, which is now signing covenants with professional organizations to report child abuse or maltreatment wherever they see it. Reducing poverty, and promoting safety and health are other and more central foci. The "liberal paternalistic" strategy of the department broadcasts a moral message that families frequently malfunction, thereby offering legitimacy for professional surveillance and electronic monitoring of every family in the country, and subsequently for intervention if the signals are strong enough. At the same time, liberal paternalism expresses support for the view that children are best cared for within their families, which provides legitimacy for policies such as the so-called "kitchen subsidy" for nonworking mothers (home care for children without strong quality criteria) and an income-related children's allowance. Thus, in their own way, liberal-paternalist child welfare politicians strive to achieve the elusive balance between care and control. Most of these family interventions are corrective in the Foucaultian way—meaning that these interventions are "productive" by seeking to support the family's autonomy instead of undermining it.

NOTES

1   The three biggest Dutch cities are considered as a province in terms of how they deal with child welfare.
2   Situations of high risk are serious suspicion of sexual abuse, immediate medical danger, and repeated serious conduct disorders of the minor.

3 Kinderrechtencollectief (Rights for Children Association) is an NGO that joins forces with Defence for Children International Nederland, UNICEF Nederland, De Landelijke Vereniging voor Kinderen en Jongerenrechtswinkels (National Association for Children and Youth Law shops), and the Nederlandse Jeugdgroep (Dutch Youth Group).

REFERENCES

Baeten, P. (2001). *Niet bij melden alleen. Achtergrond van de meldcode kindermishandeling voor beroepsgroepen* [Not only reporting. Background of the reporting code child maltreatment for professional groups]. Utrecht: NIZW.

Baeten, P. (2002). *Meldcode kindermishandeling. Richtlijnen voor het handelen van beroepskrachten* [Reporting code child maltreatment, Guidelines for professionals]. Utrecht: NIZW. Expertisecentrum Kindermishandeling.

Dekker, M., & Volaart, M. (2008). *Beroepskrachten missen in hun opleiding aandacht voor kindermishandeling* [Professionals lack of attention for child maltreatment in their curriculum]. *Tijdschrift voor Kindermishandeling*, landelijke enquête, mei 2008.

Dingwall, R., Eekelaar, J., & Murray, T. (1983). *The protection of children: State intervention and family life.* Oxford: Basil Blackwell.

Dutch Statistics. (2008). *Statline*, Voorburg/Heerlen. Retrieved August 14, 2008 from http://statline.cbs.nl/statweb/

Hermanns, J., & ter Meulen, M. (2007). *Het Regio Raak Experiment* [The regional Raak Experiment]. Woerden/Amsterdam: Eindverslag.

van IJzendoorn, M.H., Prinzie, P., Euser, E.M., Groeneveld, M.G., Brilleslijper-Kater, S.N. van Noort-van der Linden, A.M.T., et al. (2007). *Kindermishandeling in Nederland Anno 2005. De Nationale Prevalentiestudie Mishandeling van Kinderen en Jeugdigen (NPM-2005)* [Child maltreatment in the Netherlands in 2005. The national prevalence study on maltreatment of children and young persons]. Leiden: Casimir Publishers.

Inspectie Jeugdzorg. (2005). *Onderzoek naar de kwaliteit van het hulpverleningsproces aan S* [Study on the quality of the support process to S]. Utrecht: Ministerie van Volksgezondheid, Welzijn en Sport, Inspectie Jeugdzorg.

Kinderrechtencollectief. (2008). *Children's rights in the Netherlands. The Third Report of the Dutch NGO Coalition for Children's Rights on the Implementation of the Convention of the Rights of the Child.* Retrieved July 29, 2008 from www.kinderrechten.nl.

de Kruif, R.E.L., Riksen-Walraven, J.M.A., Gevers-Deynoot-Schaub, M.J.J.M., Helmerhorst, K.O.W., Tavecchio, L.W.C., & Fukkink, R.G. (2008). *Pedagogische kwaliteit van de opvang voor 0–4 jarigen in Nederlandse kinderdagverblijven in 2008* [Pedagogical quality of the care for 0 to 4 years old in Dutch childcare centres]. Leiden/Amsterdam: Nederlands Consortium Kinderopvang Onderzoek.

Lamers-Winkelman F., Slot, N.W., Bijl, B., & Vijlbrief, A.C. (2007). *Scholieren over Mishandeling. Resultaten van een landelijk onderzoek naar de omvang van kindermishandeling onder leerlingen van het voortgezet onderwijs* [Pupils and maltreatment. Results of a national study on the degree of child maltreatment among pupils of secondary schools]. Amsterdam/Duivendrecht: PI Research.

MOgroep. (2009). *Brancherapportage 2008* [Sector report 2008]. Utrecht: MOgroep.

Nijnatten, van C. (1988). Discourses in Dutch child welfare inquiries. *British Journal of Criminology, 28*, 494–512.

Nijnatten, van C. (2007). Balancing care and control: Good practice in assessing an allegation of child sexual abuse. *Social Work and Social Sciences Review, 12*, 29–47.

Programmaministerie voor Jeugd en Gezin. (2008a). *De kracht van het gezin. Nota gezinsbeleid 2008* [The strength of the family. White paper on family policy 2008]. Den Haag: Programmaministerie voor Jeugd en Gezin.

Programmaministerie voor Jeugd en Gezin. (2008b) *Alle kansen voor alle kinderen. Programma Jeugd en Gezin 2007–2011* [All chances for all children. Program Youth and Family 2007–2011]. Den Haag: Programmaministerie voor Jeugd en Gezin.

Roelofs, M.A., & Baartman, H.E.M. (1997). The Netherlands: Responding to abuse–compassion or control? In N. Gilbert (Ed.), *Combatting child abuse: International perspectives and trends*, pp. 192–211. New York/Oxford: Oxford University Press.

Rouvoet, A. (2009). *Antwoorden op kamervragen van Langkamp over het bericht dat vanaf 1 augustus jeugdigen met een machtiging voor gesloten jeugdzorg alleen nog maar kunnen worden aangemeld en opgenomen in een gesloten jeugdzorginstelling* [Letter to the Dutch Parliament (7-7-2009). Den Haag: Tweede Kamer der Staten Generaal.

Staatsblad. (2004). *Wet op Jeugdzorg* [Youth care act]. Den Haag: Staatsblad 306.

TK 2001–2002: 28169. *Regeling van de aanspraak op, de toegang tot en de bekostiging van jeugdzorg (Wet op de jeugdzorg)* [Regulation of the right on and the access to youth care and its costs (Youth Care Act)]. Den Haag: Tweede Kamer der Staten Generaal.

TK 2006–2007, 31 015, nr. 16 *Actieplan Aanpak Kindermishandeling: Kinderen veilig thuis.* [Action Plan tackling child maltreatment. Children safe at home]. Den Haag: Ministerie van Jeugd en Gezin.

Vermeer, H.J., van IJzendoorn, M.H., de Kruif, R.E.L., Fukkink, R.G., Tavechio, L.W.C., Riksen-Walraven, J.M.A., & Van Zeijl, J. (2005). *Kwaliteit van Nederlandse kinderdagverblijven: Trends in kwaliteit in de jaren 1995–2005* [Quality of Dutch childcare centres: Trends in quality from 1995 to 2005]. Leiden/Amsterdam: Nederlands Consortium Kinderopvang Onderzoek.

Wal, G.V.D. (2009). *Brief aan Minister Rouvoet over de oprichting van Centra voor jeugd en Gezin* [Letter to Minister Rouvoet on the introduction of Centres for Youth and Family]. Den Haag: Ministerie van Volksgezondheid, Welzijn en Sport, Inspectie voor de gezondheidszorg.

PART IV

CONCLUSION

12

CHANGING PATTERNS OF RESPONSE AND EMERGING ORIENTATIONS

NEIL GILBERT, NIGEL PARTON, AND MARIT SKIVENES

As noted in the introduction, the purpose of this book is to analyze how child protection systems have developed in ten countries since the mid-1990s, building on the work originally reported in *Combatting Child Abuse: International Perspectives and Trends* (Gilbert, 1997). Within this general purview, we have sought to assess the extent to which the child protection and family service orientations still reflect the differences previously identified in the countries studied and whether their characteristics continue to provide a helpful framework for analyzing and comparing different systems. How have the changes analyzed over the intervening 15 years impacted the structure and functioning of child welfare arrangements designed to guard against maltreatment? Have the changes in particular countries been such that some countries previously characterized as oriented toward child protection may now have many of the characteristics of the family service orientation, and have other countries moved in the opposite direction? Can we identify the emergence of any new orientations that cannot be easily accommodated within child protection or family services orientations, and does this alter the balance between private and public responsibility for children?

CHANGING CONTEXTS

Before we address these questions in the light of the data and analyses in this volume, it is important to be aware of some of the most significant changes in the social, political, and economic contexts that have impacted all the countries included in our study. This is not to suggest that such changes were not evident before the mid-1990s, nor that they have effected all countries equally. However, it is notable that many of our contributors have discussed the nature and impact of these developments and their implications for child welfare policy and practice. A number of chapters refer to the growing significance of neo-liberal ideas, the influence of globalization, and the increased awareness of uncertainty and insecurity in a "risk society" (Beck, 1992). The past 15 years have seen an intensification of global competition, wide-ranging mobility of capital and labor, the speeding up of economic processes, and the increasing interdependence of national economies, which have contributed to the erosion of states' abilities to control their economies. The massive global downturn since 2007, following the "credit crunch" and the crisis in the global banking and financial sectors have demonstrated this very starkly.

The nature and pace of change varies and the way governments have responded differs. Although some countries, such as Canada, have been particularly influenced by a neo-liberal doctrine, others—including England, Denmark, Finland, and Germany—have attempted to combine an emphasis on both liberal individualism and a more conservative communitarianism: what some have described as a "liberal communitarian" policy mix (Jordan, 2006). The approach has brought together an emphasis on individual autonomy and the mobility of market relations with elements of a socially conservative view of the "family" and civil society, and lends particular importance to individual "responsibility." The shift from public to private responsibility has transformed the collectivist legacy of the "welfare state" (Gilbert, 2004). The neo-liberal doctrine assumes that not only do individuals want more consumer freedom and choices, but that they will also be required to become more self-reliant and "active." Instead of expecting collective solutions to issues arising from the life cycle and the economy, citizens are required to develop personal resources and material property to cope with all eventualities. The best way of overcoming "social exclusion" is seen as encouraging/requiring that everyone actively engage with the labor market.

In analyzing how child welfare systems have responded to the problems of child abuse and neglect over the last 15 years, we first examine the common themes and developments that have appeared and then turn to the broader question of whether any new orientations have emerged within the larger context of social, economic, and political change during this period.

SOME COMMON THEMES AND DEVELOPMENTS

The rapid and often dramatic pace of organizational, policy, and legislative change is evident everywhere and is, in itself, a compelling development in child protection systems. In sorting out these changes, we reviewed specific policies and programs in the ten countries, grappling with a whole range of definitional issues prompted by both linguistic and cultural translation, together with the different histories, and organizational boundaries and remits. Despite these differences, we have identified a number of common themes and developments that mark this period, which are discussed below.

The Challenge of Operating in the Public Spotlight

In many of the countries studied, child welfare and child protection have taken on a high public and political profile, due in large measure to intense media coverage of what Best (1990) describes as "atrocity tales." Stories of human suffering and fatal cases of child abuse have in some countries played a key role as drivers for change in publishing these tragedies and holding child welfare professionals and senior managers and, increasingly, politicians to account, often in a vindictive way. The cases of the "Maas-girl" and the "Nulde girl" in the Netherlands, for example, led to an official inquiry that instigated legal proceedings against the child welfare supervisor; fatal cases of abuse in Germany drew widespread public attention and led to charges brought against child protection workers; in the late 1990s, charges of negligent homicide were brought against a child welfare worker in Canada. The Dutroux case in Belgium incited 300,000 people to march in the streets expressing their outrage, which led to a National Commission report that contained 63 recommendations for change. The suicide of a 15-year-old girl in Sweden the day before a court hearing on her sexual abuse case prompted a public outcry against social authorities for being too lenient and too hesitant to intervene in cases of abuse. The death of "baby Peter" in England put tremendous pressure on the government Minister to initiate wide-scale change, the full results of which remain to be seen.

The child protection field is a realm of public policy that draws considerably more gripping media attention than other spheres of social welfare that address, for example, problems of aging, disability, and unemployment. Public attention clearly has an important impact on the culture in which the work is carried out and might put particular pressure on politicians to show they are "doing something." The vulnerability to explosive media response to tragic cases of abuse lends a high degree of volatility and uncertainty to this field. England, Canada, Sweden, and Germany report major challenges to the professional workforce, as the high profile of child protection opens practice to public scrutiny and often to criticisms about the qualifications, skills, and quality of work carried out by front-line professionals—particularly social workers. In some countries—with England being perhaps the most extreme example—there are major challenges in recruiting and retaining staff and the turnover is considerable.

The Expansion of Child Welfare Systems

All the countries have experienced a general expansion in their child welfare systems since the mid-1990s, although the degree of expansion is uneven and varies among countries and types of child welfare system. The expansion is manifest in the broadening definitions of need/risk, and the number of children and families that are in receipt of services, that come to the notice of statutory child welfare agencies, and that are placed out of home. However, as with all the different figures we are comparing, these numbers and rates are fraught with crucial definitional and interpretive problems. Thus, as we will return to in the discussion below, the data cannot be assumed to reflect any definitive differences in policy and practice among the countries.

Countries that were previously designated as having a family service orientation, whether they had a mandatory reporting system or not, have shown a notable increase in the number of children seen as needing child protection services—whether they have had a high-profile "scandal" or not. In contrast, the United States, which was previously identified with the child protection orientation, appears to be moving in the other direction, as the number of children receiving prevention services increased five-fold from 10.1/1,000 children in 1997 to 50.7/1,000 children in 2007. Although this increase is partly attributable to a change in the method used to count those receiving services, the United States now seems to offer a much more differentiated response, with a greater emphasis on preventive family services. It is also notable that in the United States, Canada, and England, neglect has become the predominant child maltreatment category, with considerable declines in cases categorized as physical or sexual abuse.

In spite of this increase in the number of children coming within the purview of child welfare and receiving a variety of community- and home-based services to both prevent harm and improve their welfare, the numbers in out-of-home care have not declined. In most countries, the number of children per thousand in out-of-home care have increased slightly, and in Finland, significantly. Even so, the rates of children in out-of-home care vary considerably among countries, as shown in Table 12.1.

Interestingly, the three countries that were categorized as having a child protection focus do not follow the same patterns in out-of-home placements. The United States showed a decline in the number of children in out-of-home care, from 8/1,000 children in 1997 to 6/1,000 in 2007. In contrast, Canada and England have had an increase in the numbers of children in care from 4/1,000 in 1991 to 9.7/1,000 in 2007 in Canada, a remarkable increase, and in England from 4.5/1,000 in 1994 up to 5.5/1,000 in 2009. To understand the meaning of this change, it is important to note that the increase is accounted for not by a rise in admissions to care, which actually fell by a third, but by a slower rate of exit, with children remaining in care for longer periods of time. However, in the United States, there's a comparatively higher rate of children who exit the system due to adoptions, whereas in Canada and England fewer children are adopted from the child welfare system. This sheds some light on the different dynamics of placement rates among the countries.

Table 12.1: Out-of-Home Care Rates Per 1,000 Children

	Before	Now
USA	8 (1997)	6 (2007)
Canada	4 (1991)	9.7 (2007)
England	4.5 (1994)	5.5 (2009)
Sweden	6 (2000)	6.6 (2007)
Finland*	8 (1994)	12 (2007)
Denmark	9.5 (1993)	10.2 (2007)
Norway	5.8 (1994)	8.2 (2008)
Germany	9.5 (1995)	9.9 (2005)
Belgium	7.9 (2004)	8.6 (2008)
Netherlands**	8.4 (2000)	10 (2009)

* Numbers are through the year
** Source: CBS Statline/Childprotection; 2010

When we then look at the countries previously categorized as having a family service orientation an interesting trend emerges. Generally—but not always— the levels of children in out-of-home care are higher (certainly than in England and the United States) or have at least been maintained at their early 1990s levels. For example, the figure of just over 10/1,000 children is more or less constant in Denmark, and has also been more or less constant in Belgium (about 8/1,000), Germany (9.7/1,000), and Sweden (6.3/1,000). Although these data suggest that those countries characterized as following a family service orientation in *the mid-1990s*, particularly the Nordic countries, seem to have a higher out-of-home placement rate than those that followed a child protection orientation, the interpretation of these figures bears close examination. The Finnish rate is twice that of England, but it represents a much broader child welfare response to "youth problems," including delinquency, than that in England, where such behaviors are more likely to be seen in terms of "youth offending" and dealt with by the criminal justice system. As a result, although in England the number of children and young people in penal custody increased from 1,415 in 1991 to 2,825 in 2005, the numbers of youngsters in Finland's penal system continued to decline—a trend accelerating since the late 1970s. By 2003, the number of young people in Finland's penal system was down to under 10 per year—as more were being directed into the child welfare arena (Muncie & Goldson, 2006). The comparable low portion of out-of-home placements in Sweden is surprising, particularly given the fact that in Sweden the out-of-home placement rate includes mental illness and delinquency, as well as child protection. Out-of-home placements are therefore noticeably lower here than most other countries. However, as Cocozza and Hort explain, Sweden has seemed reluctant to take concerns about child abuse and neglect seriously, which reflects an effort to distance itself from the reputation it had by the early 1980s of being the "Kinder Gulag" (Gould, 1988). In Denmark and Finland, a proportion of the higher out-of-home placement rates is accounted for by the higher numbers "in care" on a voluntary basis, with the agreement of the parents.

Another important dimension in the analysis of out-of-home placement rates involves the differences in age. The United States, England, and Canada typically have younger children placed out-of-home, whereas the Nordic countries tend to have older children in care. These findings are in accordance with the child protection orientation, making removals at a given risk level and based on a premise that younger children are more vulnerable than older children. In countries with a family service orientation, interventions mostly take the form of services to the family and to the child—only if these services do not help is the child removed. For example, the Norwegian Child Welfare Act first requires that in-home services must be tried, or it must be proven that in-home services will not be useful (article 4–12). Hence, children will be older before they are removed. We would expect that as countries like the United States increase their emphasis on preventive services, they will experience a jump in age level for children in out-of-home care.

Recognizing these important variations, the point we wish to make is that all countries have expanded their child welfare services. Does this expansion reflects more incidents of child maltreatment, broader definitions of abuse combined with lower threshold for interventions, or simply more awareness related to child abuse and children's rights? The data do not provide any hard, proven answers. We do, however, find reasons to believe that children's positions in society have become more important. Hence, the expansion of the child welfare system can, on one hand, be seen to reflect serious attempts to improve prevention and early intervention for children in need. On the other hand, they can signify a broadening of systems of social surveillance toward families. Whichever interpretation is most plausible, they both imply a changing set of relationships among the state, parents, and children—an issue to which we will return.

Foster Homes and Kinship Placements

Most countries, with the possible exception of Denmark, have experienced a continued shift in the type of out-of-home placements used. Foster care has clearly become the placement of preference, with residential care taking on secondary role, a trend that is also evident in many other countries (Courtney, Dolev, & Gilligan, 2009). Part of the explanation for the continued higher-than-average number of residential placements in Denmark, and to a lesser extent in the other Nordic countries, is the high numbers of teenagers accommodated because of their "challenging behaviors." There has also been increasing interest in the use of "kinship care" for children accommodated in care, particularly in the United States, and a much greater range of the types of providers, including the private and nongovernmental sectors, as well as the state itself. At the same time, there are significant differences in the use of adoption. The United States and England have clear policies stating that adoption is the second best option if reunification with biological parents is not possible. In the United States, about

7/10,000 children are adopted from the child welfare system, and in England and Canada, this number is about 4/10,000. Finland does not allow adoptions, and in the other six countries, adoptions are not often used. However, in both Norway and Denmark, there are tendencies toward increased use of adoption.

For all these important variations, a common objective underlies children's out-of-home placements—the establishment of a new family base for children that aims for stable and permanent relations for the child. Kinship care, foster homes, guardianship, and adoptions are different paths to achieving this objective.

Growth in Formal Procedures and Evidence-Based Initiatives

A distinction between the child protection and family service orientations identified in *Combatting Child Abuse* was that the child protection orientation tended to be much more legalistic, emphasized a more investigatory approach, and placed much greater bureaucratic demands upon the front-line worker, which allowed less room for professional discretion. At its most extreme, this seemed to be exemplified by the imposition of mandatory reporting—even though it was recognized that a number of countries operating within a family service oriented approach also had their own versions of mandatory reporting.

Developments in all ten countries demonstrate an increase in the formal procedures that regulate child protection work, which is not restricted to those systems marked by a legalistic child protection orientation. This is accompanied by the pervasive spread of bureaucratic mandates and the introduction of a range of different tools and technologies to make front-line professionals and others in child welfare organizations more formally accountable both for what they do and how they do it. These developments are intimately connected with the parallel growth in efforts to legitimate and support what has come to be known as evidenced-based practice, an approach that emphasizes the importance of scientific knowledge and documentation of results—as opposed to tradition, history, anecdotes, or workers' personal judgments. Although still in its early stages of development and open to much critical debate, the increasing emphasis upon evidence-based policy and practice is reflected in the rationale, structure, and content of the new assessment tools that have been introduced—whether focusing on "risk" or "need"—and also in a range of new intervention programs being used. These developments have been supported by the introduction of information communication technologies (ICTs) into the mainstream of the child protection work. Although the spread and intensity of these initiatives vary among countries, their implementation is evident everywhere and is often closely associated with the growing significance of managerial approaches.

In the mid-1990s, a defining characteristic of the child protection orientation was its emphasis on the use of risk assessment tools. Since that time, child protection and family service oriented countries have experienced a significant increase in the use of a whole variety of assessment tools, whether these focus primarily on risk or need, and whether their rationale is driven primarily by a concern to identify the nature and level of risk to a child, or to improve a child's well-being (Parton, 2009). In addition, programs such as Multi Systemic Therapy (MST), Multidimensional Treatment Foster Care (MTFC), Parent Management Training (PMT), and Incredible Years are now increasingly being used in many of the countries. Such programs are, typically, developed and "validated" in the United States, then exported to other countries. The widespread introduction of these measures certainly gives the impression that serious attempts are being made to scientifically inform policy and practice. At the same time, how child abuse is understood and framed in policy and practice has also drawn on scientific explanations, which recognize that individual, family, and community factors all play a role. This has given rise to a broader and more complex range of explanatory models than were evident in either the child protection or family service orientations discussed in *Combatting Child Abuse*.

It is notable that, although many countries now recognize the importance of the interprofessional nature of child protection work and the necessity for different organizations and professionals to "work together," social work continues to exercise the primary responsibility in this field. The introduction of evidenced-based practice, along with the training and support of social workers, has thus become key to advancing the scientific base of professional practice.

Race and Ethnicity

Race and ethnicity are particularly emphasized as issues in the United States, England, Canada, and Germany. In the United States, there is a significant over-representation of African American and Native American children in all levels of the child welfare system, which has given rise to a number of initiatives investigating the causes of racial and ethnic disproportionality and seeking to address the consequences of disparities. In Canada, the effects of the longstanding practice of forced placement of Aboriginal children in residential schools, together with the physical and sexual abuse that was rampant in those institutions, continues to reverberate, together with the destruction of the many families and communities that resulted. Despite this history, Aboriginal children remain highly overrepresented in the Canadian child welfare population. In England, children of mixed ethnicity are the proportionately largest single minority ethnic grouping looked after in state care. Although a very diverse category, this group consists mostly of children of African Caribbean/white parentage. However, it is only in recent years that disparities have been recognized in England. Such issues have also grown in significance in all the Nordic and North European countries. In the context of the increased mobility of labor and the growth of claims for asylum, all Nordic countries have become more ethnically diverse over the last 15 years.

In sum, several trends have shaped the development of child protection systems since the mid-1990s. First, these systems have expanded their domain. More children, and hence more families, receive services and interventions from the child welfare system. This is evident in all ten countries. Second, child protection operates in a highly volatile atmosphere, where without warning, practices can come under critical public scrutiny, challenging the qualifications and quality of front-line professionals; this has posed problems in the recruitment and retention of social workers. Third, due in part to professional vulnerabilities, as well as to the highly sensitive and complex nature of this work, increased emphasis has been placed on legalistic and systemic thinking in most child welfare systems. More tools are based on procedural manuals, and methods are increasingly evidence-based. Finally, there has been a growing recognition of the issues posed by racial and ethnic disparities in child welfare systems.

It is clear, therefore, that not only have the last 15 years seen significant and rapid change, but that there are many similarities in the challenges, themes, and developments among the ten countries studied. However, there also continues to be important differences among the countries in the ways in which child welfare systems respond to child abuse and neglect. The main difference continues to be whether, or to what extent, the primary gate-keeping threshold for determining who receives a service and is seen as a priority for response is driven by concerns about child abuse and neglect. For example, although child abuse and neglect continue to be the main organizing categories for child welfare work in the United States and Canada, this is not the case elsewhere. In Finland, the terms "child abuse" and "child neglect" barely exist in the child welfare vocabulary, indicating an alternative approach to child welfare thinking. Belgium and the Netherlands are related in their approach to formal reporting and professional responsibility to intervene and take care of a child in need or at risk. Neither of the countries has mandatory reporting, but instead gives each professional a responsibility to handle suspicions of maltreatment.

However, regarding the extent to which contemporary child protection arrangements effectively safeguard children against maltreatment and neglect, none of the countries describe systems that overall are able to ensure the present or future well-being of children at risk.

In the concluding section, our analytic focus shifts from the identification of common themes and developments that have appeared since the mid-1990s to address the overarching orientations that we see emerging in this area of the welfare states.

THREE ORIENTATIONS: BLENDING ALTERNATIVE APPROACHES

The findings suggest that the current approaches to protecting children from maltreatment have become much more complex than those operating in the social, economic, and political contexts of the mid-1990s and described in *Combatting Child Abuse*. The child protection and family service orientations outlined then no longer offer an adequate representation of the current situation, which has been altered by important changes during the intervening years. Countries previously identified with the child protection orientation have taken on some of the elements of the family service orientation. For example, a number of states in the U.S. have developed "differential response" systems, so that not every report is perceived in the context of a potentially serious case of child abuse. Meaningful attempts are made to respond to cases in qualitatively different ways depending on the level and nature of risk to the child. There has similarly been considerable investment in services that attempt to offer early support, work in partnership with parents, and maximize cultural and community continuity. Similarly, in England, there is clear evidence of official policy aimed at refocusing practice in such a way that, wherever possible, family support is maximized. At the same time, there is also evidence that those countries that had previously operated according to a clear family service orientation have made resolute efforts to respond to increasing concerns about harm to children. This is well illustrated in all the Nordic countries, with the possible exception of Sweden, and in all the northern European countries studied.

In addition to the various attempts to strike a new balance between the child protection and family service orientations, we discern the emergence of an alternative approach, which we identify as a *child-focused orientation*. This alternative orientation concentrates on the child as an individual with an independent relation to the state, and hence is an approach potentially opposed to the family. It is not restricted to narrow concerns about harm and abuse; rather, the object of concern is the child's overall development and well-being. This is evident in many of the countries' policies and programs that target children, as important means to advance the welfare state and levels of social expenditure. These programs seek to go beyond protecting children from risk to promoting children's welfare. We see this, for example, in Finland and Norway, where polices are directed toward creating a "child friendly" society and in the comprehensive child-focused programs in the United States, England, and Germany. In this context, concerns with harm and abuse become relevant as one set of factors that might affect a child's development and well-being. If, for any reason, concern exists about a child's development, the state seeks to intervene to offer support and/or more authoritative intervention. With a child-focused orientation, the state takes on a growing role for itself in terms of providing a wide range of early intervention and preventive services. This role represents the state's paternalistic interests in children's needs and well-being. Interestingly, by addressing the child as a separate entity in the family, the state promotes policies that lead to defamilialization, as it reduces families and parents responsibilities (risks and burdens) in raising children. The child-focused orientation often involves arrangements adjusted to meet children's needs, competencies, and maturity by viewing situations from the perspective of the child. For example, Canada, Sweden, and Norway make institutional arrangements, such as children's homes, to ensure the child's needs are taken care of in cases of criminal acts. Finnish social workers are trained to consider the child's perspective. In Germany and Belgium, the child welfare systems are described as being "wrapped around" the child and his or her needs.

Although this emerging orientation borrows elements from both the child protection and family service orientations, we suggest that it has a qualitatively different character, which is shaped by two major and somewhat contrasting lines of influence. On the one hand, the child-focused orientation to social policy is influenced by ideas related to "the social investment state," and on the other hand, it is influenced by the growing priority allotted to the importance of "individualization." However, these two lines of influence do not sit easily together and can lead to tensions, which signifies that the child-focused orientation can take somewhat different forms in different countries.

The idea of "social investment" has emerged in recent years as an ideal promoted by the Organization for Economic Cooperation and Development (OECD) and the European Union (EU), among others. The term "social investment state" was first coined by Anthony Giddens as an alternative to the traditional welfare state. It conveyed the notion of a shift in the role of state welfare from compensating individuals for their hardships, suffered through the vagaries of the market, to investing in human capital in order to maximize individual and social wealth creation and to integrate the individual into the market (Giddens, 1998). According to this view, investment in children takes on a strategic significance for a state keen to equip its citizens to respond and adapt to global economic change, in order to enhance individual and national competitiveness. In this respect, trying to ensure that all children maximize their developmental opportunities, educational attainment, and overall health and well-being becomes a key priority for social and economic policy.

Although investment in children involves a whole range of services, particularly those that will enhance prevention and intervention in problems at an early stage, these services are accompanied by an increased emphasis on regulating the behavior of both professionals who are given the responsibility for implementing the policies and also the parents and children themselves. Regulation is designed to ensure that the investment pays off and that everyone— particularly parents—fulfils his or her responsibility. This is a future-oriented approach, one which considers childhood as a preparation for adulthood, so that investment in children now is designed to ensure that they later will develop into productive and law-abiding adults. The state has taken on this new proactive and preemptive role primarily because the challenges now are so great that "the family" is no longer seen as adequate, on its own, for carrying out the tasks expected of it.

The degree to which states hold parents responsible for ensuring children's well-being varies. Some states are willing to put strong constraints on the private sphere; in Denmark and Germany, for example, parents can lose economic support if they fail to comply with standards set by the state. These standards say that parents have an obligation to promote their children's best interest, and develop skills and competencies. It's not sufficient to prevent harm, but it's also expected that parents give their children a good childhood.

In contrast is the rationale and genealogy of policies and practices that perceive children as individuals here and now, as something different from, but equally valuable, as adults. These policies are concerned with the quality of children's childhood, stating as Finland and Norway do, that it's a social justice issue to make sure children are treated with respect and are given a loving upbringing. These states promote a happy and caring childhood, securing children the same rights granted others, aiming to give children in the child welfare system the same opportunities as other children in society.

Children are seen not so much as future workers, but as current citizens. This perspective reflects the fact that all of the countries studied in this book, except the United States, have ratified the UN Convention of Children's Rights (CRC) of 1989, which on a formal level implies that children have social, political, and legal rights. Since the mid-1990s, a number of countries have made particular efforts to secure national legislation that is in accordance with the CRC, as in Netherlands in 2001 and in Norway in 2003. Belgium considers all legislation in accordance with the CRC, and the Supreme Court in Canada made it illegal to use physical discipline on children (spanking laws) due to the CRC. Such efforts make sure children's rights are not merely varnish, but have real impact on how decisions are made in courts and in front-line child protection agencies.

The strong standing of children's rights is particularly evident in the right to participate, understood as children's active input and involvement in decisions that concern their lives. All of the countries in this book have legislation that gives children opportunities to participate and for their voices to be heard in matters concerning them. For example, in Norway, the views and opinions of children aged 7 years and older are taken into account, as are those of all children in England who are capable of expressing their opinions. Interestingly, even though the United States has not ratified the CRC, children's right to participate has a strong standing in the child welfare system. Children have a right to their own lawyer to make sure their voices are heard. In addition, several arrangements have developed (e.g., guardian ad litem, next friend) to make sure the child's best interests are taken into consideration (cf. Peters, 2007). Child participation is a matter that has gained increased attention in research and is becoming an important aspect in child welfare work. This implies that decision-makers shall both hear children and "weigh" their views according to age and maturity, and hence that formal rights are intended to have an impact on practice. From our point of view, this is a strong indicator that more states are treating children as individuals with opinions about their own life, and not only as a part of a family. Although children are seen as important in their own right and clearly having an existence independent of the family, the reasons and rationale for perceiving them as future workers or as current citizens are different and have different implications for policy and practice. In particular, these perspectives influence how much priority and influence is seriously allotted to the views of children.

The child-focused orientation puts children's rights above parents rights, and emphasizes parents obligations as caregivers. The child welfare system provides services to promote children's needs and well-being, but in return demands change and results on behalf of the child. In Table 12.2, we outline the dimensions of the child-focused orientation together with those of the family service and child protection orientations.

We are not suggesting that these dimensions form discrete models, hence our preference for the idea of "orientations." The orientations can be seen to range along a continuum from a more laissez-faire neo-liberal approach that emphasizes the watchdog functions of government to the more social democratic approach that advances policies associated with defamilialization. However, although some countries might emphasize one of the orientations more than another in their approaches to child maltreatment, all of the countries contain

Table 12.2: Role of the State Vis-à-Vis Child and Family in Orientations to Child Maltreatment: Child Focus, Family Service, and Child Protection

	Child Focus	Family Service	Child Protection
Driver for intervention	The individual child's needs in a present and future perspective; society's need for healthy and contributory citizens	The family unit needs assistance	Parents being neglectful and abusive toward children (maltreatment)
Role of the state	Paternalistic/ defamilialization–state assumes parent role; but seeks to refamilialize child by foster home/kinship care/adoption	Parental support; the state seeks to strengthen family relations	Sanctioning; the state functions as "watchdog" to ensure child's safety
Problem frame	Child's development and unequal outcomes for children	Social/psychological (system, poverty, racism, etc.)	Individual/moralistic
Mode of intervention	Early intervention and regulatory/need assessment	Therapeutic/needs assessment	Legalistic/ investigative
Aim of intervention	Promote well-being via social investment and/or equal opportunity	Prevention/social bonding	Protection/harm reduction
State–parent relationship	Substitutive/partnership	Partnership	Adversarial
Balance of rights	Children's rights/parents' responsibility	Parents' rights to family life mediated by professional social workers	Children's/parents' rights enforced through legal means

some mix of these orientations. This suggests that, rather than trying to place countries somewhere on the line of a continuum from child focus to family service to child protection, we might think of where they might fall within a three-dimensional framework—closer to some planes than others.

These orientations highlight the reality that many of the key issues relating to how child welfare systems respond to child maltreatment are primarily about how different systems strike the balance between the rights and responsibilities and the nature of the relationships among children, parents and the state. These relationships are influenced in part by the size of the state and the range of services it provides, as well as by the sociopolitical character of the state and the types of connective bonds it has with its citizens—both children and adults. The mixed orientations of different systems reflect the values and philosophies of policy and practice and the culture(s) within which professionals operate as much as, if not more than, the specific services they deliver.

As a final observation, we should keep in mind the volatile character of child welfare systems. In any of the countries studied, the focus and orientation of these systems might quickly change, particularly in times of crisis. Any system, when placed under severe pressure resulting from financial constraints, increased demand, or political and media opprobrium, might revert "to type" and adopt a default position that carries many of the hallmarks of its previous orientation. For example, although England has spent over 10 years trying to refocus its child welfare work, in the light of the dramatic political and public furor arising from the death of Baby Peter, there is clear evidence of it reverting to a much more defensive, risk-averse, and forensic approach to the work, which is very consistent with a narrow child protection orientation. Therefore, while having identified some clear developments and the emergence of new approaches, we should never underestimate the fragile and uncertain nature of this area of policy and practice.

REFERENCES

Bauman, Z. (2001). *The Individualized Society*. Oxford: Polity Press.

Beck, U. (1992). *Towards a new modernity*. London: Sage.

Best, J. (1990). *Threatened children: Rhetoric and concern about child-victims*. Chicago: University of Chicago Press.

Cooper, A., Hetherington, R., Bairstow, K., Pitts, J., & Sprigs, A. (1995). *Positive child protection: A view from abroad*. Lyme Regis: Russell House Publishing.

Courtney, M., Dolev, T., & Gilligan, R. (2009). Looking backward to see forward clearly: A cross-national perspective on residential care. In Mark E. Courtney, Dorota Iwaniec, (eds). *Residential care of children: Comparative perspectives*. Oxford University Press. Kindle version.

Franklin, B. (Ed.). (2002). *The new handbook of children's rights: Comparative policy and practice*. London: Routledge.

Giddens, A. (1998). *The third way: The renewal of social democracy*. Cambridge: Polity Press.

Gilbert, N. (2004). *Transformation of the welfare state: The silent surrender of public responsibility*. New York: Oxford University Press.

Gilbert, N. (Ed.). (1997). *Combatting child abuse: International perspectives and trends* /New York: Oxford University Press.

Gould, A. (1988). *Control and conflict in welfare policy: The Swedish experience*. London: Longman.

Hetherington, R., Cooper, A., Smith, P., & Wilford, G. (1997). *Protecting children: Messages from Europe*. Lyme Regis: Russell House Publishing.

Hill, M., Stafford, A., & Lister-Green, P. (2002). *International perspectives on child protection. Appendix B of Scottish Executive: It's everyone's job to make sure I'm alright. Report of the Child Protection Audit and Review*. Edinburgh: Scottish Executive.

Jordan, B. (2006). *Social policy for the twenty-first century*. Cambridge: Polity Press.

Muncie, J. & Goldson, B. (Eds.). (2006). *Comparative youth justice: Critical issues*. London: Sage.

Parton, N. (2006). *Safeguarding childhood: Early intervention and surveillance in a late modern society*. Basingstoke, UK: Palgrave/Macmillan.

Parton, N. (2009). Challenges to practice and knowledge in child welfare social work: From the "social" to the "informational"? *Children and Youth Services Review, 37*(7), 715–721.

INDEX